Chinese Higher Education Reform and Social Justice

In place of a distributive justice perspective which focuses simply on equal access to universities, this book presents a broader understanding of the relationship between Chinese higher education and economic and social change. The necessity for research on the place of universities in contemporary Chinese society may be seen from current debates about and policy towards issues of educational inequality at Chinese universities. Many questions arise as a consequence: What are the limitations of neo-liberalism in higher education policy and what are the alternatives? How has the Chinese government met the challenges of educational inequality, and what lessons may be learned from its recent initiatives? How may higher education enhance social justice in Chinese society given economic, social and cultural inequality? What may be learned from the experience of Macau, Hong Kong, and of Taiwan in terms of achieving social justice in Chinese universities? These questions are considered by a group of leading scholars from both inside and outside China.

Bin Wu is a Senior Research Fellow in the School of Contemporary Chinese Studies at the University of Nottingham, UK.

W. John Morgan is a Professor in the School of Education at the University of Nottingham, UK.

China policy series

Series Editor:
Zheng Yongnian
China Policy Institute, University of Nottingham, UK

Chinese Higher Education Reform and Social Justice

**Edited by Bin Wu
and W. John Morgan**

Routledge
Taylor & Francis Group

LONDON AND NEW YORK

First published 2016
by Routledge
4 Park Square, Milton Park, Abingdon, Oxon OX14 4RN

and by Routledge
605 Third Avenue, New York, NY 10017

First issued in paperback 2017

Routledge is an imprint of the Taylor & Francis Group, an informa business

British Library Cataloguing in Publication Data
A catalogue record for this book is available from the British Library

Library of Congress Cataloging-in-Publication Data
Chinese higher education reform and social justice / edited by Bin Wu, John Morgan.
   pages cm. – (China policy series ; 39)
   1. Educational sociology–China. 2. Social justice–China. 3. Education, Higher–Economic aspects–China. 4. Educational equalization–China. 5. Educational change–China. I. Wu, Bin.
   LC191.98.C6C55 2015
   378'.0150951–dc23   2015002423

ISBN 13: 978-0-8153-5498-7 (pbk)
ISBN 13: 978-0-415-71122-7 (hbk)

Typeset in Times New Roman
by Wearset Ltd, Boldon, Tyne and Wear

Contents

Figures

Tables

Contributors

Jason K.Y. Chan is Head of Information Technology at the College of Professional and Continuing Education, The Hong Kong Polytechnic University, and Vice-President of the Hong Kong Public Administration Association.

Kai-yan Choi is Associate Master and Chief of Students, Moon Chun Memorial College, University of Macau.

John Cribbin is Deputy Director (Academic Services) at the HKU School of Professional and Continuing Education (HKU SPACE), The University of Hong Kong.

Yanbi Hong is an Associate Professor at the Department of Sociology, School of Humanities, Southeast University, Nanjing, People's Republic of China.

Ngok Lee is Vice-President (Education) at UNESCOHK, having the responsibility to develop sustainable education at the school and higher education level in Hong Kong.

Stephanie W. Lee is a Lecturer and Programme Leader at the School of Professional Education and Executive Development, The Hong Kong Polytechnic University.

Fengliang Li is an Associate Professor at the Institute of Education, Tsinghua University, Beijing, China.

Junfu Li is an Associate Professor at the School of Humanity and Social Sciences and Capital Society-Building and Collaborative Innovation Centre, Beijing University of Technology.

Zhen Li is an Assistant Professor in the School of Education, University of Nottingham, UK.

Dian Liu is a PhD candidate at the Faculty of Education, The University of Hong Kong.

Ning Rong Liu is an Associate Professor and Associate Director, School of Professional and Continuing Education, University of Hong Kong.

John Lowe is an Associate Professor in the School of Education, University of Nottingham Ningbo, China.

W. John Morgan is Professor and UNESCO Chair of the Political Economy of Education, School of Education, and Senior Fellow, China Policy Institute, University of Nottingham, UK. He is also Honorary Professor, School of Social Sciences, Cardiff University.

Bernadette Robinson is Honorary Professor, School of Education and Associate Fellow, China Policy Institute, School of Contemporary Chinese Studies, University of Nottingham, UK.

Cheng-Yen Wang is Dean of the Graduate Institute of Adult Education and the Office of Academic Affairs, National Kaohsiung Normal University, Kaohsiung City, Taiwan.

Bin Wu is Senior Research Fellow, School of Contemporary Chinese Studies, and Convenor of the Centre for Chinese Migration Studies, University of Nottingham, UK.

Peter P. Yuen is Dean of the College of Professional and Continuing Education, The Hong Kong Polytechnic University, and Chairman of the Hong Kong Federation for Self-financing Tertiary Education.

Yandong Zhao is Deputy Director of the Institute of Science, Technology and Society, at the Chinese Academy of Science and Technology for Development, Beijing, China.

Acknowledgements

The idea for this book came from the positive responses from readers and reviewers to our first edited book, *Higher Education Reform in China: Beyond the expansion* (Routledge, 2011 (hbk) and 2013 (pbk)). We identified a knowledge gap about issues of social justice and higher education in the context of China and Chinese societies. The idea was discussed on a number of occasions, including the *Fifth International Forum for Contemporary Chinese Studies* (IFCCS5, Beijing, August 2012) and a *Society for Research into Higher Education* (SRHE) network event on Chinese students' perspectives on higher education in China and in the United Kingdom (London, March 2014). It was then encouraged and supported by Peter Sowden, our editor at Routledge, and by Professor Yongnian Zheng, academic editor of the *China policy series*. We express our sincere thanks to all contributors for their commitment, cooperation and patience over the past two years. Finally, we thank Helena Hurd and Huiping Bai for their assistance, and Joyce Morgan who prepared the index.

Abbreviations

CA	Capacity Approach
CCP	Chinese Communist Party
EGM	Emerging Global Model
GER	Gross Enrolment Ratio
GSSLP	Government-Subsidized Student Loan Programme
HE	Higher Education
MoE	Ministry of Education
NBS	National Bureau of Statistics
OECD	Organisation for Economic Cooperation and Development
RC	Residential College
SAR	Special Administrative Region
SRL	Self Regulated Learning
UGC	University Grants Committee, Hong Kong
UNESCO	United Nations Educational, Scientific and Cultural Organization

Introduction

Chinese higher education reform and social justice

Bin Wu and W. John Morgan

It is remarkable that the number of university students in China (including those in part-time higher adult education) reached 34.6 million in 2013. The gross enrolment ratio (GER) has risen from less than 10 per cent in 1998 to 34.5 per cent in 2013 (MoE, 2014). China is an exceptional example of post-school education in many ways, such as in absolute (student population) or relative (access opportunity) terms or in quantitative (growth rate) or qualitative (global impact) terms. Such a rapid expansion has been accompanied by unexpected and even negative consequences. The number of Chinese graduates is expected to reach 7.27 million in 2014 (SUNDXS, 4 June 2014) and the greatest challenge is the difficulty of finding them suitable jobs in the labour market, with the phenomenon of over-education becoming more apparent (Li *et al.*, 2011).This affects most strongly those from rural or poor family backgrounds who lack resources and social support in their job hunting. In addition, there is a growing educational inequality arising from the uneven distribution of higher education resources by geographic region and social group. This has resulted in barriers to higher education access by students from inland regions and from rural families, especially to key national universities. The achievements and the challenges described above indicate a new era in China's higher education reform and development. This may be seen in the new edition of the *National Strategy for Higher Education Reform and Development* for 2010 to 2020 (see MoE, 2012). This emphasises quality, structural adjustment and, importantly for this book, educational equality. Since the accession of the new leadership of President Xi Jingping in 2012, new policies have been adopted or at least signalled, with a focus on educational equality at all levels and in higher education in particular.

This process of policy adjustment provides an opportunity to rethink the relationship between social justice and Chinese higher education reform. This is because China is an interesting case in terms of both the achievements and limitations of its expansion driven by the neo-liberal approach. There is also the issue of the unevenness of China's economic and social development over the past three decades. This has rapidly created a highly stratified and unequal society, which has had a profound impact on educational inequality in China (Sheng, 2014). In these circumstances, relatively little attention has been paid to the question of whether higher education has a responsibility for promoting social justice and achieving a fairer and more harmonious society in China (Wang and Morgan, 2012). This book attempts to fill this gap through initiating a debate about Chinese higher education and social justice. Here we pose the following questions: What research has been done on the relationship between higher education and social justice internationally? What may be learned from the development of Chinese higher education in recent decades? In what ways does this book contribute to the debate on these issues?

Social justice and higher education

The term *social justice* is a popular but vague concept which changes in meaning depending on place and time. The current interest in it as a policy option has been stimulated by the dominance of neo-liberalism which regards human capital investment as the key to meeting skill shortages, and enhancing economic growth and competition in global markets (Brown and Tannock, 2009). Furthermore, higher education is regarded as the key vehicle for such human capital development through its capacity to produce knowledge, stimulate innovation and develop high-level skills (Valimaa and Hoffman, 2008; Singh, 2011). This has led to higher education expansion or so-called 'massification' of provision globally, and not least in China. This process has been described and analysed frequently (Trow, 2006). More recently, the concept of an *Emerging Global Model* (EGM) has emerged which identifies a top rank of research universities as being key to 'economic and social development' (Mohrman *et al.*, 2008). In particular, Marginson (2004: 234) suggests that 'the old equality of opportunity project is now in terminal crisis, and will continue to be undermined by heightened status competition, markets, cross-border leakages of people and resources, and global commercialisation'. It should also be noted that quality assurance through various evaluations or table leagues has spread rapidly with the objective of social justice unlikely to be prominent in such formal evaluation templates (Singh, 2011: 487–488). Indeed, depending on many local factors, it seems that such growth in provision and, according to the European Science Foundation, 'does not automatically reduce social inequality and may in fact benefit those who are already socially advantaged' (ESF, 2008: 10). This should not be surprising in that we often see a process beginning with an emphasis on social justice (or inclusion) end with the enhancement of elite reproduction.

It is in practice difficult to find an interpretation of social justice that is appropriate in terms of access to higher education. According to Sen (1992), different social groups may have different interpretations of the concept of equality of opportunity. For working-class families, access to higher education offers opportunities to enhance their potential and eventually to improve their standard of living. For middle-class families, the quality of education obtained is important and, if necessary, additional investment is made to secure not only access to higher education generally, but to one of the more prestigious universities. For the upper classes, an élite higher education is a means of status and privilege for the next generation. Such differing interpretations maintain the stratification of higher education according to the class-based demands of the population (Furlong and Cartmel, 2009: 7).

The importance of the social structure may be understood from Bourdieu's theory of social reproduction which is applied through the mechanisms of 'habitus' or through the conversion of social and cultural capitals (Bourdieu, 1977, 1986). As Marginson notes:

> Neo-liberal marketisation raises sharper questions about social inequality in higher education in two dimensions: equality/inequality of access to opportunity, and equality/inequality of the opportunities themselves. All else being equal, economic markets are associated with great social inequalities of access in systems mediated by the private capacity to pay so that access is more steeply stratified on social lines; and with a steeper hierarchy of institutions, so that what is accessed is also increasingly stratified.
>
> (Marginson, 2004: 234)

However, neo-liberals do not necessarily reject intervention for social justice. In their terms social justice is often presented as *distributive justice* or matters of benefits and resources or, simply, 'who gets what' (Vincent, 2003: 3). According to Young (1990: 15), the distributive approach tries to avoid the more fundamental questions about 'the social structure and institutional context' which determines the 'distributive patterns'. It emphasises instead community regeneration, social inclusion, and the building of a network of social capital at the micro level. This is close to the Chinese state's aspiration of a stratified but *harmonious society* mentioned above. By contrast, the *social justice* approach focuses on the relationship between patterns of domination and oppression in the social structure, and in the institutional context which influences the nature of distribution (Vincent, 2003: 3). Young (1990) identified 'five faces of oppression': exploitation, marginalisation, powerlessness, cultural imperialism and violence. These, it is said, combine the 'distributional *and* cultural or relational dimension of social justice' (Vincent, 2003: 3–4).

Addressing the same theme of higher education and social justice, McArthur (2010) argues that three terms symbolise the approach of a critical pedagogy which is motivated by a belief that society is structured unfairly and that this may be changed. These are: *exile* or the experience of 'being outside the mainstream' in both positive and negative ways; *sanctuary* or a safe space 'wherein one can explore and challenge ideas', and *diasporas*, or 'non-identity', a term taken from Adorno (1973) and intended to 'encourage multiple senses of belongings that can potentially free one from mainstream or normalizing forces'. This critical perspective broadens the concept of social justice in three ways. First, by registering the existence and difference of vulnerable, disadvantaged and social groups which are marginal to mainstream society. Second, through fostering effective dialogue or debate between different groups. Third, through the creation of an inclusive society based on equal and mutual respect among different groups in resistance to the hegemonic and homogenising forces of globalisation (Braziel and Mannur, 2003: 10).

The advocates of critical pedagogy believe that 'education and society are intrinsically inter-related and that the fundamental purpose of education is the improvement of social justice for all' (McArthur, 2010: 493). However, educational and social change is not a simple process and is influenced by many complicated factors. Marxists and other radical modernists emphasise the need for structural economic and social change, while postmodernists emphasise the multiplicity of identities found among groups and individuals (Morgan, 2003; McArthur, 2010). Consequently, the understanding and use of the concept of social justice varies greatly, according to how policy goals are conceptualised and prioritised (Singh, 2011: 482). It is argued by Sen (2010), for instance, that there are two dimensions to social justice: the theoretical and the normative, which together create a vision of the just society; and advocates practical engagement with the elimination of social injustices. There is also a longstanding debate on the purpose or functions of higher education. According to Trow (2006: 243), three categories may be identified. First, an *élite* system for the ruling class. Second, a *mass* system which develops selected students for a wide range of technical roles. Third, a *universal* system for the 'whole population' aimed at enabling rapid economic and social change. It is argued that: 'These different views about the purpose of higher education mean that for different stake-holders social justice is not a primary concern'. Furthermore, the principle of social justice is more central to higher education policies in some countries, such as in Scandinavia, than in others (Furlong and Cartmel, 2009: 9).

Social justice and Chinese higher education

The debates about social justice and higher education in China must obviously be considered within the changing contexts which the country has experienced since 1949 when the Chinese Communist Party (CCP) came to power. The evolution of the higher education system has had four stages hitherto: the era of Mao Zedong from the 1950s to the mid-1970s, including the Cultural Revolution of 1966 to 1976; the reforms of Deng Xiaoping from the late 1970s to the mid-1990s; the period of higher education reform from the mid-1990s to 2010; and continuing adjustment since.

This is not the place to consider the history of Chinese higher education in republican China. We note that with contributions from Western society, notably Protestant religious organisations, China had, during the first half of the twentieth century, developed a significant higher education system (Hayhoe, 2006). By 1948 there were some 210 institutions which were public and private funded, comprehensive and vocational, national and regional, and with a student total of some 155,000.[1] This system was reconstructed completely from 1952 according to the 'Soviet Union Model'. This considered higher education to be part of the national planned economy under the direction of the CCP. This meant that higher education, like education generally, was provided by the Chinese state.

This financed the entire system, with allocations made according to the requirements of the CCP. In the same way, graduates of the system were allocated jobs according to the demands of the planned economy. Higher education students and their teachers were expected to show loyalty to the CCP and to its ideological vision for social justice in China; and to work to acquire expertise in their assigned field. The purpose of universities was to produce a knowledgeable and skilled population with a revolutionary class consciousness. The national industrialisation strategy stimulated an expansion of student numbers which had reached 674,000 by 1965.[2] This was four times as many as in 1948. This trend was interrupted by the upheavals of the Cultural Revolution which saw the effective closure of almost all institutions of higher education in China. Again, this is not the place for a discussion of the complex and still contentious history of the Cultural Revolution and Mao Zedong's motives in encouraging it. We note only that it was a fundamental experience in both the intellectual and the institutional history of Chinese higher education, not least because of its radical ideological view of social justice (Yang, 2011).

In the next stage, from 1978, as an important part of Deng Xiaoping's strategy in economic reform and policies for opening China to the world, higher education institutions were reopened and developed. There was no fundamental change in that state control was maintained and higher education continued according to the national central development plan. However, a series of gradual reforms or adjustments was made to China's higher education system throughout the 1980s and in the first half of the 1990s. These included: a high value assigned to scientific knowledge, innovation and application, as compared with traditional knowledge; the de-politicization of university curricular and of direct political control over student recruitment and behaviour (although each institution continued to be monitored by its internal CCP organisation); the opening to international higher education through academic exchange and a state-funded programme through a China Scholarship Council for visiting scholars abroad (Welch and Cai, 2011); the introduction of tuition fees; and autonomy for universities to recruit a small proportion of students outside the national plan. It should also be noted that this period saw the decline of local community engagement with higher education institutions which had social justice implications. For instance, most urban students who entered universities directly did not now visit the countryside to undertake farming work. As a result, they knew little about rural poverty and its impact on their counterparts from rural families, resulting in a social divide within classrooms. By 1998, with over one million new students each year, there were some 23 million students in the higher education system and the gross enrolment ratio (GER) was 9.76 per cent compared with 1.55 per cent in 1978. In contrast with the Maoist era, the most significant change is that higher education institutions are now essentially centres for the production of political, economic and social élites, in the manner of such institutions in the capitalist economies. The acquisition of university credentials through degrees and other certificates was emphasised and became a key criterion for recruitment or promotion in the dominant public sector and in the emerging private sector.

Beginning in the late 1990s, China's higher education system entered a new era, with the introduction of new policies which changed the principles that had hitherto guided the organisation and provision of higher education. It began with the state's decision to develop so-called world class universities through its 211 projects (involving the top 100 universities since 1995) and 985 projects (involving the top 40 universities since 1998)[3] (Zha, 2011). This led to strict ranking of higher education institutions and to a centralisation of state financial support. It was followed by the devolution of responsibility for around 300 other universities to provincial governments. This was indicative of a transition from the national plan's responsibility for the recruitment, training and employment of graduates, to a system of graduate labour markets (Li *et al.*, 2011). The most significant change was the introduction of a funding system which saw an expansion of public universities on the one hand and the emergence of private higher education on the other (Li and Morgan, 2011).

Bearing in mind uneven regional economic development, local fiscal capacity and the growth of socio-economic inequality, such neo-liberal reforms have had serious consequences if considered from a social justice perspective. The most serious is the considerable difference in higher education resource distribution geographically and socially. For instance, the number of universities administered by central government fell from more than 400 in the mid-1990s to around 100 by early 2002; and many provinces are without a national key university. The unevenness in the distribution of higher education resources may also be seen in the difference of average revenues among the different types of higher education institutions (shown in Table I.1). It shows that the ratio of revenues between core 985 members and 211 universities, local universities and higher vocational colleges was as high as 45:26:10:4:1 in 2006. The share of tuition fees in institutional revenue increased by 14.3 per cent, 21.1 per cent, 27.0 per cent, 37.9 per cent and 50.3 per cent over the same period (Zha, 2011: 758).

Given similar tuition fees (related to strict government control)[4] and differences in state funding, such policies intensify the competition among Chinese students and their families for access to highly ranked universities. The stratification of China's higher education system also had an impact on secondary and

Table I.1 Institutional revenues and share of tuition fees by types of HE institutes (2006)

Item	Core 985 universities	Other 985 universities	211 project universities	Local universities	Vocational colleges
Number	9	28	68	588	712
Mean revenues (million Yuan RMB)	2,028.6	1,153.0	456.8	188.1	45.2
Ratio of revues	45	26	10	4	1
Tuition fees in the revenues (%)	14.3	21.1	27.0	37.9	50.1

Sources: Zha (2011: 758).

even elementary education. Students from the élite groups have significant advantages compared with those from other groups because of their possession of economic, social and cultural capital (Sheng, 2014). For example, evidence suggests that the percentage of rural students in universities such as Peking and Tsinghua universities fell, from over 30 per cent in the 1990s to only 10 per cent in 2010, while the percentage in higher vocational education in Hubei province increased from under 40 per cent in 2002 to over 60 per cent in 2007.[5] In short, students from rural and/or poor urban families are now more likely to attend higher vocational colleges or low-tier universities. Furthermore, there is very limited opportunity for students to engage with the wider communities and to acquire local knowledge. As a result, students know less and less of society in general and commonly lack work experience, or a sense of citizenship and social responsibility (Wu and Morgan, 2011).

In recognition of these problems compensatory policy initiatives have been introduced by the Chinese Communist Party and state in recent years, particularly by the current President Xi Jingping. These include but are not limited to:

- An increase in the share of students from inland provinces, poor counties and rural communities accessing national key universities through strong administrative intervention by the State Council.[6]
- Additional government investment to improve teaching conditions in higher vocational education and certain universities in the disadvantaged west of China.
- Allow students from migrant workers' families to attend the national higher education entrance examination at their current place of residence rather than in their place of family origin.
- Improve state financial support for students from poor families.
- Promote entrepreneurship and community engagement for the purpose of enhancing employability.
- Improve education equality in secondary education level by abolishing key schools and key classes at different levels.[7]

It remains to be seen how effective such policies will be in reducing educational inequality in China given that they are dependent upon administrative measures. It seems that fundamental issues have yet to be considered through research which can guide policy debates. For instance, what should China do to build a knowledge economy and develop the professional expertise that this requires, while simultaneously maintaining social justice and harmony? Can the tensions between the stratification strategy (for world-class universities and élite education) and the massification of higher education be resolved? What should be the social responsibilities of higher education, especially in terms of citizenship and social justice among its students? The following section presents a framework for considering these questions.

Rethinking higher education in China

The uneven pattern of China's higher education reforms over the past half century encourages a rethink about its purpose and structure. We suggest that there are two aspects which need to be considered. The first is knowledge creation and diffusion, or global (or universal) vs. local (or indigenous) knowledge. The second is its value system which is fundamental to the purpose of higher education if it is to go beyond functionalism. These are not separate issues, but may be seen in China's higher education development since the 1950s. Figure I.1 shows that there have been different views of the purpose of higher education in China. In the Maoist era, for instance, a collective spirit and local knowledge were valued by communist ideology (1). However, this was pushed to the radical extremes of the Great Proletarian Cultural Revolution and its consequences. Deng Xiaoping's reform led to an increasing emphasis on the value of science and technology, on knowledge productivity, and on the contribution of professionals. The rapid changes since the late 1990s accelerated this trend and led to stratification at the institutional level and to marketisation at the student level: a fundamental adjustment of the mission of higher education (2). If China is to build a fair and sustainable society, a balance is needed between global and local knowledge and between individualism and collectivism. The key question is: Does China have the social and political will to achieve such a balance? Furthermore, what are the dynamics favouring this, as well as the constraints?

This, in turn, raises the following questions:

1   What are the limitations of neo-liberalism in higher education policy and what are the alternatives?
2   How has the Chinese government coped with the challenges of educational inequality, and what lessons may be learned from its recent initiatives?
3   What can higher education do to enhance social justice in Chinese society given the severe challenges of economic, social and cultural inequality?
4   What can be learned from the experience of Macau, Hong Kong and Taiwan in terms of promoting social justice in Chinese higher education?

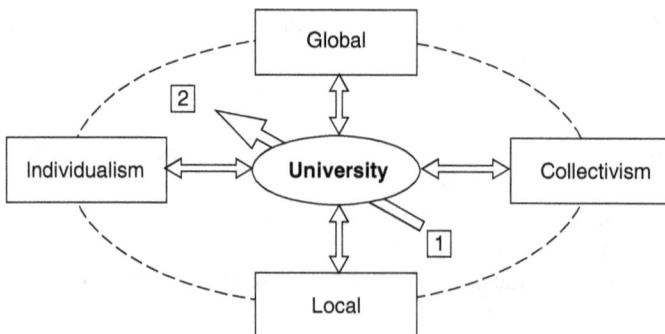

Figure I.1 Framework for analysis.

The structure of the book

This book considers these and related questions through detailed empirical studies and analysis. In addition to this Introduction there are nine further chapters. In Chapter 1, Li and Lowe consider how the capabilities approach of Sen and Nussbaum may assist Chinese higher education in addressing wider social issues which lie beyond a narrow human capital approach. They examine the social justice implications of recent higher education policies in China from a capabilities perspective. These include the emergence of a hierarchy of élite institutions; the prioritising of academic fields; changes to admissions procedures; and the devolution of organisational powers to local and institutional levels.

In Chapter 2, Wu and Robinson consider the replacement of state funding with cost sharing which has made heavy demands on the family finances of poor students, despite the introduction of government grants and subsidies to support students in need. The chapter explores this issue through a questionnaire survey of 1,547 students at six universities in Shaanxi province conducted in 2011. It examines the distribution of financial support to students from different socio-economic backgrounds, together with students' perceptions about equality of opportunity and fairness in the distribution of resources in higher education.

Li, Wu and Morgan (Chapter 3) explore the development of university teachers as a professional community in contemporary China. They use a survey conducted in Beijing in 2011 with the participation of 1,692 teachers from 18 universities to examine the key factors behind the distribution of incomes among university teachers, together with their perceptions of and demands for decent pay and conditions which should reflect their qualifications and professional status.

Liu and Hong (Chapter 4) focus on the influences of cultural capital in the process and outcome of job search. They use evidence from an empirical study comprising interviews with 60 fourth-year students, from four disciplines, at two top-tier Chinese universities in Wuhan in 2011/2012. The authors argue that the job search is based on a joint work of delicately constructed individual 'excellence' comprising the capitalised cultural assets, family socio-economic support and parental intervention in keeping the student job searcher on the right track.

Using a national survey of postgraduate employment conducted by the Chinese Academy of Science and Technology for Development (CASTED), Li, Zhao and Morgan (Chapter 5) analyse the effect of migration on starting salaries, job matching and the potential over-education of postgraduates. The empirical results indicate that migration employment does not bring significantly positive benefits. The authors suggest that higher education institutions should establish guidelines for the migration employment of postgraduate students. The authors conclude with a discussion of the significant implications of their findings for social justice in access to higher education opportunities in China.

Choi (Chapter 6) examines the rationale of various kinds of residential college systems at selected universities in China to analyse how the general education components, including social responsibility, are addressed in the specific college education curricula, and how these components are brought to general college activities. The educational rationale behind residential colleges and the extent to which they have achieved their goals, such as whole-person development and citizenship education, and the different kinds of opportunities and challenges faced in the context of higher education reforms, are discussed in the chapter.

Liu and Cribbin (Chapter 7) show that the provision of adult, higher and continuing education in mainland China and in the Special Administrative Region (SAR) of Hong Kong have both similarities and differences. They explore these different traditions and influences, their impact in terms of social justice and the extent to which this has been an aim or objective of policy, or whether what has developed was simply a reaction to market pressure. In the context of a comparative review of adult and higher continuing education in China and Hong Kong, the authors consider the latter's efforts to serve the needs of the former.

In Chapter 8, Yuen, Lee, Lee and Chan examine the three modes of education services in Hong Kong with a view to determining whether the government's proposed measures and existing instruments are adequate in meeting the key attributes of a pillar industry. The three modes are: (1) cross-border trade, including supply of books, education-related equipment and online education; (2) an education hub, including student hub, workforce hub and knowledge hub, and (3) foreign participation and ownership of education institutions. The authors argue that Hong Kong's quality assurance experiences can be a model for mainland institutions in the current neo-liberal educational management environment.

Moving geographic focus to Taiwan, Wang (Chapter 9) points out that the values of lifelong learning and of social justice have been the essence of culture since the age of Confucius. Accordingly, from the constitution to major acts concerning education, assuring the right to learning and to social justice has been endorsed by law. Wang considers self-regulated learning (SRL) as a key competency through which to achieve the ideal of education for all, with a focus on adult learners' literacy. Using evidence from a questionnaire survey and semi-structured interviews, the author analyses Taiwan's experiences and suggests ways of supporting adult learners' literacy and self-regulated learning to protect and enhance social justice in education. The author suggests that the Taiwanese experience may be helpful to other education systems, especially those with a Confucian cultural background.

Notes

1 For details, see http://club.kdnet.net/dispbbs.asp?boardid=2&id=1780706 (in Chinese) (accessed 23 August 2014).
2 See www.360doc.com/content/13/1101/19/642066_325919653.shtml (accessed 23 August 2014).
3 For the detailed background and list of universities, see www.chinaeducenter.com/en/cedu/ceduproject211.php (accessed 17 August 2014).
4 Despite the introduction of the share of financial costs for higher education since the late 1990s, the Chinese government has not relinquished its control on the growth of

tuition fees in all public universities to ensure that the share of tuition fees is not too high for low-income families. As a result, there is a little difference between public regular universities and colleges, regardless of rank and geographic location.

5 See 'For social justice, more opportunities should be given to rural students to be able to access to national key universities' (in Chinese) at www.chsi.com.cn/z/jygp/index. jsp (accessed 27 August 2014).

6 The State Council (国务院) denotes the central government in China, the chief administrative authority of the People's Republic of China. Chaired by the Premier, it supervises all ministries, including the Ministry of Education.

7 The evidence suggests that unequal distribution between national key and other universities among students from different social groups is closely related to uneven distribution of education resources in primary and secondary schools to which students from the disadvantaged groups have fewer opportunities to access key schools as well. To alleviate education inequality at tertiary level, the central government has decided to abolish the distinction between key and normal schools to ensure more equal distribution of education resources. Whether the new government policy is effective in practice remains to be seen.

References

Adorno, T.W. (1973), *Negative Dialectics*, London: Routledge & Kegan Paul.

Apple, M.W. (2004), Creating difference: Neo-liberalism, neo-conservatism and the politics of educational reform, *Educational Politics*, 18(1): 12–44.

Bourdieu, P. (1977), Cultural reproduction and social reproduction, in Karabel, J. and Halsey, A.H. (eds) *Power and Ideology, Society and Culture*, London: Sage, pp. 487–511.

Bourdieu, P. (1986), The forms of capital, in Richardson, J. (ed.) *Handbook of Theory and Research for the Sociology of Education*, New York: Greenwood, pp. 241–258.

Braziel, J.E. and Mannur, A. (2003), Nation, migration, globalisation: Points of contention in diaspora studies, in Braziel, J.E. and Mannur, A. (eds) *Theorizing Diaspora*, Malden, MA: Blackwell, pp. 1–22.

Brown, P. and Tannock, S. (2009), Education, meritocracy and the global war for talent, *Journal of Education Policy*, 24(4): 377–392.

Brubaker, M.D., Puig, A., Reese, R.F. and Young, J. (2010), Integrating social justice into counselling theories pedagogy: A case example, *Counsellor Education and Supervision*, 50: 88–100.

European Science Foundation (ESF) (2008), Higher education looking forward: An agenda for future research. Available online at: www.esf.org/fileadmin/Public_documents/Publications/HELF_01.pdf (accessed 16 September 2014).

Furlong, A. and Cartmel, F. (2009), *Higher Education and Social Justice*, Maidenhead: Open University Press.

Harkavy, I. (2006), The role of universities in advancing citizenship and social justice in the 21st century, *Education, Citizenship and Social Justice*, 5: 5–37.

Hayhoe, R. (2006), *Portraits of Influential Chinese Educators*, CERC Studies in Comparative Education 17, Hong Kong: Comparative Education Research Centre.

Jacob, W.J. (2006), Social justice in Chinese higher education: Regional issues of equality and access, *International Review of Education*, 52(1/2): 149–169.

Klein, J. (2011), *Tertiary Education: A global report*, EdStats, Education Advisory Service, World Bank.

Li, F. and Morgan, W.J., (2011), Private higher education in China: Problems and possibilities, in Morgan, W.J. and Wu, B. (eds) *Higher Education Reform in China: Beyond the expansion*, London and New York: Routledge, pp. 66–78.

Li, F., Morgan, W.J. and Ding, X. (2011), The labour market for graduates in China, in Morgan, W.J. and Wu, B. (eds) *Higher Education Reform in China: Beyond the expansion*, London and New York: Routledge, pp. 99–108.

Lunt, I. (2008), Beyond tuition fees? The legacy of Blair's government to higher education, *Oxford Review of Education*, 34(6): 742–752.

McArthur, J. (2010), Achieving social justice within and through high education: The challenge for critical pedagogy, *Teaching in Higher Education*, 15(5): 493–504.

Marginson, S. (2004), Competition and markets in higher education: A 'glocal' analysis, *Policy Futures in Education*, 2(2): 175–244.

Marginson, S. (ed.) (2007), *Prospects of Higher Education: Globalisation, market competition and public goods and the future of the university*, Rotterdam: Sense Publishers.

Ministry of Education (MoE) (2012), Ministry of Education's guidance and measures for a comprehensive improvement of the quality of higher education in China (in Chinese). Available online at: www.hie.edu.cn/zcfg_detail.php?id=845 (accessed 17 September 2014).

Ministry of Education (MoE) (2014), Annual statistical report of national education development in China 2013 (in Chinese). Available online at: www.moe.gov.cn/publicfiles/business/htmlfiles/moe/moe_633/201407/171144.html (accessed 21 August 2014).

Mohrman, K., Ma, W. and Baker, D. (2008),The research university in transition: The emerging global model, *Higher Education Policy*, 21: 5–27.

Morgan, W.J. (2003), *Communists on Education and Culture 1848–1948*, London and New York and Basingstoke: Palgrave Macmillan.

Ryan, J. (ed.) (2011), *China's Higher Education Reform and Internationalisation*, London and New York: Routledge, pp. 34–47.

Sen, A. (1992), *Inequality Re-examination*, Oxford: Oxford University Press.

Sen, A. (2010), *The Idea of Justice*, London: Penguin.

Sheng, X. (2014), *Higher Education Choice in China: Social stratification, gender and education inequality*, London and New York: Routledge.

Singh, M. (2011), The place of social justice in higher education and social change discourses, *Compare*, 41(4): 481–494.

Stehr, N. (1994), *Knowledge Societies*, London: Sage.

Sunny Daxuesheng Network (SUNDXS) (2014), Situation of Chinese graduates in job hunting in 2014 (in Chinese), 4 June 2014. Available online at: www.sundxs.com/dxslz/jiuye/8197.html (accessed 21 August 2014).

Trow, M. (2006), Reflection on the transition from elite to mass to universal education access: Forms and phases of higher education in modern societies since WWII, in James, J., Forest, F., Phillip, G. and Altbach, P. (eds) *International Handbook of Higher Education*, Amsterdam: Springer.

Valimaa, J. and Hoffman, D. (2008), Knowledge society discourse and higher education, *Higher Education*, 56: 265–285.

Vincent, C. (2003), *Social Justice, Education and Identity*, London and New York: Routledge.

Wang, N. and Morgan, W.J. (2012), The harmonious society, social capital and lifelong learning in China: Emerging policies and practice, *International Journal of Continuing Education and Lifelong Learning*, 4(2): 1–15.

Welch, A. and Cai, H. (2011), Enter the dragon: The internationalisation of China's higher education system, in Ryan, J. (ed.) *China's Higher Education Reform and Internationalisation*, London and New York: Routledge, pp. 9–33.

Wu, B. and Morgan, W.J. (2011), There's more to life than textbooks!, *The China Daily: European Weekly*, 18–24 November, p. 11.

Yang, R. (2011), Chinese ways of thinking in the transformation of China's higher education system, in Ryan, J. (ed.) *China's Higher Education Reform and Internationalisation*, London and New York: Routledge, pp. 34–47.

Young, I.M. (1990), *Justice and the Politics of Difference*, Princeton, NJ: Princeton University Press.

Zha, Q. (2011), China's move to mass higher education in a comparative perspective, *Compare*, 41(6): 751–768.

1 Social justice and Chinese higher education

What can the capability approach offer?

Zhen Li and John Lowe

Introduction

In this chapter we critically examine whether the capability approach to human development, as proposed by Sen and developed by Nussbaum and others, offers analytical insights or policy guidance in identifying and addressing issues of social justice in higher education in China. We can think of two good reasons for not attempting to do this.

The first reason is that the capability approach has evolved into multiple forms that differ in their interpretation and elaboration of Sen's original principles. There is no single capability approach to be addressed except, perhaps, at the level of basic concepts and principles, and even these have been subject to diverse interpretations. Two distinct names for the approach have emerged: the capability approach and the capabilities approach. These names reflect different heritages to some extent – Sen in the first case and Nussbaum in the second. We will draw upon both instances and, unless it is important to distinguish them, we will use 'CA' as a generic acronym; readers are welcome to read 'CA' in whatever way they wish. Associated with this diversity and debate is a daunting volume of literature on almost every aspect, interpretation or application of the approach. We cannot do full justice to this literature here and will be quite selective in the authors we cite; fortunately, the limited literature on CA in higher education makes this more justifiable.

Our second 'good reason' for being wary about adopting a critical perspective on CA is that politically and philosophically we have sympathy with the broad formulations of its underlying principles expressed in terms of enhanced individual freedom, agency and 'capability to live the sort of life and be the sort of person one has reason to value' (Sen, 1999). CA is closely associated with the human development challenge to narrowly economistic approaches to national development and their replacement or supplementation by a fuller, more humane conception of human existence, expressed in terms such as 'well-being' and 'human flourishing'. Furthermore, in their respective paradigmatic formulations of CA, both Sen and Nussbaum are guided by a fundamental concern for the equitable distribution of development outcomes; that is, a concern for social justice. We intuitively endorse these aspects of CA and its association with social justice and the human development approach, and are loath to appear reactionary in adopting too critical a stance.

Paradoxically, this second source of our reluctance is also a stimulus to engage with CA to analyse China's higher education development and reform. It is a simplification that nonetheless captures much of the truth to state that China's historically unparalleled development over the past 30 years or so has been driven by a single-minded focus on economic development, notably GDP expansion. We might question, however, whether China's economic success has been at the expense of measures of human well-being that are valued in the human development approach and which underpin CA; or, alternatively, whether China's success presents a challenge to CA and the human development approach as an effective basis for development policy and the measurement of developmental achievement. These are very broad questions and higher education may seem to be an inappropriate context for addressing them. We will try to show, however, that moving away from what are undeniably the most important human development issues, such as health, basic education, security and nutrition, leads us to challenge aspects of both CA and China's recent development path.

Capability/capabilities approach: a critical overview

At the heart of the capability approach is the recognition and celebration of the diversity and complexity of human beings and of how they wish to build lives that are meaningful to themselves. To encompass this human diversity and complexity, Sen (1999: 18) argues that individuals must have the freedom to do the things and live the kind of life that they have reason to value; the extent to which all members of a society enjoy the freedom to do so is a measure of its 'success'. This position provides the *normative* component of the capability approach, but Sen further argues that the possession and exercise of such individual freedoms is the most effective means of engaging people in social development: 'Greater freedom enhances the ability of people to help themselves and also to influence the world' (ibid.). This is his *effectiveness* argument for the validity of the approach. Three points emerge from Sen's discussion of freedom as both the source and the measure of development. The first is his emphasis on 'positive' freedoms to do what one chooses over 'negative' freedoms from undesirables such as hunger and disease. Second, positive freedoms are seen as the means of releasing individuals' powers of agency to control their own lives. Finally, the combination of these two and the normative stance of the capability approach means that the CA is inevitably concerned with developing a more equitable world; that is, with issues of social justice.

The attention to positive freedoms leads us to the most distinctive concepts in the capability approach: those of 'capabilities' and 'functionings'. These are the operationalisations of Sen's notions of freedom and individual agency. Functionings are 'the various things a person may value being or doing', while an individual's capabilities are 'the alternative combinations of functionings that are feasible for her to achieve' (Sen, 1999: 75). So far so good, but Sen sows some seeds of confusion in his further use and elaboration of the terms. He goes on to write about 'realized functionings', which are the *actual* achievements of the individual and which he confusingly describes as 'what a person is actually able to do'. He contrasts this with the 'capability set' or 'her real opportunities', and he gives an example in which 'functioning achievement' seems to mean just 'what you do' rather that 'what you value doing' (ibid.: 75). Essentially, an individual's capability set provides her with options and the freedom to choose from alternative functionings, and an expansion of that capability set represents an increase in her personal freedom. Sen argues that actual functionings (by which he seems to mean 'achieved' functionings or simply 'what you do') indicate freedom only if they are the intended result of a 'free' choice of something the individual wishes to do or be, and this freedom of choice arises from the possession of an enhanced capability set. The size and diversity of one's capability set is a measure of the degree of one's personal freedom; the functionings that one achieves – as long as they are the result of choices of what one has reason to value – are an indicator of one's personal powers of agency.

Nussbaum's capabilities approach (in which the plural form is deliberately chosen) shares Sen's basic concepts but differs in key respects that to some extent reflect their different academic origins in philosophy and economics respectively. Her fundamental concern is 'human dignity': its definition, development and distribution. She has ventured where Sen has been reluctant to tread by endorsing a particular ideology – political liberalism – and developing a list of ten central capabilities with minimum threshold levels that reflect 'a life worthy of human dignity' (Nussbaum, 2011: 32).[1] Sen's reluctance to develop lists of capabilities reflects his more pragmatic policy and practice orientation, in which he wishes to leave room for capabilities to be chosen to meet specific contextual needs and to respect the diversity of priorities among different agents (Alkire, 2005). Similarly, he insists that CA is relevant to and applicable across a wide range of political ideologies and systems, although these must, presumably, all observe his primary insistence upon respect for individual agents' choice in forming their own lives.

Gasper (2002) helpfully proposes three distinct meanings of 'capabilities': what he calls S-, O- and P-capabilities. S-capability refers to 'an everyday meaning: capacity, skill, ability, aptitude' (p. 446). O-capability denotes 'the set of life paths attainable for a given person ... options and opportunities' (ibid.). P-capability is referred to as 'potential', presumably implying innate capacities that require some form of training or nurturing to turn them into S-capabilities. Somewhat similarly, Nussbaum makes a distinction between 'internal' (Gasper's S- and P-) capabilities and 'external' (O-) capabilities, although we are less convinced that her central capabilities are actually all capabilities and not functionings, or even, as she suggests, 'a species of human rights' (Nussbaum, 2000). It is important to distinguish between these possible meanings, as they each denote different ways in which a capability may be denied or become unrealisable in practice. As we will see, the distinction is particularly important when we consider CA and education.

One of the reasons for the rather cavalier use of certain terms in both Sen's and Nussbaum's work is that neither version of CA is grounded in an adequate theorisation of society and the social. The operation of society is largely portrayed as an aggregation of individuals – more or less free agents – engaged in processes of 'choosing' to suit their own preferences and to achieve some individually desired form of living. 'Institutions' do appear in their accounts but largely as inhibitors of free agency. There are clear family resemblances between Sen's model and rational choice theory, which is perhaps not surprising given his background in economics. There is a huge difference in the object of the choice-making in the two accounts, with rational choice theory based on a one-dimensional model of *homo economicus*, but the processes by which social life operates (to the extent that the social is recognised) are remarkably similar. We endorse Sayer's opinion that such accounts 'reduce [the social world] to a few basic structures and are oblivious to the complexity, openness and ambiguity of social action' (Sayer, 2000: 30).

It is revealing to note that Sen feels obliged to explain that he uses the term 'agency' not with a meaning that economists might commonly recognise but in the sense that sociologists would take for granted: that of the power of an individual to act and bring about change of a form that she intends (Sen, 1999: 19). Despite this, an element of the conventional economistic approach remains in Sen's interpretation of agency in his emphasis – both analytical and normative – on the individual as a 'free' agent. Discussions of 'institutions' – or 'structures', in the common terminology of sociologists – tend to focus on those that limit the capacity of individuals to choose and act in a way that they wish, frustrating the goal of individual freedom. There is little recognition of the capacity for social structures to empower the individual agent as well as to constrain, or of the fact that both agents and their capabilities – options – are dependent on society for their very existence. We are not advocating any form of social determinism here – far from it – but rather an engagement of CA with some of the theorisations of the structure–agency relationships that have exercised sociologists for many years.

Capabilities and social justice

The notion of social justice is fundamental to CA, whichever version we examine. Sen's work has returned ethical considerations to the heart of economics; ethical considerations and the nature of 'a good life' have always been at the core of Nussbaum's intellectual work. Both Sen and Nussbaum maintain that human capabilities are the preferred 'currency' (Kaufman, 2006: 2) of social justice and distributional equity, rather than 'utility' or 'resources', although Nussbaum (2003: 35) maintains that Sen's reluctance to commit himself on the substance of core capabilities limits the guidance his approach offers in operationalising social justice. We would add a further observation that the primacy afforded to 'freedom of choice' in CA fits perfectly with Hayekian neo-liberalism, but Hayek himself rejected the term social justice as a 'mirage', 'devoid of meaning or content' (Hayek, 1976: 96); unlike Nussbaum, Sen's lack of commitment to even a broad ideological position leaves his version of CA open to subversion of its ethical foundations.

Both Sen and Nussbaum insist that it is the distribution of capabilities and not functionings that is important for social justice; they wish to leave individuals with the option of not realising a capability in practice *if they so wish*. They issue some caveats about this primacy of individual choice and of capabilities over functionings, however. First of all, the non-realisation of capabilities must be a 'reasonable' and 'reasoned' choice on the part of the individual and not based on some sort of false consciousness or lack of reasoning capacity. This easily leads us into 'grey areas' and questions about who judges whether a choice is reasonable, where there is considerable scope for cultural and intellectual arrogance and paternalism (Deneulin, 2002). Nussbaum does, however, argue for exceptions in which governments should demand actual functionings, among which is education up until the age of at least 16 (Nussbaum, 2011: 156). It is 'childhood' which allows this exception, as children are deemed not only to be incapable of making independent, reasoned choices but are also open to economic exploitation by their parents. This is an interesting exception for two reasons: first of all because the definition of 'childhood' is open to cultural variation; and second, because she advocates that the decision-making be taken away from parents or other family members and handed over to the 'institution' of government.

There are difficulties with taking capabilities rather than functionings (that is, capabilities turned into actions) as the currency of social justice. One is simply practical: how does one measure capability in order to determine whether it is equitably distributed if it remains unrealised in practice? Functionings can be observed; capabilities cannot – at least, not directly. Sen and Nussbaum wish to allow individuals to make their own choices and so they must be allowed *not* to turn a capability into a functioning if they so choose. Suppose, however, that a large proportion of a subgroup in a society – ethnic, religious, social class, gender, or some combination of these characteristics – were observed not to be taking up a particular functioning, even though the capability (at least the formal O-capability, or opportunity) is deemed to exist. An example of this would be the low take-up of higher education by working-class boys in the UK, even though the 'external' (Nussbaum) or O- (Gaspar) capability exists and even in many cases when the internal or S-capability exists in the form of appropriate qualifications. In response we may suspect that there is a previously unidentified impediment to participation in operation – some version of 'culture' is a common target – that actually denies the capability that was assumed to exist. The point is that it is the absence of actual functionings of the group that alerts us to the absence of genuine capability.

An alternative reaction to such a situation may be to deny that there is a breach of social justice: 'they could if they wished, but obviously they don't want to'. We have heard this argument presented about scheduled castes in India and minorities (*shaoshu minzu*) in China in relation to their relatively poor representation in education. Even if we were to accept this position, should we feel obliged to question the rationality or 'reasoned nature' of the choice that such a group has made? But on whose grounds would we judge the reasoning behind the choice, which may reflect particular cultural values that are not shared by others? Do we encourage or compel such groups to make different choices on our understanding that it is to their advantage to change, or do we respect the 'freedom to choose' above all other considerations? These are not fanciful questions but ones we will exemplify in our consideration of higher education in China and whether or not CA provides an adequate basis on which to answer them.

CA provides us with a currency in which to measure social justice: the freedom 'to choose a life one has reason to value' (Sen, 1999: 74). In Nussbaum's version this appears as the freedom to live a life of dignity and self-respect, but, through their (more or less) shared subscription to the concept of 'capability', these two are largely the same. Any model of social justice must also adopt a position on how the currency is to be distributed: do we attempt to maximise everyone's holdings at roughly equal levels, or do we define a 'sufficient' level for all and not concern ourselves with distribution beyond this level? In terms of the distribution of capabilities, Nussbaum appears to be primarily concerned with identifying minimum 'sufficient' levels of her ten basic capabilities, with less concern for what happens beyond these levels. Sen's position is more ambiguous, as reflected in his reluctance to specify capabilities or to endorse a particular political position. This question of distribution can be particularly difficult when we are dealing with education because of its dual position as a capability in itself and as a means of access to other capabilities, as we shall see.

The capability approach and higher education

The lack of adequate recognition of 'the social' in CA that we referred to earlier in general terms emerges in its treatment of education. Formal education in modern society serves purposes other than those of individuals. It is an essential component in the operation and management of complex modern societies, contributing to their maintenance but also potentially providing a means for their transformation. If we step outside CA and consider the relationship between education and 'opportunity' from a society's perspective, we see that it plays a powerful role in the regulation of access to opportunity. From a CA stance this 'regulation' might be portrayed and condemned as restricting personal freedoms, but this is naïve. Opportunities/capabilities are not limitless; they are often finite in number and, as a general rule, the fewer they are, the more desirable they are (Hirsch, 1977). We cannot assume that the distribution of the diversity among individuals in what they value will match the distribution of actual opportunities available, so that a naïve interpretation of CA implying that everyone should have the capability to choose what they value may be unachievable in practice. In this situation there must as a minimum be some form of selection, with its necessary accompaniment of rejection. Since frustration among a large proportion of the population to achieve that which they (have reason to) desire is potentially highly destabilising, some form of 'desire management' is likely to be developed or to emerge. Formal education in most societies has been given a central role in both selection/rejection and desire management – of 'legitimating exclusion' and 'cooling out ambition', in Broadfoot's (1996) terms. Note that the nature of these selection and management processes will depend on the political system in place, since they are a manifestation of the distribution of power in a society (Bernstein, 1971), but the need for them is uniform, whether organised as a 'free' market or through a more or less authoritarian form of government. For those of us working in education, these observations and consequences are not new, having been expounded from a variety of perspectives for more than 40 years.

The most concise summary of the status of education in CA is a five-page section of Nussbaum's 'Creating Capabilities' (2011: 152–157). Among the more significant points in Nussbaum's account is the recognition of education as occupying a special position in the CA canon for two reasons: education is both a valuable capability in itself and 'pivotal to the development and exercise of many other human capabilities' (ibid.: 152). This recognition of the role of education in developing other capabilities leads Nussbaum to place particular importance on the content of education – on curriculum and pedagogy. She provides a general goal for education in keeping with the principles of CA as being that of 'creating young adults who are free to engage with life in a wide range of ways'. Elsewhere she expresses a strong commitment to the inclusion of 'liberal arts' or 'humanities' in the education of all young people, as part of educating for a democratic society, critical citizenship, global citizenship and creativity, and as a counterblast to human capital-driven higher education policy and practice (Nussbaum, 2010).

This is also a point of departure for Walker (2012a), who has researched and written extensively on the critical application of CA to higher education, notably in South Africa (Walker, 2010, 2012b, 2012c). She laments the dominant human capital 'idea that a university education is instrumentally a means to something else' (Walker, 2012a: 452), but it becomes clear that what she objects to is the narrowly economic nature of this 'something else' rather than the instrumentality per se. Instrumentality is after all what is implied by recognising that education is a means to develop other capabilities; that is, education is a means of access to a form of living that one has reason to value and which one 'freely' chooses. This is emphasised in Walker's insistence in the same article that, despite 'Nussbaum and Sen's emphasis on capability', it is functionings – 'how people actually spend their lives' and 'what [students] actually do and are' – that are the measures of development (Walker, 2012a: 453).

If we ask what contribution CA can make to considerations of social justice and higher education, there would appear to be two options. The first is to accept that higher education is a capability in itself and to query the distribution of access to it. Nussbaum's position on this seems to offer little new information. Although education at any level is likely (if it is any good) to contribute to the development of capabilities on her list of those that 'must' be available to ensure human dignity, her commentaries on the list make it clear that she does not expect anything higher than 'basic education' (perhaps up to the age of 16) to be part of her threshold capabilities. Her political and philosophical writings make it clear that she would wish to see 'group-blind' access to higher education, but she does not appear to address how this might be achieved. For CA advocates of maximising capabilities for all, the question arises as to whether the expansion of higher education should be 'allowed' or even encouraged to take place until demand is satisfied, or whether some means of regulating demand should be imposed or allowed to develop.

An alternative approach is that advocated by Melanie Walker and her colleagues, in which social justice is to be promoted *through* rather than directly *in* higher education. This entails trying to develop critical social awareness among university students and 'hoping' that they will go on to act on this awareness in their subsequent professional roles, becoming 'caring' professionals and choosing to act for the benefit of society as a whole but particularly for the most disadvantaged rather than acting simply in their own interest. It is a trust in critical reflexivity as an additional, internal capacity that will somehow address the external structural limits to the equitable distribution of capabilities more generally; ultimately, it hopes that the exercise of power that comes with such professional positions will be benevolent.[2]

Working from a CA perspective, Walker and her colleagues must avoid any hint of indoctrination in their approach as this would compromise the capabilities of the students. They are aware of this and the consequential loss of control over the longer term outcomes that they seek. Apart from this inherent uncertainty in its long-term effectiveness in achieving its action goals and not just its consciousness-raising goals, we have other concerns about this approach. It is an inversion of Freire's 'conscientisation' approach to education, aiming to raise awareness of social inequities in the consciousness of the future élite rather than the 'oppressed' (Freire, 1972). As such, it advocates using the current inequitable distribution of power to address that same inequity. Whereas the dispossessed have little to lose in a struggle to gain human dignity, élites may be more cautious about dispersing and dissipating the power which they enjoy. At the very least it runs the risk of promoting a paternalistic attitude among these future professionals, dispensing largesse when it does not compromise their own position and their ability to hand on their advantage to their own children.

Capabilities and higher education in China

Adopting the view of both Nussbaum and Sen, namely that education is a capability in itself and a means of accessing other capabilities, leads us to ask two related questions about social justice in higher education in China: Is access to higher education equitably distributed and does it provide equitable access to subsequent capabilities for all those who do gain access to it? It is not realistic, given the current level of development in China, to ask the first question in the form 'Is higher education available to all?', but we can ask whether there are any systematic differences in access rates that are based on group membership. The second question is partly about the distribution of educational quality across higher education institutions but also involves something more than this, as we will try to show.

The huge expansion of HE enrolments that has taken place in China since the late 1990s – from under 4 per cent to over 20 per cent of the age cohort since 1990 – is an undoubted extension of capability to a greater proportion of young people, but this extension has not been uniformly shared across various population groups. It has also gone hand-in-hand with a deliberate accentuation of a hierarchy of quality and esteem across Chinese universities, as highlighted by the '985' and '211' projects, which has tended to counteract the potential for greater social justice in such an expansion of access (Zha, 2011). The key 'dimensions' of inequity in both access and quality of provision have been variously identified as location (East–West, rural–urban), social class, 'national' identity (sometimes expressed as Han-minorities, although this dimension is more complex than this simple dichotomy), differences in wealth (private and provincial) and gender (Yang *et al.*, 2014; H. Wang, 2011; L. Wang, 2011; Guo *et al.*, 2010; Yao *et al.*, 2010; Liu and Li, 2010; Jacob, 2006). Among others, both Wang (2010) and Yao *et al.* (2010) identify aspects of recent higher education reform as being largely responsible for a deepening of inequality and social injustice, notably decentralisation and marketisation.

As an illustration of how CA might provide further insight into the nature of social injustice in Chinese higher education, we will look at just two of these dimensions of inequity: gender and nationality status. We recognise that there is very considerable overlap and interaction between the various dimensions however, and our purpose is simply that of examining possible insights available from a CA approach rather than offering a complete analysis of the manifestation of inequities in Chinese higher education. We will also look at the potential in the Chinese context of the approach advocated by Walker and her colleagues for addressing social injustice through rather than in higher education.

Gender

By 2012, over half (51.2%) of students in tertiary education in China were female (NBS, 2013). Given the predominance of young males in the Chinese population as a whole, this figure suggests that females are 'over-represented' in higher education in China and, if there is gender-based inequity of access, currently it would appear to act against male students. Closer examination of the data – when the data can be located – and of research into the experiences of female students makes it clear, however, that the situation is more complicated than this overall figure for enrolment would suggest.

First of all, if we look at different levels of higher education, we find a slight but significant predominance of female students for both undergraduate and taught postgraduate (Master's) degrees: 51.35 per cent and 51.46 per cent respectively in 2012 (NBS, 2013). But something happens after Master's level, with women accounting for only 36.45 per cent of doctoral degree students – not only a reversal of apparent advantage but a massive swing in favour of male students. This does not appear to be simply due to a delay in the improved position of women working its way up the degree hierarchy, since the same pattern has persisted for many years.

Second, if we look at the distribution across different subjects by gender we get a rather different picture. Drawing upon data from 2005 (Guo *et al.*, 2010), reveals significant disparities in the gender distribution of students by major being studied. We have been unable to locate more recent data but have reason to believe that the broad picture is unlikely to have changed very much since then. The 2005 data reveal considerable over-representation of women in liberal arts (62.4%), a slight majority (52.0%) in social sciences, a minority (42.5%) in science and technology subjects, and a massive under-representation (22.5%) in engineering. Furthermore, Guo *et al.* reveal that the female students who did take engineering significantly out-performed their male classmates 'in both general course grades and English proficiency tests' (Guo *et al.*, 2010: 234; Liu and Li, 2010).

What might we make of these brief statistical indicators from a CA perspective? The overall enrolment rates and the existence of a national directive against gender discrimination in recruitment (Sharma, 2013) indicate that if we take participation in higher education as a capability in its own right, then it is a capability that is equally available to both men and women. It also appears to be a capability that is being equitably converted into an 'achieved functioning'. Looking at the gender distribution across different majors however, we might come to a different conclusion: the directive against gender discrimination in enrolment applies uniformly across all majors, so we may conclude that there is equal capability (in its O- or external sense) among men and women to choose their study major. The unequal distribution of actual choice (unequal conversion to actual functioning) still remains to be explained however. Is it a 'free' choice based on actual preferences? Does it reflect 'natural' gender-based inclinations? Or are there other forces at work which mean that actual capabilities (options) are not gender-blind? We need to probe more deeply.

The high level of achievement by female engineering students certainly suggests that there is no 'natural' shortage of aptitude or ability to engage with engineering as a subject. In some universities at least however, this superior female performance may be predictable from the admissions procedures: despite regulations and a specific directive to the contrary, some universities are openly using gender-differentiated admissions criteria by setting significantly higher cut-off scores for the recruitment of female students in some subjects (Sharma, 2013). These universities include many of the elite '211' and '985' institutions. It is possible that the observed differences in achieved functionings may indeed reflect reduced capability sets for women in higher education brought about by the operation of differential admissions criteria. We need to probe deeper still.

In addition to the different take-up rates in study majors, Guo *et al.* (2010) also found that, despite their superior degree grades, female graduates in engineering had significantly lower employment rates and lower starting salaries than male graduates. Several studies have reported similar gender discrimination in employment and the ways in which it operates across a wider range of special-isms (Liu and Li, 2010; Turner, 2006). Sharma (2013) reports a project leader from the Chinese NGO, Media Monitor for Women Network declaring that some universities deliberately discriminate against female applicants in subjects where they outnumber men 'because male graduates are more employable than their female counterparts'.[3] This and other research into the experiences of female university students in China suggests very strongly that the 'formal' equity in higher education as a 'capability' is something of an illusion.

To understand better why this is so, we must look at the wider discourse on gender and, in particular, the discursive production of gender identity in con-temporary China, which challenges to the point of subversion the formal, state-declared position on gender equality. This is a vast area that still requires much more critical research to be carried out in a wide range of fields, and all we can do here is pick out a few pointers. A good starting point that has particular relevance to this discussion of women in higher education is the widely used term 'leftover women' (*sheng nü*). This is used to denote women who remain unmarried after the age of 27.[4] It is difficult to underestimate the pressures that Chinese women face from their family, friends, the media and even the state to get married while they are still 'young'. Any desire to prolong their education and delay marriage is seen as almost pathological. Fincher (2014) quotes the website of the All-China Women's Federation, an organ of the Party charged with protecting women's rights and interests, which contained the following post in March, 2011:

> Pretty girls don't need a lot of education to marry into a rich and powerful family, but girls with an average or ugly appearance will find it difficult. These kinds of girls hope to further their education in order to increase their competitiveness. The tragedy is, they don't realize that as women age, they are worth less and less, so by the time they get their M.A. or Ph.D., they are already old, like yellowed pearls.
>
> (Fincher, 2014: 9)

Women know that they will find it harder than men to get started on a career and may strive both to outperform men at university and to extend their education to a postgraduate degree in order to make up for their 'inherent disadvantage' in the labour market, but at the same time they are constantly reminded of the 'necessity' to marry as soon as they can and start a family. The way in which female univer-sity enrolments 'drop off a cliff' in comparison with male enrolments at doctoral level now makes sense: doing a PhD will take one beyond the 'cut-off' age of eli-gibility for marriage. Besides, it is widely held that men will not want to marry a woman who is 'too highly educated': a commonly repeated aphorism is that there are three kinds of people in China: 'men, women and women with a PhD'.

This brief account cannot do justice to the complexity of issues of gender in Chinese (or, indeed, any) society and how they impinge upon opportunity/capability – in this case in higher education. We have suggested how social discourses and other 'structures' influence both access to higher education as a capability in itself but also those 'capabilities' (work and family life, as well as others) that higher education may be expected to open up. There are perhaps two points which we believe this discussion illustrates: the need to be aware of 'functionings' as the uptake of capabilities and not just capabilities themselves, and the need for a CA perspective to engage with an in-depth, nuanced (and theorised) understanding of the operations and interactions of social structures and individual agencies in specific contexts, if it is to provide useful insights (Allen, 2012; de Herdt and Deneulin, 2007).

'Nationality status'

A significant source of inequity in HE and in China more broadly is minority ethnic group membership (*shaoshu minzu*).[5] Inequalities in HE access and achievement among China's ethnic minority groups are an interesting case to examine from the CA perspective because they instantiate a problem with CA's focus on individual 'choice' as the ultimate freedom. The protection and preservation of minority cultures is written into the Chinese Constitution, although the interpretation of this in practice is largely limited to 'language, art and festivals' in a 'Disneyfication' of these cultures.[6] Minorities are allowed to be educated through the medium of their own language if they wish, although they must also learn Mandarin (*Putonghua*). There are 'minorities universities' offering both cultural studies and mainstream courses, and lower entry requirements are set for minorities compared with those for Han students. This is presented as evidence of respect for and promotion of minority linguistic and cultural rights; indeed, a Han student told one of us that allowing minority students to go to university with lower college entrance examination (*gaokao*) scores is evidence of the absence of racism in China. Furthermore, minority student graduates are more or less guaranteed employment in local government administrations in their home areas.

In CA terms these educational arrangements clearly promote an important capability set related to identity and citizenship among minority group students. They do so, however, at the expense of a capability set of economic opportunity and national political power. In a study of students at the Central University of Nationalities, Clothey (2005) found that the students often internalised a sense of their own backwardness from experiences in the education system. This led them to believe that only by adapting – or trying to adapt – to the dominant Han social structure could they hope to 'succeed' in wider Chinese society. That is, only by abandoning their cultural capabilities could they hope to share in the economic and political capabilities of the Han majority.

In contrast, Yi and Wang (2012) studied the experiences of Tibetan students who had followed the *neidi ban* programme in which they opted for Putonghua-medium high school education – thereby compromising their connections to their own linguistic and cultural heritage – and went on to study in a Han-dominated university outside of the Tibetan Autonomous Republic in which Putonghua is the medium of instruction and dominant social language. The *neidi ban* programme is intended to promote wider economic participation by minority students but this is very limited in practice. Once again, the overall experience for these Tibetan students tended to reduce their sense of self-worth and they sought to regain 'biographical continuity' and 'ontological security' by re-engaging with Tibetan culture through their own initiative. Yi and Wang (2012) comment that these 'Tibetan undergraduate students lacked adequate support from the social system that tends to reduce diversity to homogeneity (usually in the name of creating a harmonious society) [and] ... the pedagogical framework of the party-state that discourages alternative forms of citizenship' (Yi and Wang, 2012: 78).

These examples emphasise the point that different capability sets may be mutually exclusive, at least when an attempt is made to turn them into functionings. The minority students in both cases are faced with a choice of fully realising either their 'cultural capability set' or an 'economic and political capability set', but not both. To some extent we might endorse Yi and Wang's comment on the inflexibility of the party-state and lay the blame for this 'clash of capabilities' there, but this is an over-simplification of a situation faced by minorities in many countries (and by governments who, often through goodwill, wish to do something about it). It is also a particular example of a wider phenomenon in which choices between incompatible capability sets must be made. We may try to take action to reduce the incompatibility – the provision of childcare facilities for mothers who do not want childbirth to interrupt their career is a commonly discussed example – but there are often only limited possibilities available, at best. CA's tendency to reduce such complex situations to the expansion of 'free choice' as the holy grail of development is ultimately neither realistic nor helpful, and a fuller appreciation of human society is needed to understand such phenomena and to inform policy and action to reduce their potential for furthering social injustice.

In a study of minority groups in different kinds of universities, Zhao (2010) points out how Chinese universities themselves are complicit in the narrowing of their role in society. He argues that universities see their role in citizenship education as promoting loyalty to the state and enhancing students' job market competitive advantages. He suggests that in the former role the universities are largely failing to meet minority students' needs for their own sense of identity, which they will increasingly seek for themselves and within their own communities, leaving the economic role of the university as its sole relevance in their lives. We would argue that, in a sense, this is the position that many students in general – not just certain minority groups – are realising. The unprecedented development of China over the past three or four decades has been primarily and intentionally economic in nature; 'opening up' to the wider world has been carefully controlled and constrained largely to serve economic purposes. The controlled but extensive neo-liberalisation of the economy has not extended to political liberalism.

There has, therefore, been a massive expansion of options for employment, in the variety of occupations available as a result of the expansion of the economy, in the possibility for people to move to other regions and cities to work and in the ability of individuals to 'choose' their occupation rather than being allocated a job. This has come, however, at the cost of redundancy and unemployment for some and a reduction in job security for many; these take on particular signifi- cance in the lives of those whom they affect because of the limited provision of social security. Our experience of discussing employment aspirations with Chinese students suggests that, for many at least, the choice of occupation (often influenced in practice by parents) has less to do with 'what I would like to do' and more to do with occupational security, which offers greater guarantees of meeting more basic needs or capabilities.

This expansion of 'choice' in individuals' economic lives is not, therefore, the unequivocal 'good' that CA might propose it to be. This new 'capability' of being able to choose one's own career path is actually the 'capability' to *engage in a competition* for work and such competitions foster both winners and losers. Furthermore, the costs of losing and the benefits of winning feed back into the system to exacerbate inequality and consequent social injustice. The universities, as the distributors of the qualifications that give access to the most desirable and highly rewarded (and often most highly rewarding) occupations, are intimately implicated in these processes. In CA terms, they play a central role in the inequitable distribution of important capability sets.

In such a situation, it is hardly surprising and surely not reprehensible that students (and, we cannot emphasise too often, their parents) see universities primarily in vocational terms, as the only route to obtaining a 'desirable' job and its attendant social benefits. But, as Sayer (2012) points out, we should not be unthinkingly critical of this instrumentalism. Work occupies a large part of our lives and it is a 'reasonable' choice to seek work that either provides high returns or makes bearable the large amount of time we must spend doing it or, prefera- bly, both. Work, like education, is itself a capability that opens up further cap- abilities – social esteem, material resources, friends, marriage partners and so on, whether directly or indirectly. A 'good' job is likely to be an important part of the 'sort of life they would like to live' for most individuals and pursuing such a job through university study constitutes a 'reasonable' choice to make. This pursuit may shut off other options – the development of other capabilities – but this is the nature of the world, not a consequence of university study itself. One must make 'choices among choices', although such a statement overplays the role that choice actually plays in social activity: where opportunities are fewer in number than those who pursue them, many will miss out and must choose altern- atives. Unless we adopt the sort of radical proposal that Sayer suggests, and which involves a sort of rotation of occupational opportunities ('everyone gets a chance at the good jobs sometime'), this is inevitable, and to promise an altern- ative is deceitful.

Addressing social justice through higher education

If we turn from inequities in Chinese higher education to look at the Nussbaum/ Walker alternative of addressing wider social injustices *through* higher education by adopting a curriculum and pedagogy for critical awareness and action, the situation is possibly even more bleak (as judged from Nussbaum's/Walker's perspective at least). Just about the last thing the Chinese government wants is to raise the critical political and social awareness of university students; any politicisation through education is expected to be tightly regulated by the compulsory 'patriotic education' course. And, on the whole, the majority of students are happy to comply and to adopt – at least in public – a position of political apathy and conformity, but one which endorses the legitimacy of the party-state and can be mobilised by the Party when required. Reporting the results of a large survey of political and social attitudes among Chinese university students, Wang (2013) is of the opinion that pedagogical improvements in political education courses (that have traditionally been seen by students as boring and irrelevant) are at least partly responsible for the finding that:

> A sizeable proportion of [students] endorse the Party's view that social stability is the most important condition for China's continuing growth, and the view that upholding Party leadership is the key to maintaining stability and defending national interests.
>
> (Wang, 2013: 348–349)

We must be careful not to over-generalise from this observation, however. Using different methodologies from those adopted by Wang, Rosen (2010) reports a lack of unity in the belief systems held by Chinese youth and a pluralism of values that often appear contradictory. Internet activities such as 'spoofing' (*egao*) reveal elements of resistance to 'authoritative voices' and 'repackaged politically correct role models' (Rosen, 2010: 171), and party membership is seen more in individual instrumental than in ideological terms, matching a switch in party emphasis in its legitimacy claims from ideology to material success criteria.

Our own, admittedly less systematic observations suggest that Chinese students are probably no less or no more possessed of a social conscience than those in many other countries. We find, for example, an enthusiasm to engage with social action volunteer programmes in order to raise the living standards of disadvantaged communities in China and abroad. Political education programmes and campaigns in China have commonly urged such activities as a means to build a sense of national solidarity (and, in Mao's time, of an international solidarity with oppressed peasants and workers), as long as this remained interpreted by and under the control of the Party.[7] In terms of raising social consciousness and encouraging social engagement, such programmes may be at least as effective as the critical awareness pedagogy promoted by Walker and others, but they are anathema to CA precisely because they are 'closed', submissive to the party line rather than critical, thereby closing off rather than expanding scope for individual choice and capabilities.

Conclusion

The capabilities approach under Sen did not claim to be a complete theory of social justice, although it has been developed, by Nussbaum in particular, to be presented as such – a 'counter-theory' to those based on a one-dimensional view of human flourishing (Nussbaum, 2011). CA is labelled an 'approach', but an approach to what? An approach to the development of human welfare is probably the best answer in Sen's foundational work. Of central importance to CA, however, is the distribution of welfare within and between societies and not just aggregate or mean values, so that we are obliged to examine the means and mechanisms by which this distribution takes place if the approach is to have practical value. To do that we need a model, an understanding, a theory of society or societies and how they 'work', and this is certainly not what CA gives or claims to give us. It provides us with a new perspective, an alternative view of the nature and constituents of human welfare – or human well-being, or human flourishing, or simply of what it is to be human, depending on whose version of CA we use. We can examine this alternative and decide whether it is superior to measures such as GDP per capita (which has been the most widely used measure of social development), but this is only a starting point, and to continue further requires much more complex analytical machinery drawn from a range of disciplines – politics, economics, anthropology and sociology, for a start. Given our own intellectual interests and backgrounds, we would point out the particular need for sociological theory to inform both understanding of the distributional processes in societies and the means by which these may be altered – although we recognise that for the latter, we inevitably move into the realm of politics at least. Above all, though, we must go beyond the simple agency and choice models of social processes that permeate much of the writing on CA. Even if we are to accept agency and choice as valid currencies for the measure of social justice, we are not obliged to do so as the basis of a model of society and social operations. The enhancement of agency and choice may be accepted as desirable outcomes without seeing them as the sole or even primary components of our models of social processes.

There is a 'real world naivety' about the core model of social processes in CA in the prioritising of 'choice'. One's choices cannot be the only basis for action in a world of limited resources, conflicting interests (choices) and power. Beneath CA is an utopian vision of the world. That is not intended to insult those who strive to bring the minimum necessary for human flourishing or just life itself to the most disadvantaged. There, CA works as well as the notion of 'rights' in setting us immediate targets. But when we look at the 'luxury' end of the market, what is the ideal world that we are trying to achieve? Are we challenging the capitalist order, particularly in its neo-liberal manifestation? If not, then competition and selection, not choice, will be what graduates face.

From a Western political liberal position it is easy to identify the restrictions on capabilities imposed by the Chinese authoritarian political system while welcoming the apparent relaxation of capability restrictions in the economy. The reality in China is that the economy – to a large extent – now operates within the power structures of capitalism and capitalist markets, whereas power in other spheres remains centralised in the hands of the Party-state. The exercise of capabilities is, in reality, not the model of 'freedom' that Sen and Nussbaum suggest, although, as Dean (2009) expresses it, their account makes CA the 'beguiling concept' about which we expressed our reluctance to be too critical. Choices are made within and are strongly mediated by power structures. The source and distribution of power may vary with life sphere and across politico-economic systems, but it is a reality for us all and will be limiting of the exercise of 'free choice' in any system. Although the limitations on personal freedoms in important aspects of life in China are commonly pointed out, and would be seen as the denial of capabilities in CA, we should also recognise that '[i]n neoliberal hands, CA provides an appealingly humanistic cover for the neoliberal naturalization of capitalist domination and exploitation' (Sayer, 2012: 593).

Notes

1 Briefly, by their headings, the ten are: Life; Bodily health; Bodily integrity; Senses, imagination and thought; Emotions; Practical reason; Affiliation; Other species; Play; Control over one's environment – (1) political and (2) material.
2 Although Walker does not seem to address directly issues of social justice in the distribution of higher education, this would presumably emerge as one aspect of the more equitable distribution of capabilities/opportunities that her approach suggests.
3 There are in fact some occupations – notably mining and some other forms of engineering – that are 'officially' closed to women, along with their relevant university programmes.
4 Originally, 30 was more commonly taken as the cut-off age and we still often hear this, but this has progressively decreased in the public media, even heading towards 25 (Fincher, 2014: 20ff.).
5 We recognise this as an over-generalisation across all ethnic minorities when the truth is that the level of disadvantage varies enormously, perhaps to be virtually unidentifiable among some groups.
6 Our thanks to Dr David O'Brien for this term.
7 The way in which recent anti-Japanese demonstrations permitted and encouraged by the Party turned violent illustrate how this control may not be as absolute as is widely portrayed – or as the Party believes: the patriotism promoted through education and the media can too easily turn into violent nationalism.

References

Alkire, S. (2005), Why the capability approach?, *Journal of Human Development*, 6(1): 115–135.
Allen, N. (2012), Individual freedom and institutional frameworks in development, *Cambridge Journal of Education*, 42(3): 425–440.

Bernstein, B. (1971), On the classification and framing of educational knowledge. In Young, M.F.D. (ed.) *Knowledge and Control: New directions in the sociology of knowledge*, London: Collier Macmillan.

Broadfoot, P.M. (1996), *Education, Assessment and Society: A sociological analysis*, Buckingham: Open University Press.

Clothey, R. (2005), China's policies for minority nationalities in higher education: Negotiating national values and ethnic identities, *Comparative Education Review*, 49(3): 389–409.

de Herdt, T. and Deneulin, S. (2007), Guest editor's introduction, *Journal of Human Development*, 8(2): 179–184.

Dean, H. (2009), Critiquing capabilities: The distractions of a beguiling concept, *Critical Social Policy*, 29(2): 261–278.

Deneulin, S. (2002), Perfectionism, paternalism and liberalism in Sen and Nussbaum's capability approach, *Review of Political Economy*, 14(4): 497–518.

Fincher, L.H. (2014), *Leftover Women: The resurgence of gender inequality in China*, London: Zed Books.

Freire, P. (1972), *Pedagogy of the Oppressed*, Harmondsworth: Penguin.

Gasper, D. (2002), Is Sen's capability approach an adequate basis for considering human development? *Review of Political Economy*, 14(4): 435–461.

Guo, C., Tsang, M.C. and Ding, X. (2010), Gender disparities in science and engineering in Chinese universities, *Economics of Education Review*, 29: 225–235.

Hayek, F. (1976), *Law, Legislation and Liberty, Volume 2: The Mirage of Social Justice*, Chicago, IL: University of Chicago Press.

Hirsch, F. (1977), *Social Limits to Growth*, London: Routledge & Kegan Paul.

Jacob, W.J. (2006), Social justice in Chinese higher education: Regional issues of equity and access, *Review of Education*, 52: 149–169.

Kaufman, A. (2006), Introduction, in Kaufman, A. (ed.) *Capabilities Equality: Basic issues and problems*, London: Routledge.

Liu, B. and Li, Y. (2010), Opportunities and barriers: Gendered reality in Chinese higher education, *Frontiers of Education in China*, 5(2): 197–221.

National Bureau of Statistics (NBS) (2013), *Statistical Yearbook 2013*, Beijing: China Statistics Press.

Nussbaum, M.C. (2000), Aristotle, politics and human capabilities: A response to Antony, Arneson, Charlesworth and Mulgan, *Ethics*, 111: 102–140.

Nussbaum, M.C. (2003), Capabilities as fundamental entitlements: Sen and social justice, *Feminist Economics*, 9(2–3): 33–59.

Nussbaum, M.C. (2010), *Not for Profit: Why democracy needs the humanities*, Princeton, NJ: Princeton University Press.

Nussbaum, M.C. (2011), *Creating Capabilities: The human development approach*, Cambridge, MA: Belknap Press of Harvard University Press.

Rosen, S. (2010), Chinese youth and state–society relations, in Gries, P. and Rosen, S. (eds) *Chinese Politics: State, society and the market*, London: Routledge, pp. 160–178.

Sayer, A. (2000), *Realism and Social Science*, London: Sage.

Sayer, A. (2012), Capabilities, contributive injustice and unequal divisions of labour, *Journal of Human Development and Capabilities*, 13(4): 580–596.

Sen, A. (1999), *Development as Freedom*, Oxford: Oxford University Press.

Sharma, Y. (2013), Top universities break rules on gender discrimination, *World University News*, 284. Available online at: www.universityworldnews.com/article.php?story=20130823114249619.

Turner, Y. (2006), Swinging open or slamming shut? The implications of China's open-door policy for women, educational choice and work, *Journal of Education and Work*, 19(1): 47–65.

Walker, M. (2010), Critical capability pedagogies and university education, *Educational Philosophy and Theory*, 42(8): 898–917.

Walker, M. (2012a), Universities and a human development ethics: A capabilities approach to curriculum, *European Journal of Education*, 47(3): 448–461.

Walker, M. (2012b), Universities professional capabilities and contributions to the public good in South Africa, *Compare*, 42(6): 819–838.

Walker, M. (2012c), The possibilities for university-based public-good professional education: A case-study from South Africa based on the 'capability approach', *Studies in Higher Education*, 37(5): 585–601.

Wang, H. (2011), Access to higher education in China: Differences in opportunity, *Frontiers of Education in China*, 6(2): 227–247.

Wang, L. (2011), Social exclusion and inequality in higher education in China: A capability perspective, *International Journal of Educational Development*, 31: 277–286.

Wang, Q. (2013), Strengthening and professionalizing political education in China's higher education, *Journal of Contemporary China*, 22(80): 332–350.

Wang, Y. (2010), Value changes in an era of social transformation: College-educated Chinese youth, *Educational Studies*, 32(2): 233–240.

Yang, J., Huang, X. and Liu, X. (2014), An analysis of education inequality in China, *International Journal of Educational Development*, 37: 2–10.

Yao, S., Wu, B., Su, F. and Wang, J. (2010), The impact of higher education expansion on social justice in China: A spatial and inter-temporal analysis, *Journal of Contemporary China*, 19(67): 837–854.

Yi, L. and Wang, L. (2012), Cultivating self-worth among dislocated Tibetan undergraduate students in a Chinese Han-dominated national key university, *British Journal of Sociology of Education*, 33(1): 63–80.

Zha, Q. (2011), China's move to mass higher education in a comparative perspective, *Compare*, 41(6): 751–768.

Zhao, Z. (2010), Practices of citizenship rights among minority students at Chinese universities, *Cambridge Journal of Education*, 40(2): 131–144.

2 Social justice through financial distribution in China's universities

A student survey in Shaanxi Province[1]

Bin Wu and Bernadette Robinson

Introduction

Two key policy goals in the reform of higher education in China over the past decade have been the expansion of higher education and the cultivation of 'world-class' universities (MoE, 1998). Since 1998, gross enrolment (GER) in higher education has risen from 9.8 per cent (about one million students) to 15 per cent in 2002, a level of 'mass' higher education, and then further to 30 per cent in 2013 (MoE). This rapid increase has been driven by government policy, market demand, the activism of local governments and the self-interest of universities (Chan and Ngok, 2011). Existing universities expanded their intake and new institutions were set up, including private colleges. As with other countries expanding their higher education systems, the diversification of institutions and levels resulted, with stratification both as a consequence and a goal. Within China's stratified system of higher education, universities are commonly placed in one of three tiers according to status and quality. Tier 1 refers to national key universities (the élite universities chosen to participate in Project 211 or Project 985, two government-funded projects aimed at strengthening selected institutions to become world-class universities and research leaders in key disciplinary areas as a national priority).[2] Tier 2 refers to key universities owned by central government agencies (such as ministries of industry or telecommunications). Tier 3 refers to all other universities, usually the responsibility of provincial and prefectural governments. The huge concentration of government funding in selected élite universities, through Projects 985 and 211,with the aim of creating world-class universities and research centres, has increased the distance between the resultant tiers of university status. Some issues of equality and social justice have emerged as a result.

The concept of social justice has proved difficult to define, leading its critics such as the economist Hayek (1976) to dismiss it as 'a mirage'. Nonetheless, it has carried meaning for many in different contexts, generally revolving around themes of fairness, equality and human rights. Attempts to define social justice lead us into a complex landscape of differing concepts and theories (Patton *et al.*, 2010). One aspect relevant to higher education is that raised by Young

(1990), who argues that the term 'social justice' has become conflated with the concept of distributive justice, that is, the distribution of material goods such as resources, income or social position (Rawls, 1971). Patton *et al.* (2010: 268) also warn that:

> we can fall into the trap of equating social justice in higher education with distributive justice by exclusively focusing on distribution questions – numerical representation of minorities bodies among faculty, students, and administrators in universities/community colleges, college access, voice in the classroom, curricula, and so on – and ignore the social structures, processes, and institutional contexts that produce these distributions in the first place.

They state that in addition we need to understand the institutional processes, social relations and cultural norms at work, that is, the relational justice which structures society at individual and organisational levels.

Other critics, such as Young (1990) and Gewirtz (1998), also argue that while the concept of distributive justice includes a focus on equality of opportunity, outcomes, access, participation and the distribution of cultural and social capital, it fails to take account of the social structures and institutional arrangements that can often determine the distribution of resources. In other words, social justice in higher education involves several concepts in order to construct full understanding and a thorough analysis. This complex task is beyond the scope of this chapter but one small part of achieving understanding is through the experience and perceptions of those engaged in higher education, and for this reason our research focuses on one constituency: the students. We also bear in mind that in China the notion of social justice (*shehui gongping*) differs slightly from that in some Western countries and literature. While Western notions of equal opportunity are more likely to recognise that it may involve different treatment according to need and make a distinction between equity and equality, the Chinese concept places more emphasis on sameness, an equal share for everybody in a group (an emphasis which emerged in some of our survey responses).

Given the social and economic inequalities in Chinese society, especially at the level of household income, this chapter explores the distribution of financial support to university students together with their views on it. Why focus on this aspect? Research has shown the effect of college costs and financial aid on educational outcomes to be strong and multi-dimensional (Avery and Hoxby, 2003; Bettinger, 2004; Long, 2008); yet communication to students about costs and aid is often inadequate (Loyalka *et al.*, 2013; Shi *et al.*, 2007). Our research examined the distribution of financial support across students from different socio-economic backgrounds together with students' perceptions about equality of opportunity and fairness in the distribution of resources for students in higher education. We begin by reviewing the policy context and current system for enabling wider access to higher education through financial support. We then move on to describe the research undertaken, its method and findings. In the final section we draw some conclusions in relation to policy implementation and issues of social justice. The chapter focuses on three questions:

- Is financial support distributed equally and equitably across different groups of students and universities?
- Do students themselves view the system as fair and equitable?
- To what extent is social justice achieved and how could the present system be made fairer?

Policy initiatives for financing wider access

The expansion of higher education from 1999 onward was accompanied by the introduction of cost sharing and the provision of financial aid (subsidies and grants for low-income students). The Chinese government has implemented various policies, both financial and non-financial, for supporting wider access to higher education. Non-financial initiatives have included the introduction of quotas and concessions in entry standards for minority students. Financial initiatives have been many and complex, involving government at national and local levels.

In response to a tripling of university fees between 1997 and 2006, the State Council introduced a new financial aid policy providing substantial funding for eligible students in four ways (Cheng, 2011; Loyalka *et al.*, 2013):

1 Expanding the national needs-based aid programme (grants and living subsidies) with the aim of reaching 20 per cent of all university enrolment.
2 Increasing the number of merit-based scholarships.
3 Waiving fees and providing stipends for students attending military colleges and normal universities for teacher education.
4 Introducing the Residence-Based Government-Subsidised Student Loan Programme for student loans through local Student Financial Assistance Management Centres affiliated with students' home county education bureaux and provided by the National Development Bank.

In 1999 the national Government-Subsidised Student Loan Programme (GSSLP) began to provide student loans to individuals through commercial banks near the student's university or college. In 2000, the 'green channel' programme was implemented to allow low-income students to enrol and begin university courses without having to undergo a needs-based financial aid assessment or having to pay tuition fees up front. Further financial support for students has come from other sources: local governments, corporations, businesses, charity organisations and universities (through merit scholarships, tuition waivers, work-study arrangements, and special need subsidies for extreme cases). Public universities were required to earmark 4 to 6 per cent of their operating revenue for the support of low-income students, and private universities were encouraged to do the same (MoF/MoE, 2007).

The amounts of finance available to any individual student are not large (smaller than in some other countries), ranging from 1,000 to 3,000 Yuan per year for government-funded needs-based grants, to 6,000 Yuan maximum a year for loans and up to 8,000 Yuan for merit-based scholarships. For poor rural families they leave a large gap in the funds required. For example, the average annual tuition cost for a four-year public university course in Shaanxi was about 150 per cent of an average rural household's yearly disposable income in 2007, even higher for the poorest families (Loyalka *et al.*, 2013). The problem of financing university education is made especially difficult for poor rural families because of the way the process of communicating about financial support is designed. Students are required to apply and register for their courses before they know if and how much they will receive in financial support. Since this information only becomes available several weeks into the course and after registration, it is not timely. It is likely that this uncertainty deters at least some school students from applying or may unnecessarily limit their choice of university or subject track (Liu *et al.*, 2011). A related obstacle is the nature of information available. Studies by Shi *et al.* (2007) and Loyalka *et al.* (2013) point to the inadequate and poor quality of information available and the jargon-laden language used in materials on China's financial aid policies for higher education students. Compared with poor rural students, those in urban schools and families with higher socio-economic status and higher levels of parental education and teacher know-how are more likely to understand and be knowledgeable about the way the application process works and the various forms of financial support available to students.

Once they have entered higher education, does financial support reach the students who need it most? From a study of students from 41 counties in Shaanxi, Loyalka *et al.* (2013) draw five conclusions:

1   Government needs-based and merit aid was spread fairly evenly across tiers and subject tracks but since students in the higher tier universities tend to be from higher socio-economic levels, poorer students were disadvantaged by this even distribution, especially since tuition fees for Tiers 1 and 2 universities are lower than those for Tier 3.
2   Government needs-based and merit aid was indeed reaching lower income and higher ability students.
3   Aid from various organisations within society was allocated more often to students in higher tier universities than to students from disadvantaged backgrounds, though the latter group was often their avowed target group.
4   University-financed aid was not generally directed to the poorer students and was also distributed according to other factors (examination scores, gender, party membership).
5   Some poor students (nearly one-third) received little or no aid.

The findings from our research provide a little more evidence to support Loyalka *et al.*'s (2013) conclusions and further explore students' experience and perceptions about equality of opportunity and financial support.

Research design and data collection

The aim of the research was to examine the experience and perceptions of students on financing their studies in higher education and in relation to equality and equity. The research was carried out through a questionnaire survey of 1,547 students at six universities in Shaanxi province in 2011. Shaanxi is a medium-sized province in northwest China with a population of 37.3 million (2010). It ranked fourteenth for economic development out of 33 provinces (or equivalent administrative areas) and its GDP per capita reached US$6,108 in 2012. Shaanxi is traditionally strong in the provision of higher education (with 77 higher education institutions in 2010). Its provincial capital of Xi'an has one of the largest concentrations of key institutions of higher education in China; ranking third after only Beijing and Shanghai. Shaanxi was selected for this survey for two reasons: its economic position could be taken to represent the national average and it allowed a sample to be drawn from a variety of universities. The sample of students came from the six universities listed, chosen to represent the different tiers of universities in China.

First tier (high level)

1 *Xi'an Jiaotong University* is a national key university under the direct jurisdiction of the Ministry of Education (MoE). It was included in Project 211 and Project 985 and has about 30,000 full-time students, including 13,000 postgraduate students. It is an active research university with a major emphasis on science and engineering.
2 *Northwest Agricultural and Forest University* is a national key university under the direct jurisdiction of MoE. It was included in Project 985 and Project 211 and is the leading agricultural university in northwest China. It has 20,000 full-time undergraduate students and about 40,673 students altogether, including those taking postgraduate and adult education courses.

Second tier (middle level)

3 *Xi'an University of Technology* was originally an Institute of Mechanical Engineering but in 1972 it became a polytechnic university. It is supported jointly by the Shaanxi provincial and national government. It concentrates on science and technology and has about 36,000 students.
4 *Xi'an University of Architecture and Technology* achieved its present form in 1994 when the MoE gave approval for the existing institute to become Xi'an University of Architecture and Technology. It focuses mainly on civil engineering and architecture. It has about 40,000 students, including 19,000 undergraduates, over 5,000 postgraduates, and about 14,000 students at the vocational and technical college level.

Third tier (low level)

5   *Shaanxi University of Technology* is a provincial-level university, established in 2001 from a combination of a teachers' college and an institute of technology as part of the expansion of university education. It offers a wide variety of courses and has about 19,000 full-time students.

6   *Xi'an University of Finance and Economics* is a provincial-level university with about 18,000 students (undergraduate and postgraduate). It is a multidisciplinary institution but with a strong emphasis on economics, management and finance.

Within each selected university two subject majors were chosen, the science and engineering track (*like*) and the humanities and social science track (*wenke*) and, with the support of student administrators (the Communist Youth League Committee), several courses were chosen. In 2011 student leaders within each selected course distributed and collected a hard copy of the self-administered questionnaire (the plan was to issue questionnaires to 300 students in each university, though there was some shortfall). Second-year students were chosen because they had some experience of university life compared with first-year students, and were less occupied with examination preparation than third-year students. The overall administration of the questionnaire was carried out with the help of a partner at Xi'an University of Technology, Professor Chen Aijuan.

The questionnaire consisted of 39 items on family background, financing of studies, perceptions of social and economic difference among their fellow students and government policy on access and support for rural and poor students. Where appropriate, space was provided for students to explain their choices. A total of 1,800 questionnaires were distributed and 1,560 were returned (a response rate of 86.7 per cent). From these, 1,547 were judged valid. The data were analysed using SPSS to provide frequency and cross-sectional tables to reveal key differences among students in terms of their background, financial support for study, distribution among universities as well as their perceptions of equality in access to higher education. Chi-square or ANOVA analysis was used to reveal relationships between different variables (tier of university, place of birth, household income, gender, parental education and occupation).

Survey findings

The results are sequenced as follows: (1) profiles of the students in the sample according to various categories (rural–urban, gender, household income, university tier); (2) students' views of poverty and equality in higher education; (3) the distribution of financial support; and (4) students' perceptions of fairness in the distribution of government financial support.

Profiles of students

The key characteristics of students are shown in Table 2.1 where students are grouped according to the tier of university they attend, place of birth, region of origin and gender. Place of birth is chosen as a proxy for the rural–urban distinction rather than the place of *hukou* registration, since the latter can change in some circumstances. As may be seen, in our sample rural students outnumbered urban students overall (53.5% to 48.5%), reflecting the relative proportions of the rural–urban population nationally. Although, at first sight, this suggests that rural students have roughly equal access to higher education, the reality is somewhat different if comparisons are made with the relevant age group (18 to 21) within the population. In a survey of senior secondary students in Shaanxi province, Wang *et al.* (2011) found that only 20 per cent of rural students entered higher education compared with the national average of 31 per cent (54 per cent in cities like Beijing, Shanghai and Tianjin), and suggest that the actual percentage may be even lower than 20 per cent since this included non-poor rural as well as poor rural students. They also found the share of poor rural students entering the Tier 1 universities of Sichuan and Xi'an Jiaotong to be even less – 6.9 per cent – disproportionately low in relation to the poor rural population.

The poor rural students in our sample did not include their peers who may have dropped out of primary school (10%), junior middle school (22%) or senior middle school (7.4%), but are the successful survivors among the 20 per cent who then passed the college entrance examination (*gaokao*), if we use figures from Wang *et al.* (2011).[3] We found that most students in Tiers 2 and 3 universities were from rural areas, and most in the Tier 1 universities were from urban areas (14.2 per cent more urban than rural students). The gender difference was greater, with 29.4 per cent more male than female students in Tier 1 universities and the opposite in Tier 3 (22 per cent more female than male students). Most students (78%) in the Tier 1 universities came from outside Shaanxi province, indicative of the strong competition for places at the best universities and the government policy for enabling student mobility between provinces.

The rural–urban division is a key factor in economic and social inequality in contemporary China. Related to this is the increasing gap in household (HD)

Table 2.1 Background and university destination of students

University tier	Total		Place of birth (%)		Region of origin (%)		Gender (%)	
	N	%	Urban	Rural	Shaanxi	Other	Male	Female
Tier 3	535	34.6	46.8	53.2	83.6	16.4	39.0	61.0
Tier 2	538	34.8	42.6	57.4	66.1	33.9	65.4	34.6
Tier 1	474	30.6	57.1	42.9	22.0	78.0	64.7	35.3
Total	1,547	100	48.5	51.5	59.4	40.6	56.5	43.5

Notes
All tables and figures shown in this chapter are based on our survey data and compiled by the authors.

income which influences both the access to high-quality secondary schools (a route to Tier 1 universities) and the quality of students' university lives under the current cost-sharing model. Table 2.2 shows household income in relation to father's employment, parental education and university tier.

Given the difficulty of gathering reliable and accurate information about household income, students were asked to make an assessment of their family economic level, their gross annual income and the relative economic position of their family to others in their local community. Based on the information provided, students were grouped into three income levels: low (gross annual income of less than 10,000 Yuan), middle (10,000 to 50,000 Yuan) and high (over 50,000 Yuan). In terms of 'father's work', three categories of employment were used: public (comprising government officers, civil servants, employees in public institutions and state-owned enterprises), private (those working in private enterprises, joint ventures and small or family businesses) and farming. Categories of parental education were designated as high (one or both parents had reached higher education); mid (one or both parents had graduated from senior middle school, Grades 10 to 12), and low (neither parent had progressed beyond basic compulsory education, school Grades 1 to 9).

As may be seen in Table 2.2, 43 per cent of students placed their families in the category of low income, 36 per cent in the middle and 20 per cent in the high income group. How much reliance can be placed on this categorisation? In the absence of accurate data in China on household income (for example, based on income tax information) self-reporting is widely used by researchers and administrators as a rough substitute (Loyalka *et al.*, 2012). University administrators determine how financial aid is to be allocated to students based on self-reported data from students on household background and income together with some other information. Provincial governments then make lump sum transfers of financial aid funds across institutions which allocate funds to individual students. The allocation is done according to national government guidelines but is interpreted by the institutions (and provinces) in their own various ways and generally on the basis of inadequate, non-standardised and sometimes inaccurate data (Loyalka *et al.*, 2012; Wang and Shang, 2005).

Nearly half (46.9%) of students from high-income households and about a quarter (23.6%) from low-income families (73.3% of them from farmers' families)

Table 2.2 Reported household (HD) income by place of birth and university tier (%)

HD income	Sector of father's work			Parental education			University tier		
	Public	*Private*	*Farm*	*Low*	*Mid*	*High*	*Tier 1*	*Tier 2*	*Tier 3*
Low	14.2	12.4	73.3	53.1	38.5	8.4	23.6	44.4	32.0
Mid	43.7	33.3	23.9	29.1	35.3	35.6	29.1	28.9	41.2
High	67.9	29.2	3.4	7.8	20.1	72.2	46.9	24.6	28.5
Total	37.6	24.1	38.3	34.9	33.5	31.6	34.6	34.7	30.7

were attending Tier 1 universities. There was relatively small variation between the percentage of students from low- and middle-income families attending Tiers 2 and 3 universities although more low-income students attended Tier 2 universities than their middle-income peers. In our sample there was only a small difference between the proportions of students from low- and middle-income families attending Tier 1 universities. Students from all income groups could be found at all university tiers, though in different proportions, but the largest difference lay at the level of Tier 1 universities where twice as many students came from high-income as from low-income families. It seems that students are more likely to attend a Tier 1 university if their family has a high income, if their father works in a public or professional sector, if at least one of their parents has participated in higher education, and if they are male.

From the above data, it seems that access to university education is available to students from both rural and urban areas, from families with high, middle and low incomes, and from professional and farming families, though unevenly distributed. The expansion of higher education has included poor and rural students, according to our data. However, our sample only includes the small percentage of poor rural students who have successfully navigated access to higher education and not those who decided against it, either because they perceived it as unaffordable or for other reasons relating to disadvantage. Once within higher education, do students see the system as an equitable one? The rest of this chapter will examine one aspect of this, namely the distribution of funding for study in higher education and student perceptions of it.

Students' views on poverty and equality in higher education

Did students think there was equal opportunity for all young people in China to access higher education? Overall, 60 per cent of the students said there was not. This negative view was more evident in rural students, those coming from outside of Shaanxi province and those whose fathers worked in the public sector (see Figure 2.1). More students attending Tier 1 universities thought there was inequality of opportunity than those attending Tiers 2 and 3 universities. Students on Humanities and Social Science courses more often said that there was unequal opportunity than those on Science and Technology courses, a view also shared by more male than female students.

Where then did the perceived inequality lie? Around a half (48.4%) of all students identified access as a source of inequality, agreeing with statements that poor and rural students have less opportunity to access higher education (see Table 2.3). Around 20 per cent disagreed and the rest (over a quarter) took a neutral position. Overall, 58.9 per cent of rural and 46.5 per cent of urban students agreed that rural students had less opportunity for higher education. Between a quarter and one-third of all students expressed no view on this issue, suggesting either a lack of awareness or indifference (interestingly, a quarter of rural and poor students fall into this neutral category). Without interviewing students, we can only guess at the reasons for this response.

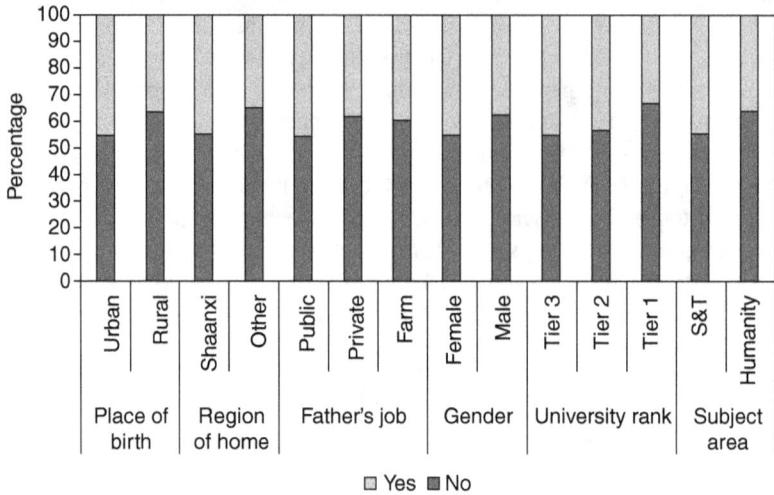

Figure 2.1 Does the current higher education system provide equal opportunities for all young people?

To explore awareness of poor students in their midst, the students were asked if there were any poor students in their classes. As Table 2.4 shows, more rural students (61.5%) said that there were. A similar difference was found for income groups and levels of parental education: fewer students from high-level income (35.3%) and better educated families (39.3%) thought there were poor students in their classes and also more responded with 'don't know' as their answer. The reasons for the size of this neutral response are open to various interpretations, both negative and positive.

Students who said that there were poor students in their classes were asked to estimate their proportion. Overall, they estimated that 30 per cent of students in their classes were poor. Students who were themselves from poor and rural families judged the proportion to be only a little more (5%) than those from urban or high-income families. This was close to the actual number of poor rural students in the sample (502; 32.4%); 631 of all students (40.7%) were in the low-income group and poor rural students constituted 79.6 per cent of these.

Were there any differences between groups in their satisfaction with university life? Did differences in the family's economic and social status influence it? Our data appear to suggest that this was the case. As Table 2.5 shows, more students from urban areas and high-income families (around 40 per cent in both cases) were satisfied with their university experience than those from rural and low-income families. As might be expected, students' satisfaction was also related to university tier, with those in the Tier 1 universities expressing most satisfaction. However, 40 per cent overall were neither satisfied nor dissatisfied. It is possible that this result may be influenced by the involvement of the universities' administrative systems

Table 2.3 Student perceptions of equal opportunity for higher education (%)

Statement		'Poor students have fewer opportunities for higher education than urban students'			'Rural students have fewer opportunities than urban students'		
Category	Item	Disagree	Neutral	Agree	Disagree	Neutral	Agree
Place of birth	Rural	21.7	25.3	53.1	17.3	23.9	58.9
	Urban	23.9	32.3	43.8	20.3	33.1	46.5
HD income	Low	22.8	26.1	51.1	17.7	24.5	57.8
	Mid	24.8	26.6	48.6	19.4	30.8	49.8
	High	18.8	35.9	45.3	19.3	33.2	47.5
Parental education	Low	21.4	26.7	51.9	17.0	25.7	57.3
	Mid	23.8	27.1	49.1	19.3	24.9	55.7
	High	23.7	32.6	43.8	20.3	35.1	44.5
Mean		22.9	28.7	48.4	18.7	28.6	52.7

Table 2.4 Are there poor students in your class?

Category	Item	Yes (%)	No (%)	Don't know (%)
Place of birth	Rural	61.5	11.3	27.2
	Urban	41.6	12.9	45.5
HD income	Low	65.0	9.4	25.6
	Mid	46.3	14.6	39.1
	High	35.3	13.1	51.6
Parental	Low	59.0	11.3	29.8
education	Mid	56.4	11.7	31.9
	High	39.3	13.6	47.1
Mean		52.1	12.1	35.9

Table 2.5 Student satisfaction by family background and university tier (%)

Category	Item	Dissatisfied	Neutral	Satisfied
Place of birth	Rural	23.2	44.5	32.3
	Urban	14.4	43.8	41.8
HD income	Low	20.4	46.5	33.1
	Mid	20.4	40.0	39.6
	High	12.9	46.5	40.6
University tier	1	12.0	41.6	46.4
	2	20.6	43.7	35.7
	3	23.2	47.6	29.2
Mean		19.0	44.1	36.9

to distribute and collect the questionnaires, causing some students to be reluctant to express any negative opinion.

Given the difficulties of some poor students in financing higher education and in accessing labour markets following graduation, students were asked whether young people from poor families should find alternatives to higher education after they left school. Opinion was equally divided among those who agreed and disagreed, and between rural and urban, and between low- and high-income family students in response to this question.

Availability and distribution of government financial support

Although the government has increased the amount of financial assistance for students, especially those from low-income families, and though social organisations, local governments and universities have also increased aid for students, it is nonetheless difficult to judge how well the financial aid is reaching the students most in need of it. About 60 per cent of the students in our survey said they were familiar with the government's policy on financial support for students in higher education. Familiarity was claimed by 10 per cent more students from rural and poor family backgrounds than from urban and high-income groups. Of the students who said they were unfamiliar with government policies, 60 per cent also said that there were no poor students in their classes. Students' claims of familiarity with government policy were not explored further, so we are unable to say what level of knowledge the students and their families had, but this area needs further research. As Loyalka *et al.*, (2013) found, many students lacked timely and adequate information about available resources.

The survey collected information about three forms of financial support to students: scholarships provided by the university or commercial companies, needs-based support, and bank loans. About half (49.2%) of students had benefited from at least one of these three forms of support. As Table 2.6 shows, 23 per cent of students received a scholarship of 2,068 Yuan on average, and of these just 3.2 per cent were sponsored by commercial companies. Compared to the scholarship funding, the needs-based funds paid out more (an average of 2,525 Yuan) to more students (29 per cent of the sample). The bank loans were bigger (6,737 Yuan on average) but were provided to fewer students (13%). About one-third (32%) of students were in receipt of more than one form of support and a small number (2.2%) received all three.

Table 2.7 provides more detail. In general, students' access to financial support varied depending upon university tier, with merit-based scholarships

Table 2.6 Type and allocation of financial support

Items	Scholarship	Needs-based subsidy	Bank loan
Number of holders	356	450	203
% of students	23.0	29.1	13.1
Mean allocation (Yuan)	2,068	2,525	5,737

Table 2.7 Distribution of financial support to students (%)

Category	Item	One or more forms of support	Merit-based scholarship	Needs-based grant
University tier	1	56.1	36.1	*33.3*
	2	49.2	21.0	*35.1*
	3	42.9	13.5	*32.5*
Place of birth	Rural	67.2	*24.1*	55.3
	Urban	30.0	*22.5*	10.4
HD income	Low	70.7	22.7	60.0
	Mid	37.8	*23.4*	20.1
	High	27.5	*22.3*	4.2
Mean		*49.2*	*22.9*	*34.4*

Note
Cells with italics denote item not passing statistical test (Chi-square).

more often given to Tier 1 university students. There was little difference between the universities in their allocation of grants.

Numerically, more students from rural or low-income groups gained financial support than their counterparts in urban and high-income groups (Table 2.7), suggesting that financial support was reaching students in need to some extent. The award of merit-based scholarships (a small percentage overall) was fairly evenly distributed among income groups. However, half of the students in our sample (50.8%) and 30 per cent of students from poor rural families received no form of financial support other than from family and personal resources.

Students' perceptions of government financial support

Did the students think that government policy on financial support was fair and adequate for their needs? Approximately 43 per cent of the students in our sample agreed that the 'current financial support system is unfair'; only 12 per cent disagreed and 45 per cent neither agreed nor disagreed. A greater proportion of the students who did not receive financial support or who did not know about government financial aid policies said that the system was unfair than those who had gained financial support or who knew about government policies. Of those who claimed familiarity with government policies, 60 per cent viewed the level of current financial support as appropriate (no difference in this opinion was found between rural and urban and between low- and high-income groups).

On the issue of fairness, the vast majority of students (92%) agreed that the government should give special support to students from poor families. Students were then asked if financial aid for poor students should be increased and whether all students were equally entitled to financial aid (see Table 2.8). About 45 per cent overall said financial aid should be increased, making comments such as 'the government should increase financial support to the poor students so that their income is equivalent to the average income of non-poor students'. Those from urban and high-income groups and not in receipt of financial aid showed lower levels of agreement (14 to 17% less). Over one-third (36.8%) of students said that all students are equally entitled to financial aid, adding comments such as 'Most students are short of funds, not just poor students, and so all students should get government support'. Students from urban and higher SES backgrounds showed stronger support for this idea. From all groups, around one-third or more of students took a neutral position.

The data in Table 2.8 indicate a division of opinion among students in relation to the fair distribution of government financial support. We can speculate that this reflects different notions of social justice. On the one hand, the students (36.8%) agreeing that all students are equally entitled to financial support appear to be operating on the principle of equality; that is, same shares for all regardless of need or difference. On the other hand, students disagreeing (28.9%) that all students should receive equal shares, or agreeing (45.3%) that financial aid for poor students should be increased, may be operating from principles of equity: that is, accepting that shares may vary according to individual need. Students

Table 2.8 Student views on governmental financial support for study (%)

Category	Item	Financial aid for the poor should be increased			All students are equally entitled to financial aid		
		Disagree	Neutral	Agree	Disagree	Neutral	Agree
Place of birth	Rural	15.0	32.9	52.1	36.4	33.4	30.2
	Urban	18.2	43.8	38.0	20.4	35.5	44.1
HD income	Low	13.4	33.3	53.3	36.1	34.4	29.5
	High	19.0	44.7	36.3	20.4	38.4	41.2
Beneficiary	Yes	12.4	32.3	55.3	42.0	35.0	22.4
	No	18.9	41.0	40.2	21.8	34.0	44.2
Mean		16.1	38.1	45.3	28.9	34.3	36.8

opting for 'equality' (just over one-third) were slightly more likely to come from urban and richer backgrounds, whereas those choosing 'equity' came from poor and rural backgrounds. These different views may also reflect differences in expectations about government responsibility for funding higher education and the low amounts of grants generally.

Although social inequality is an increasing concern of the Chinese government and the public, a concern with social justice issues was not highly visible in our survey. Students' views on equality and equity varied, as might be expected, and a large number of students expressed no views at all. Two-thirds of the students in our sample agreed that there were inequalities in access to higher education but this recognition differed according to the university tier, subject track and gender of students. Views on the equitable distribution of financial support may be influenced by the low level of awareness in some students about student poverty or the significance they attached to it. About 60 per cent of students were aware that some of their fellow students were poor. The 30 per cent who were unaware tended to be from urban backgrounds, with higher levels of income or with parents with higher education, suggesting some urban or class bias. Student views of social justice were divided and sometimes not clear-cut. For example, half of the students said that family background and students' income levels did not affect a student's life at university, while at the same time, two-thirds of students said that poor students were not able to study as well as their richer peers.

Conclusion

This chapter has attempted to shed light on the distribution of financial resources for higher education in the context of one province, Shaanxi, and from a perspective of social justice. Government policy has opened access to students from a wider range of socio-economic backgrounds and provided earmarked support for poor and rural students. However, while access has greatly expanded and government financial support is spread fairly widely, if thinly, inequalities persist. As Ding and Liang (2012) observe, while there has been a decline in inequality of access to higher education (the quantitative dimension), the degree of qualitative inequality (the type and quality of education accessed) has increased. Socio-economic status remains influential in determining which university a student will attend. Attendance at Tier 1 universities is regarded as having a significant impact on social mobility, hence its importance in promoting equal opportunity. In our sample, twice as many males as females attended Tier 1 universities.

The participation of poor and rural students in Tier 1 universities is lower than that of students from urban and higher income families. Not only do Tier 1 universities have twice as many students from high-income as from low-income families, the Tier 1 universities themselves receive more government funding and charge lower fees than Tiers 2 and 3 universities. Although Wang *et al.* (2013) found that financial aid for poor students who gain access to Tier 1 universities 'is currently sufficient and accessible for poor rural students', it is not the case for poor rural students in Tier 3 universities, which often provide no financial aid. As Li (2007: 734) concludes: 'There is therefore a reverse relationship between family affordability and cost burdens. Lower income families are taking on much higher burdens for their children's education than higher income families.'

Looking beyond the indicators of distributive social justice, it seems that systems and structural arrangements are not yet working well enough to ensure equality and equity if we define social justice as the activity of 'ensuring systemic and structural social arrangements to improve equality' (National Pro Bono Resource, 2011: 2). Persistent inequalities remain, reaching well back into the school system which feeds the universities. As Wang *et al.* (2011) found in their sample of Shaanxi upper secondary students, there was no statistical difference in the school grades achieved by poor and non-poor students or in their college entrance *(gaokao)* examinations, yet poor students were underrepresented in higher education, a gap attributed to inequalities in earlier stages of education.

The distribution of financial resources is, as Young (1990), Gewirtz (1998) and Patton *et al.* (2010) have argued, determined by the processes and institutional arrangements involved, key agents in shaping social justice. Processes which limit opportunity for poor rural families include the flow and quality of useful information, the timing of financial information about grant awards to students and their families, and inflexibility in the process of choosing and registering for an institution and course. Some institutional arrangements could be more equity-focused and less merit-focused. Although the government issues general guidelines about the distribution of financial support, the universities can interpret them as they wish. While this provides useful flexibility to meet local circumstances, it also allows unfairness in the system. University practices raise questions about the role of universities in promoting social justice within and beyond their campuses and their approaches to fostering equity for disadvantaged students and groups. Fairer distribution requires better targeting of available funds to avoid the drift of financial support towards Tier 1 universities and higher SES groups. This would result in more loans and fewer grants for those in higher socio-economic groups, and more and larger grants and fewer loans to those in lower ones. Greater equity would also be achieved by shifting more aid to lower tier universities and to poor rural students, including those who receive no aid at present. However, we agree with Yang's (2010: 568) conclusion that 'pumping more money into the student aid system is not the single best solution. It is the structure rather than the scale of aid system which makes the biggest difference in access to aid.' To this we would add the need for a stronger focus on social justice values.

Notes

1 The empirical data of this chapter are based on a questionnaire survey in six universities across Shaanxi province in 2011. Special thanks are due to Professor Chen Aijuan

from Xian University of Technology who participated in the design of the question-naire and was in charge of the survey implementation.

2 Two projects were launched by the central government in 1995 and 1998 respectively. The 211 project refers to the financial support to 100 top universities towards 'world-standards' in the twenty-first century while the 985 project is named after the date in May 1998 when the government decided to provide special financial support to a number of top universities to create 'world-class universities' (Zha, 2011).

3 Wang *et al.* (2011) estimate that only 4 per cent of rural children who begin primary school enter university.

References

Avery, C. and Hoxby, C.M. (2003), Do and should financial aid packages affect students' college choices?, NBER: working paper 9482.

Bettinger, E. (2004), How financial aid affects persistence, in Hoxby, C. (ed.) *College Choices: The economics of which college, when college and how to pay for it*, Chicago, IL: University of Chicago Press and NBER, pp. 207–238.

Chan, W.K. and Ngok, K. (2011), Accumulating human capital while increasing educational inequality: A study on higher education policy in China, *Asia Pacific Journal of Education*, 31(3): 293–310.

Cheng, B. (2011), *Student Loans in China: Efficiency, equity, and social justice*, Lanham, MD: Lexington Books.

Ding, X. and Liang, Y. (2012), Changes in the degree of equalization in opportunities for entering higher education, *Chinese Education and Society*, 45(1): 22–30.

Gewirtz, S. (1998), Conceptualizing social justice in education: Mapping the territory, *Journal of Education Policy*, 13(4): 469–484.

Hayek, F. (1976), *Law, Legislation and Liberty: A new statement of the liberal principles of justice and political economy* (Vol. 2, *The Mirage of Social Justice*), Chicago, IL: University of Chicago Press.

Li, H., Meng, L., Shi, X. and Wu, B. (2013), Poverty in China's colleges and the targeting of financial aid, *The China Quarterly*, 216: 970–922.

Li, H., Loyalka, P., Rozelle, S., Wu, B. and Xie, J. (2013), Unequal access to college in China: How far have poor rural students been left behind?, Working paper, rural education action projects, Stanford University.

Li, W. (2007), Family background, financial constraints and higher education attendance in China, *Economics of Education Review*, 26: 725–735.

Liu, C.F., Shang, L.X., Luo, R.F., Wang, X.B., Rozelle, S. and Sharbono, B. (2011), Early commitment on financial aid and college decision making of poor students: Evidence from a randomised evaluation in rural China, *Economics of Education Review*, 30(4): 627–640.

Long, B.T. (2008), What is known about the impact of financial aid? Implications for policy, National Centre for Postsecondary Research Working Paper.

Loyalka, P., Song, Y. and Wei, J. (2012), The distribution of student financial aid in China: Is aid reaching poor students?, *China Economic Review*, 23(4): 898–917.

Loyalka, P., Song, Y., Wei, J., Zhong, W. and Rozelle, S. (2013), Information, college decisions and financial aid: Evidence from a cluster-randomized controlled trial in China, *Economics of Education Review*, 36: 26–40.

Ministry of Education (MoE) (1998), *Action Plan to Vitalize Education in the 21st Century*, Ministry of Education, Beijing: PRC.

Ministry of Finance (MoF) and Ministry of Education (MoE) (2007), Regular HEI and vocational HEI national student financial and management interim procedures (in Chinese), *MoF/MoE joint document*, No. 92, Beijing.

National Pro Bono Resource Centre (2011), What is social justice? *Occasional Paper* No. 1, University of New South Wales, Australia.

Patton, L.D., Riyad, A.S. and Osei-Kofi, N. (2010), Introduction to the emergent approaches to diversity and social justice higher education, *Equity and Excellence in Education* (Special Issue), 48(3): 265–278.

Rawls, J. (1971), *A Theory of Justice*, Cambridge, MA: Harvard University Press.

Shi, Y.J., Zhang, L.X., Bai, Y.Y., Luo, R.F., Sylvia, S. and Sharbono, B. (2007), Taking the next step: Are information and financials holding poor rural students back?, Northwest Socioeconomic Development Research Centre (NSDRC), Working Paper, WP-07-E4 Xi'an.

State Council (2007), *Opinions on establishing and improving the policies for subsidizing students in universities of regular undergraduate education, post-secondary vocational schools and secondary vocational schools from families with financial difficulties*, Beijing: State Council.

Wang, F.Z. and Shang, H.C. (2005), Questions and counter-measures of poor students' subsidy in universities in West China – Take Shanxi as an example, *Journal of Soft Science*, 19(3): 91–93 (in Chinese).

Wang, X., Liu, C., Zhang, L., Yue, A., Shi, Y., Chu, J. and Rozelle, S. (2013), Does financial aid help poor students succeed in college?, *China Economic Review*, 25: 27–43.

Wang, X., Liu, C., Zhang, L., Luo, R., Glauben, T., Shi,Y., Rozelle, S. and Sharbono, B. (2011), What is keeping the poor out of college? Enrolment rates, educational barriers and college matriculation in China, *China Agricultural Economic Review*, 3(2): 131–149.

Yang, P. (2010), Who gets more financial aid in China? A multilevel analysis, *International Journal of Educational Development*, 30: 560–569.

Young, I. (1990), *Justice and the Politics of Difference*, Princeton, NJ: Princeton University Press.

Zha, Q. (2011), China's move to mass higher education in a comparative perspective, *Compare*, 41(6): 751–768.

3 Employment equality in China's universities

Perceptions of 'decent work' among university teachers in Beijing[1]

Junfu Li, Bin Wu and W. John Morgan

Introduction

In recent years there has been an increase in awareness of social justice, equality and rights issues among Chinese citizens including university teachers (Li, 2011). The higher education (HE) sector is an important example of this because of its potential for developing and disseminating new ideas about a just society, and in influencing policy-makers. An example is the role of university teachers in influencing students, both directly and indirectly, through their lectures, public statements and personal behaviour. University teachers influence the younger generation of Chinese professionals, the future leaders of the nation, in their understanding, development and use of the concept of social justice in China. It is important for us to observe and understand this process as a key to the development of a professional community in a post-socialist society where there is tension between the different understandings and expectations of 'professionalism' (Kaurin and Morgan, 2014). In this chapter, we consider specifically the term 'decent work', which is often used by Chinese university teachers to reflect on their employment and, especially, on their working conditions, which are often seen as unfair or unjust. Based on a survey of a number of universities in Beijing, we examine the distribution of incomes among university teachers, together with their perceptions of and requests for 'decent work'.

The demand for 'decent work'

The growth of demands for 'decent work' or employment equality in China's HE sector may be seen through the online spread of reports and comments on the 'strike' of university teachers[2] which took place at Chongqing Business and Management University on 15 March 2013. This was caused by the inadequacies of a consultation process about a proposal for wage system reform prepared by the university administration. A number of teachers, dissatisfied with the proposal and with the consultation process, came together to declare spontaneously their objections, both within the university and at the campus gate. This demonstration was reported immediately and was disseminated widely online, attracting much support and sympathy, and stimulating debate nation-wide (Liu, 2013). Such an event drew public attention to the working conditions of teachers in China's universities about which many discussants expressed their concern. Below is a quote from the online comments:

> It may not be too bad if you take a university teacher post as a second job, because the income from a full-time post is certainly not enough to support a family [feed a child].... Among university staff, teachers are at the bottom and nobody cares about them. What can we do?... What we, university teachers, want is not just the livelihood security, but even more importantly, respect and dignity, we want more respect for universities in society.[3]

This quote suggests that what university teachers are concerned about is not merely pay, but also fair treatment, working conditions and the distribution of rewards and benefits (e.g. workload, performance-related pay and promotion opportunities) among teachers, and between teachers and other staff within universities. It seems that the term 'decent work' has three dimensions. First, it is about a fair balance of income and other opportunities between teachers with administrative titles and those without. This is because there is a general perception that the former are rewarded unfairly because of the centralisation of resources (including teaching, research and other opportunities) under the control of the university administration (Shi and Zhang, 2012a). This determines resource distribution and rewards without the adequate participation of university teachers generally and a transparent process of decision-making. Second, the income gap between senior and junior teachers is also seen as being too great (Zhao, 2013). This places extra pressure on the younger academic staff to cope with various challenges of teaching, research and social life. Third, there is comparison of working conditions, welfare and pay between university teachers, and those equally well qualified, for instance, with a doctoral degree, who work in other sectors such as government and other public agencies. Such comparisons may make young teachers even more dissatisfied with their working conditions, incomes and long-term career prospects (She, 2001; Li and Shang, 2009).

This chapter asks the following questions: Why is decent work, or employment equality, a concern for university teachers in China? What is their pattern of terms and conditions of work? How do they perceive these issues and how do they think they may be addressed?

We offer some answers to these questions using data collected through secondary information and an empirical survey conducted in Beijing in 2011. The survey involved 1,692 teachers at 18 universities. The following section provides an explanation of the evolution of the 'decent work' concept in China. This is followed by the research design and data collection method. The data are then presented and analysed in two further sections: the distribution of the pattern of incomes; and the perceptions of respondents. Among a number of factors contributing to income inequality in the HE sector, we draw attention to the bureaucratisation and negative impact on the professionalism among teachers and perceptions of social justice among students. The chapter ends with a set of conclusions and policy implications.

'Decent work' in the Chinese context

The meaning of the term 'decent work' (体面劳动) may differ according to the individual, while it also changes according to social contexts or times. In this chapter we use the concept both subjectively, referring to the perception of group members and others in society, and objectively, according to economic and social indicators. We consider three dimensions: job opportunity and security, fair pay, and respect and dignity. Prior to economic reform, there were generally no big differences in China in terms of economic incomes, social welfare and security, or even in political hierarchy, between different groups and individual members. A Chinese term, the '*iron rice bowl*', was created to refer to those who were employed in state-owned enterprises or public sectors with long-term job security, relatively high wages, welfare and social security, and protected by the state via the national planned system. It was used in contrast with rural farmers and employees in local collectively owned enterprises in urban areas whose income and social welfare standards were relatively lower. However, generally speaking, there was no significant difference between different industrial sectors, occupations and job titles given the dominant ideology which emphasised loyalty, equity and collectivism among citizens. This has influenced many Chinese people, including university teachers, to compare their current pay and conditions of work with others (Sun, 1996).

Since the economic reforms of the mid-1980s, a fundamental change has taken place in China in terms of the principles and working mechanisms of the public sector, including universities generally. This has not only reshaped the wage and welfare systems, but also the perceptions of people about their group interests and position in the Chinese social system. As a result, the concept 'decent work' has changed in meaning, context and extent. In particular, three changes may be identified compared with three decades ago.

First, all urban sectors, including government offices, public agencies and state-owned enterprises, have experienced restructuring to match the principles of market economics which gives priority to efficiency rather than to equity. This has resulted in significant differences among urban employees in incomes, welfare and social security, depending upon sectors, departments and the nature of enterprises. The uneven distribution of incomes among urban employees is related to the still inchoate nature of market reform (e.g. the continuing monopoly of state-owned enterprises in many economic sectors (Sun, 2009)) and partly to delayed political reform, which is responsible for the high level of government control of various economic and social resources (P. Wang, 2011; Xu, 2012). As a result, unlike the homogeneous 'iron rice bowl' of the past, there are no common criteria for 'decent work' which can be applied to all sectors or employees in urban China. This is because people may have different expectations or interpretations about what is fair pay which varies among sectors, departments and industrial areas. It is agreed, however, that civil servants in government or other public agency employment and employees in a few monopolised state-owned enterprises have 'decent work'. This may be seen in the high demand for such employment in the graduate labour market each year (Wang and Yu, 2014; Y. Wang, 2011; Li *et al.*, 2011; Xiong, 2010a). In other words, 'decent work' in China today is dependent upon the specific sector, industry or department.

Second, instead of an equal distribution of income and welfare among social members within 'iron rice bowl' sectors as in the past, a hierarchical system has been established, determined by occupation and job title, even in the same sector or organisation. A significant gap may be seen between different ranks in which manual workers are at the bottom and senior managers at the top in terms of pay, welfare and respect, and which also determines political power or influence in terms of resource allocation (Feng and Xiu, 1993).

Third, besides official wages, informal income, referring to occasional or irregular income, has become an important part of real income among employees in the public and state-owned enterprise sectors, and which is not available in official statistics. There are also many 'grey' incomes which are intermediate between 'white' (regulated) and 'black' (illegal) which have no clear definition in the current regulation system. Taking into account the uneven distribution of economic, social and political resources among urban employees, unsurprisingly, informal income (including grey income) varies greatly according to sector, occupation and job title (X. Wang, 1997; Xiong, 2010b).

This chapter offers fresh light on a particular aspect of social justice through its focus on the perceptions of university teachers about fair pay and conditions of work. The following should be noted. First, university teachers are more secure compared with other sectors, which allows a focus on fair pay, respect and dignity. Second, university teachers comprise a highly professionalised sector which offers insight into the tension or conflict between professionalism and political centralism (*guan-ben-wei* in Chinese). Third, 'decent work' as shown at the beginning of this chapter has been increasingly a matter of concern to university teachers (Tong, 2007; Yang, 2010; Zhao, 2009; Xie, 2011). By focusing on the distribution of incomes, both formally and informally, this chapter offers an insight into the challenges and dilemmas facing the continuing reform of the higher education sector (Liu *et al.*, 2012). Fourth, understanding the perception of university teachers of 'decent work' could influence students in their conception of social justice. Finally, it should be noted that concern about decent work or fair pay is not limited to higher education only in China, but is also significant for the international academic community. Altbach *et al.* (2012), for instance, conducted an international comparison of wages and social welfare among university teachers across 28 countries worldwide, in which it was found that Chinese university teachers came at the bottom.

Empirical data collection

It is not easy to demonstrate the distribution of real income among university teachers in China because of the complexity of the wage system. Generally, the total income (TI) of university teachers comprises two parts: formal and informal income. The former consists of basic wages (BW), performance-related pay (PRP), bonus, book and reference allowances, and transport subsidies. The BW does not change much nationwide since it comes from the state financial budget. However, the PRP varies greatly from university to university since it is the institution which decides how much to pay and how it is distributed among administrative staff, teachers and support staff. Compared with formal pay, informal income is much more difficult to identify since it comes from a variety of sources such as overtime teaching, research projects, references and publications, consultancy fees, etc. Furthermore, informal income is distributed highly unevenly among teachers. A good example of 'grey income' is that of the allowances accompanying research projects commissioned by external users with or without a contract. Most teachers don't have such opportunities, while different universities have different regulations about the appropriate use of such funds (Zhang and Mao, 2013). In this chapter, we use the term 'formal income' (wages) to include BW and PRP and exclude 'grey income'.

In 2011, a survey was conducted at 18 universities in Beijing (Liu *et al.*, 2012; Zhao, 2013) which aimed to understand the complexity of the wage system and its impact on the perceptions and performance of university teachers. Seven of the universities were funded by central government (Ministry of Education) and 11 by the Beijing municipal government. A stratified sample was used based on the pay lists of all staff at the universities. This enabled us to identify the candidates for the questionnaire survey which 1,692 teachers completed. In addition four focus groups and 21 semi-structured interviews were held enabling us to triangulate the data.

The aim was to identify the perceptions of respondents to the issue of fair pay using three dimensions: (1) a personal perspective about whether income matched effort; (2) an organisational perspective on fair pay through comparing views of respondents with different ranks and job titles across sampled universities; and (3) a sector perspective referring to a comparison of incomes with counterparts in sectors outside HE. We believe that our survey findings presented in this chapter reflect common issues among university teachers regarding the increasing income gaps found in China. The survey, however, may not be entirely appropriate to represent the position and pay of university teachers throughout China because of the exceptional economic circumstances found in Beijing, especially for junior-rank teachers (e.g. the high cost of housing).

Employment conditions, income composition and distribution

In the current HE system of China, university teachers are graded according to four ranks: professor, associate professor, lecturer and assistant lecturer. Generally, there is a decline in the numbers of assistant lecturers, the lowest rank which requires postgraduate education experience. This is because a doctoral qualification has become common practice for academic employment at almost all regular universities in China. The possession of a doctorate enables academic staff to apply for a promotion to associate professor rank after two years' teaching experience, subject to the availability of posts and competition against other qualified applicants within the university. In reality, promotion may take much longer to achieve. There are also significant differences among different types of institutions. For example, at national key universities the distribution of university teachers according to rank is likely to be 20 to 30 per cent, 40 to 50 per cent and 30 to 40 per cent between professor, associate professor and lecturer or below respectively. This is in contrast with 10 per cent, 30 per cent and 60 per cent at the majority of standard universities. The posts for senior ranks (professors and associate professors) are much fewer than in standard universities (Wang, 2012).

According to the survey, the average income of respondents in 2010 was 74,687 Yuan (£7,500), which may be grouped according to job title (professional rank): 126,730 Yuan (£12,700) for professors, 83,624 Yuan (£8,400) for associate professors, 63,365 Yuan (£6,300) for lecturers and 46,616 Yuan (£4,700) for assistant lecturers. Table 3.1 shows that formal incomes (basic wage plus performance-related pay) account for just over three-quarters (76%) of total incomes, while other incomes (excluding 'grey incomes') account for nearly a quarter (23.3%). Interestingly, an increase may be seen in the share of formal incomes in total incomes from 67.9 per cent for a professor to 83.9 per cent for an assistant lecturer. This is associated with the decline of other incomes from 32.3 per cent for a professor to only 16.1 per cent for an assistant lecturer. Two conclusions may be drawn from Table 3.1. First, it is confirmed that other incomes have become an important part of the current wage system. Second, income gaps among university teachers are not caused by formal incomes but by other sources of income. For instance, the difference in total income between professors and assistant lecturers is 2.68 as much, comprising two parts: 2.12 as much formal income and 5.32 as much other income. The higher the academic rank, the higher the other incomes in both absolute and relative terms.

It is worth noting that Table 3.1 is likely to underestimate the income gaps. According to our interviews and focus group meetings the questionnaire survey most likely under-reported real incomes. In particular, it was unlikely that, for various personal reasons, they provided any information on 'grey income'. The higher the total incomes the more likely it was that they were under-reported. Participants in the interviews and focus groups expressed concern about the increasing share of other incomes and the impact on income inequality within universities. For instance, one professor stated:

> In my opinion, the informal incomes are a major factor driving income inequality in our HE system, because not everyone has the opportunity to access grey income. In fact, most teachers are dependent upon university wages with little chance of earning opportunities outside. This is particularly so for those who are in charge of basic course teaching whose other incomes are even less.

Table 3.1 Composition and distribution of incomes among respondents by rank (2010, Yuan/year)

Rank	N	Total incomes (TI)	Basic wages (BW)	BW in TI (%)	Other	Other in TI (%)
Professor	284	124,730	84,692	67.9	40,038	32.3
Associate professor	603	83,624	66,063	79.0	17,561	21.0
Lecturer	656	63,365	49,045	77.4	14,320	22.6
Assistant lecturer	114	46,616	39,911	83.9	7,525	16.1
Total	1,657	74,687	57,285	76.7	17,402	23.3

Source: all tables in this chapter are based on the survey project 'University teachers' income distribution and stimulation mechanism in Beijing' (2011).

A younger lecturer showed his payslip to us: basic wage 1,100 Yuan, performance-related pay 2,500 Yuan. 'It is a shame that my income is less than that of a migrant worker in Beijing, although I have a PhD and 20 years' teaching experience.'

It is reasonable to assume that people of similar age, qualifications, work experience and job titles should have similar incomes. However such an assumption was not supported by the empirical survey. In fact the income gaps within the same rank were even greater than between ranks (as shown in Table 3.1). Table 3.2 shows an uneven distribution of total incomes among respondents who are of the same rank and divided equally into ten groups according to mean total incomes. Two conclusions may be drawn from Table 3.2. First, it shows the unevenness of income distribution among university teachers measured by both the ratios of standard deviation to mean incomes; and the gaps between Group 1 and Group 10. Taking professors as an example: the mean of total incomes at the top (Group 10) is 5.4 times higher than at the bottom (Group 1). Second, the uneven distribution of incomes is caused by a few people in the top income group (Group 10) whose incomes are almost twice as high as the next group (Group 9). The existence of such a high-income group, although very small in population, gives an image about income distribution in the HE sector that has two negative impacts. For the public it may lead to the false perception that the incomes of university teachers are very high and comparable with other highly qualified groups. For the vast majority of university teachers it exaggerates the unevenness of income distribution within the universities.

An important factor explaining the uneven distribution of incomes is the university bureaucratic structure which determines the distribution of resources within universities. According to our survey a quarter of professors, holding an administrative post of Head of Department, had incomes of 137,120 Yuan per

Table 3.2 Distribution of total incomes by academic rank and income group

Variable	Professor	Associate Professor	Lecturers
Mean	124,730	83,624	63,365
Std. Dev.	98,629	48,978	50,441
Ratio (%)	79.1	58.6	79.6
Group 1	59,195	42,525	32,126
Group 2	70,302	51,146,	41,041
Group 3	77,620	57,437	45,359
Group 4	90,548	62,335	49,686
Group 5	101,350	68,231	52,680
Group 6	110,560	73,377	56,935
Group 7	119,340	81,266	61,887
Group 8	131,030	92,119	68,023
Group 9	156,080	109,330	79,744
Group 10	322,650	174,580	132,720
G 10/G 1	*5.4*	*4.1*	*4.1*

year, compared with 115,600 Yuan for those without such an administrative title or duties. For associate professors, the figures were 100,700 Yuan for the same post. Furthermore, income from research is related closely to administrative title or rank. For instance, the mean incomes from research were 34,174 Yuan for professors with administrative titles and 15,719 Yuan for those colleagues without an administrative title. In addition, the higher the administrative rank, the greater the incomes from such research projects. For instance, the mean income for all respondents at the level of Head of Department was 11,250 Yuan compared with 6,359 Yuan at the level of Head of Group (a subsection of the Department).

Perceptions of the distribution of incomes

This section examines the comments of respondents. In respect of satisfaction with incomes, almost half (49.2%) of respondents said 'no' with only 13.6 per cent saying 'yes' and a surprisingly high 35.8 per cent as 'neutral'. Clearly, the number of those dissatisfied was higher than satisfied respondents.

From a personal perspective, we asked respondents whether their current income level matched their perceived contribution: 28.9 per cent said 'matched' or 'very matched', 24.3 per cent were 'neutral', with 46.7 per cent saying 'unmatched' or 'very unmatched'. As a result, nearly half (46.7%) of respondents feel 'unfairly treated' (unmatched), and was much higher (15%) than those who feel 'fairly treated' (matched) (28.9 per cent). We note, furthermore, that there were differences among respondents according to rank. Table 3.3 shows that about half of lecturers or assistant lecturers chose 'unmatched', 20 per cent more than professors, as 40 per cent of the latter chose 'matched'. Clearly, and not unexpectedly, younger teachers are more sensitive to unfair pay issues than their colleagues in senior ranks.

We also asked respondents about the income gaps between teachers with administrative titles and ordinary teachers without administrative titles. The result shows that 19.0 per cent of respondents felt the difference was 'too big', 34.8 per cent said 'big', 40.3 per cent said 'OK', with only 3.8 per cent and 1.2 per cent saying 'small' or 'very small' respectively. In other words, over half of respondents (53.8%) feel the distribution of income to be unfair, 14 per cent higher than those who believe the current system to be acceptable (40 per cent). Furthermore, nearly half (48.1%) of teachers without administrative titles feel it

Table 3.3 Are your incomes matched with your performances (%)?

Job title	Matched	Neutral	Unmatched
Professor	40.2	26.0	33.8
Associate Professor	30.2	23.0	46.8
Lecturer or below	23.9	24.7	51.4
Total	28.9	24.3	46.7

to be unfair, which is 20 per cent higher than those who believe it to be 'acceptable' (28.1%). However, surprisingly, among respondents with administrative titles only 30.8 per cent said it was 'acceptable', with 44.7 per cent saying it was 'unfair'. It seems that a large number of respondents in administrative roles are also concerned about unfair distribution of incomes in the HE sector.

It seems that, for the participants in the survey, the distribution pattern of incomes among university teachers was not only an internal matter within the HE sector, but involved a comparison with counterparts in other sectors. For this reason, we asked respondents how their incomes compared with professionals in other sectors. Unsurprisingly, over 60 per cent of respondents said 'unfairly', with only 7.5 per cent saying 'fairly'. Such a high level of dissatisfaction was due to their perception that the average incomes of university teachers, comparative with other sectors, was lower across Beijing. According to official statistics, the mean wage of all employees in both public and private sectors across Beijing was 65,700 Yuan in 2010 (BBS, 2011), about 15 per cent and 40 per cent higher than the average wages of university teachers and lecturers in our survey (57,285 and 49,045 Yuan) respectively. In 2011, the mean wage of all employees in Beijing was 75,834 Yuan, of which 198,409 Yuan were for finances, 114,168 Yuan for IT services, 101,033 Yuan for research and development, 84,897 Yuan for health and social security, and only 77,566 Yuan for education (including HE). Given such comparisons, unsurprisingly, many participants and in particular the younger ones felt that being university teachers was not economically rewarding.

Bureaucratisation: an explanation for the uneven distribution of incomes in the HE sector

A further question arises: Why has such an apparently unfair system emerged and been maintained despite the dissatisfaction of large numbers of university teachers, including those with administrative titles? We do not think it can be explained by specific parameters such as gender, age, qualifications or personal capacity as some scholars have suggested (Wu *et al.*, 2005; Zhao, 2013). Instead it is explained by the various economic, social, political and cultural factors driving the reform and expansion of China's HE sector since 2000. In particular, we identify *bureaucratisation* as a major factor responsible for the uneven distribution of incomes within universities.

The term 'bureaucratisation' refers to the centralisation of key resources in administrative departments, schools and staff, leading to the marginalisation of the vast majority of teachers. The consequence of bureaucratisation is that the distribution of resources and incomes is skewed to administrative staff, including those academic staff with administrative job titles (Zhao and Zhu, 2010). Bureaucratisation is not, of course, new to China's modern universities which were developed on the Soviet model. What is new is the unexpected scale and impact on university management in an era of marketisation, decentralisation and increasing government investment. This means that senior managers in universities via the administrative departments have much more power to decide or manipulate the allocation of various resources among different departments, disciplines and groups, without a proper procedure of consultation. This has resulted in an uneven distribution of incomes, leading to increasing dissatisfaction among university teachers in general and young teachers in particular (Shi and Zhang, 2012b). The process and consequences of bureaucratisation since the expansion of HE sector are shown below.

- Distribution of key resources by the administrative system without academic participation. Universities allocate scarce resources via their administrative departments such as Planning, Personnel, Research and Development, and Teaching, resulting in a total control of university teachers. A good example is the selection and distribution of various government allowances, such as 'Yangze Scholarship' and 'Trans-Century Talents', which permit allowance holders to use a large proportion of the funding for personal expenditure. Given the absence of an open and transparent competition, the process has caused contradictions and debates within universities (Wang, 2002).
- An uneven distribution of university resources to a few subjects and professors. This is similar to state policy which focused government investment on key universities via its '985' or '211' programmes, where a few subjects are selected as university priorities while senior academic staff with administrative titles become 'super-bosses' who control most of the resources, which leaves little for young teachers who depend upon such 'bosses' for research opportunities and publications. The competition is intensified by the connection between project funding and the incomes of project holders and participants (an important part of informal pay or grey income) directly. An interviewee complained: 'Some professors in my view are just like project contractors who do nothing but exploit young colleagues and postgraduate students. For the same project, he may apply and gain financial support from 12 different sources. It is really corrupt indeed!'
- All administrative departments are likely to have their own 'research' budgets, which allow them to conduct 'research' or to commission academic staff to do so, which induces academic staff to become administrators. This is why informal incomes are more likely to be secured by teachers with administrative titles than those without.

Many consequences follow such bureaucratisation. The most salient is perhaps the erosion of professionalism, since nothing is more important than political value or administrative assessment, to which academic research or publications become a means for either a share of resources or for earning more informal income. This is why access to or distance from administrative power become key factors in determining income distribution among university teachers. Success in access to political resources or administrative power without high professional standards, however, may not win respect from students, but will instead have a negative impact, because less attention is paid to teaching students than to 'research' or 'publications'. Again, priority is given to the quantity of research rather than to its quality, contributing to human knowledge and our understanding of the world. It gives a message to students about professionalism and about the reward system in society which erodes the social function or responsibility of universities in terms of social justice in China.

Conclusion

This chapter has shown the uneven distribution of incomes in Beijing's universities and perceptions of teachers. What conclusions may be drawn from its empirical survey and analysis?

First, the unevenness of income distribution has become a serious issue facing China's HE sector today. This is shown by the income differences among those with the same job rank which is greater than between those with different job ranks. A few people in the top income group have not only distorted the structure of income distribution, but also given a wrong impression about the general level of university teachers' incomes.

Second, income inequality in universities is caused mainly by informal incomes which are distributed very unevenly among university teachers. Bearing in mind that no 'grey income' was included in the survey, the real situation is even more serious than is shown by our statistics. Abolishing or regularising 'grey income' (by increasing the transparency of financial management) and reducing the proportion of other informal incomes in total incomes (by increasing formal incomes) are important tasks for the further reform of the HE sector in China.

Third, income inequality has serious consequences for the younger generation of teachers in universities, not only because they have fewer resources and opportunities to earn informal or grey incomes, but also because they are facing heavy pressure to access housing markets in Beijing and other major cities of China. It seems that a large increase of basic wages is an important condition for the development of a high standard of professionalism in China, which would enable academics to concentrate on research quality and teaching performance, without worrying too much about informal income.

Fourth, employment equality or decent work for university teachers, which is related to fair pay or fair distribution of incomes within universities, can hardly be achieved unless the bureaucratisation controlling resources is broken. This requires the development and enhancement of professionalism which emphasises professional standards, quality of research and teaching on the one hand, and collegial procedures, equal opportunity, and respect and dignity for all staff on the other. The desire for employment equality is not limited to the HE sector, but requires political reform in China which would reduce the control of the political system over its organisation and direction.

Finally, apart from income distribution and job satisfaction among university teachers, employment equality in the HE sector would influence, directly or indirectly, the mission of universities in promoting social justice in the wider society. Further research is needed to identify the links between employment equality, professional standards and the perceptions of students about social justice.

Notes

1 The empirical data used by this chapter are drawn from a questionnaire survey conducted in a number of universities in Beijing. With a theme of income distribution and stimulation mechanism among university teachers, this survey was sponsored by the Education Department of Beijing municipal government, and implemented by a team, including Professor Zhang Jing, Professor Shi Xiuying, Dr. Li, Junfu, Dr. Zhao Weihua, Dr. Liu Jingwei, among others.
2 The media report is available online at: http://epaper.oeeee.com/A/html/2013–03/18/ content_1823118.htm (accessed 27 August 2014).
3 More online comments on this event are available at: http://news.sciencenet.cn/html/ comment.aspx?id=275744 (accessed 27 August 2014).

References

Altbach, P.G., Reisberg, L., Yudkevich, M., Androushchak, G. and Pacheco, I.F. (2012), *Paying the Professoriate: A global comparison of compensation and contract*, London and New York: Routledge.

Beijing Bureau of Statistics (BBS) (2011), Annual Report of Economic-Social Statistics in Beijing. Available online at: www.bjstats.gov.cn/.

Feng, T. and Xiu, X. (1993), The inner relations and structure of China enterprise in the move to a market economy (in Chinese), *China Social Science*, 3: 101–120.

Kaurin, D. and Morgan, W.J. (2014), The changing expectations of education for the professions in post-socialist Serbia: The views of lawyers and of university teachers, *International Journal of Continuing Education and Lifelong Learning*, 16(2): 59–74.

Li, F., Morgan, W.J. and Ding, X. (2011), The labour market for graduates in China, in Morgan, W.J. and Wu, B. (eds) *Higher Education Reform in China: Beyond the expansion*, London and New York: Routledge, pp. 93–108.

Li, K. and Shang, L. (2009), On the external equity: A case study of post subsidy systems in colleges and universities (in Chinese), *Journal of Zhejiang Education Institute*, 2: 19–25.

Li, Z. (2011), Labour right and protection of teachers: A perspective of decent work (in Chinese), *Theory and Practice of Education*, 5: 30–32.

Liu, J., Zhang, J., Li, J. and Zhao, W. (2012), An analysis of the pay satisfaction and its influential factors of university faculty in Beijing – based on the sample survey of 18 universities in Beijing (in Chinese), *Fudan Education Forum*, 2: 72–77.

Liu, W. (2013), Performance appraisal programme was censured that discriminate against teaching staff (in Chinese), *Nanfang City Daily*, 18 March, A20. Available online at: http://epaper.oeeee.com/A/html/2013-03/18/content_1823118.htm.

She, Y. (2001), The influence of income disparity on university staff and countermeasure (in Chinese), *Journal of Architectural Education Institutions of Higher Learning*, 1: 69–71.

Shi, X. and Zhang, J. (2012a), Marketization reform of university and university staff, *Beijing Social Development Report* (in Chinese) (2011–2012): 93–112.

Shi, X. and Zhang, J. (2012b), University management and university staff in transformation (in Chinese), *Annual Report on of Beijing Society Building* (2012): 133–154.

Sun, H. (2009), The analysis of uneven of income distribution in China: An institutional perspective (in Chinese), *Study and Exploration*, 1: 133–136.

Sun, J. (1996), The cause of perception of unfairness of distribution and its strategies of adjustment (in Chinese), *Jiangxi Social Science*, 9: 60–63.

Tong, L. (2007), Are you happy, university teachers? (in Chinese), *Henan Education* (Higher Education Edition), 7: 8–9.

Wang, C. (2002), How much are incomes of university staff? (in Chinese), *Social Science Weekly*, 26 December.

Wang, J. (2012), Analysis of the title structure of college teachers at different levels and types of colleges, A Master degree dissertation (in Chinese), Wuhan: Wuhan University of Technology.

Wang, M. and Yu, N. (2014), The cause of graduates' and civil servants' frenzy and countermeasures (in Chinese), *Journal of Changchun University of Science and Technology* (Social Sciences Edition), 2: 172–184.

Wang, P. (2011), Analysis of depth reasons of unfair individual income distribution in China and the countermeasures (in Chinese), *Journal of China University of Petroleum* (Social Sciences Edition), 1: 51–55.

Wang, X. (1997), Grey incomes enlarge the gap of income (in Chinese), *China Reform*, 7: 9–12.

Wang, Y. (2011), The sociological analysis of the frenzy to register for civil servants' examination (in Chinese), *Journal of Changchun University of Technology* (Higher Education Edition), 2: 84–92.

Wu, S., Chen, Q. and Yang, Q. (2005), A survey on teachers' satisfaction with their income in research-led universities (in Chinese), *Science Research Management*, 5: 152–156.

Xie, X. (2011), University teacher is not a decent profession (in Chinese), *Education*: 35.

Xiong, B. (2010a), Happiness and sorrow for the first choice of graduates employment is SOE (in Chinese), *Career Development*, 18: 25.

Xiong, B. (2010b), There are shady regulations in scholar's income (in Chinese), *People's Tribune*, 27: 40–41.

Xu, Y. (2012), Distribution of incomes in China and cause analysis (in Chinese), *Reformation and Strategy*, 10: 30–33.

Yang, X. (2010), The Marxist concept of labour and university teacher decent work, *Higher Education Forum*, 8: 97–99.

Zhang, Z. and Mao, J. (2013), Research of scale, structure, level and effect factors of research income in universities (in Chinese), *Modern Education Management*, 6: 25–30.

Zhao, H. (2009), Decent work and right protection for teaching staff (in Chinese), *Trade Union Tribune*, 4: 54–55.

Zhao, L. and Zhu, J. (2010), China's higher education reform: What has not been changed?, *East Asian Policy*, 2(4):115–125.

Zhao, W. (2013), Analysis of factors influencing income distribution in universities: Based on the data of 18 universities in Beijing (in Chinese), *Fudan Education Forum*, 2: 66–67.

4 The career prospects of university graduates from urban families

A cultural perspective

Dian Liu and Yanbi Hong[1]

Introduction

The past decade has witnessed a rapid expansion in Chinese higher education with a sharp growth in both student enrolment and, consequently, in the number of graduates. In 2003, there were 1.88 million graduates entering the Chinese labour market and this had reached 6.99 million by 2013. In the meantime the problem of graduate unemployment in China began to grow. This is shown by the steady fall in the graduate employment rate. This fell from 64.7 per cent in 2002 to 50 per cent in 2003 and continued to fall in subsequent years (MoE, 1998–2007, 2003–2009). The Ministry of Human Resources and Social Security admitted in early 2013 that graduate employment continued to be a severe problem. In the Beijing region alone, less than one-third of the total graduates had signed job contracts by April 2013.[2]

This situation has led to research and policy interest in the factors affecting graduate unemployment. Researchers have found that students from urban households, with higher family income, parental educational level and occupational status, are more likely to obtain higher socio-economic status (SES) jobs and secure a higher salary in the labour market (Min *et al.*, 2006; MyCOS, 2009; Wen, 2005).[3] The research literature attributes the better chances of students from such higher SES households to the valuable job information offered by their higher status contacts embedded in their social network and that job-seekers depend largely on their family networks in order to be employed (Bian and Huang, 2009). This literature adapts the social network job search framework developed by Granovetter (1995) to the Chinese context and examines functioning mechanisms of social ties in the Chinese society (Bian, 1994; Li *et al.*, 2012). However, this literature has largely ignored the gradually established market mechanism in the graduate labour market with formalised recruiting procedures. Thus the older generations now use their influence in a more indirect manner rather than simply introducing good contacts to their relatives. Therefore, this chapter argues for a more comprehensive explanation of the SES–job chance linkage by introducing the cultural capital explanatory framework. This uses Bourdieu's idea of maintaining the cultural experiences at home as a means by which to facilitate students' passage in their later life trajectory. According to this framework, chances in the job market in terms of higher SES occupations and salary level are improved by a cultural definition of excellence that derives from middle-class parental intervention to keep children 'on the right track'.

In order to test this theory in practice, 30 senior fourth-year students from urban middle-class families[4] were interviewed between 2011 and 2012 at two universities in Middle China. Drawing upon the data collected, it first argued that the characteristics and skills intensively cultivated by the parents at an early stage have a strong influence on students' career perspectives. Second, focus is given to the direct parental involvement and family influences at each stage of the job search. Urban middle-class parents always keep their children 'on the right track' of a standard middle-class career path, and sometimes even take on a stronger role to 'correct' students' inclinations to move away from this path. This chapter first reviews the cultural capital studies related to social exclusion and show how this explanatory framework is applied in this study. It then demonstrates how parental involvement at the early stage and at the job search stage influences students' chances in the labour market. In conclusion, it is emphasised that parental practices bind together the urban Chinese middle-class cultural system which is oriented to personal advancement and which effectively excludes underprivileged students in the labour market.

Middle-class and cultural capital

As early as the 1920s, Alfred Marshall observed that middle-class parents, 'while generally eager to save some capital for their children, are even more alert for opportunities of investing it in them' (Marshall, 1920: 562). In the decades that followed, such family-based inequality has been identified by sociologists as vital to the reproduction of the middle class. Some of the most influential work on this issue has been conducted by Pierre Bourdieu in France.[5] He developed the concept of cultural capital to examine the 'affinity between class cultural habits and the demands of the educational system or the criteria which define success within it' (Bourdieu and Passeron, 1979: 22). The core idea of cultural capital is the direct or indirect 'imposition' of evaluative norms favouring the children or families of a particular social milieu (Lareau and Weininger, 2003: 598). It has been useful with regard to the idea of cultural capital to understand how individuals and families from middle-class backgrounds are able to capitalise on their cultural assets in ways that those from disadvantaged backgrounds are not (Brown, 1995; Crozier *et al.*, 2011; Demerath, 2009; Demerath *et al.*, 2008; Hardaway and McLoyd, 2009; Lareau and Horvat, 1999).

Lareau's (2003) research shows that parents from different class backgrounds have very different perceptions of their roles in facilitating their children's development of cognitive and non-cognitive skills. Middle-class parents adopt a 'concerted cultivation' style of parenting which involves a deliberate cultivation of children's skills and talents; while working-class parents engage in an 'accomplishment of natural growth' style of parenting which allows children to grow up in a more spontaneous manner.

How does this affect contemporary China? The dramatic expansion of China's higher education since 1999 has increased the educational opportunities for students from all social strata. Together with the booming economic development, this higher education expansion has been producing a large number of *potential* middle-class members from every sector of Chinese society (Lin and Sun, 2010). Although the exact size of the Chinese middle class is still an open question, its increasing number and the important role in current Chinese society is beyond doubt (Li, 2010). However, this does not imply that middle-class parents can pass their social status on to their children automatically. In the reform period, with the marketisation of the *danwei* unit and its planned employment policy, the principle of meritocracy has become more popular in the more open labour market than before (Wu, 2002). Hence very few middle-class families can now maintain their social positions through direct inheritance, or through monopolistic control over the market for best jobs. With the dramatic higher education expansion, many college graduates from middle-class families experienced difficulty in finding jobs (Li, 2010: 4). The perceived 'risks' associated with unemployment and educational change since the mid-1970s have made parents more aware of the uncertainties of success and the consequences of failure. They turn to more specific strategies to facilitate the excellence of their children to succeed with the heightened 'competition for a livelihood' in the modern society (Weber, 1978).

The students from middle-class families surely enjoy better opportunities than those from lower class families, but the successful transmission also requires the involvement of students themselves. In the Wisconsin Model of educational and occupational attainment, parental expectation and students' self-expectation play crucial intermediate roles in social reproduction and mobility (Sewell *et al.*, 1969).[6] In other words, agency and aspiration cannot be ignored. In the Wisconsin Model significant others play an important role in shaping students' educational and occupational expectations. Family members of course comprise the majority of significant others in Chinese society. In middle-class families, such expectations are an important goal of cultivation. Expectation cultivation sometimes involves parents' direct intervention in children's choices and activities.

In China such social class differences and parental involvement persist throughout the whole of children's education and their transition from the education system to the job market. Current literature analysing Chinese graduates' job search processes relies mainly on social capital (Xue, 2009; Meng *et al.*, 2012; Li *et al.*, 2012), while relatively few studies pay attention to influencing mechanisms of family cultural capital. In fact, child-rearing and parenting is a cultural practice (Lareau, 2003: 4–5), and broadly includes educational expectations and participation in high-status cultural activities (Roksa and Potter, 2011). Hence, Lareau's class-differed parenting thesis can be extended to undergraduates' experiences and helps in understanding educational outcomes.

Cultural capital and social capital are often intertwined with each other. In his analysis of how social capital affects the function of credentials, Bourdieu (1977: 506) emphasised that social capital is sometimes transmitted through cultural capital. In educational studies, Modood (2004) points out that the majority of

American researchers subsume Bourdieu's concept of cultural capital within social capital in their analyses; while British researchers prefer to adopt both concepts in a complementary way. In the job search processes on the one hand, the social capital approach emphasises the resources parents provide to facilitate graduates' employment; on the other hand, the cultural capital approach pays more attention to parents' perceptions, the cultural dispositions and the cultural abilities of the individuals.

By comparison with the theoretical approach of social capital, this chapter argues that the functioning of cultural capital represents a more subtle and sophisticated means of class reproduction, resulting in selective university graduates' occupational attainment. By extending Lareau's concepts of 'concerted cultivation' parenting of the middle class and the 'accomplishment of natural growth' parenting of the working class, this chapter argues that such class differences continue during higher education and during the transition from education to society – a key point of the life course. The job searches of students from middle-class backgrounds are more planned and monitored by their parents compared with those of their counterparts from working-class families.

How was our data collected?

The data were collected from October 2011 to March 2012 with a group of 30 final-year middle-class students from two universities in Wuhan, Middle China. Urban middle-class students were identified through their parental occupations following the classification of the Chinese middle class by Lu Xueyi (2003, 2012). Students were invited to participate in the interviews on a voluntary basis. There were two rounds of interviews in the data-collection process: the first round was conducted prior to December 2011 to collect students' first-hand job search experience. The second round interviews finished in March 2012 to trace students' follow-up job search behaviours. Key questions in the first round included student background, early childhood education, job preparation and job search difficulties encountered. The second round of interviews focused on the students' job search experiences, their compromises and parental involvement during the job search. All the informants are referred to by numbers, and all the names used here are pseudonyms.

Parental involvement and practices during the early stage

According to cultural capital theory, students from higher socio-economic backgrounds are exposed to socially valued knowledge and cultural cues much earlier than those from lower social strata (Bourdieu, 1977). For example, they may possess more cultural goods and media, such as works of art and instruments, and also develop the ability to understand and appreciate those cultural goods at quite an early age. In much research, scholars have found that the initial differences in cultural dispositions have been reinforced during schooling, resulting in the greater achievement of middle-class students (Graham, 1992; Hardaway and

McLoyd, 2009; Rothstein, 2004). Certain types of cultural dispositions, such as reading ability (Burgess, 1997; Ujiie and Krashen, 1996), calligraphy practice and piano playing (Kraus, 1989) have long been recognised as the middle-class ways of cognitive development, later being translated into individual advances in their life trajectory. The following section evaluates the two types of cultural assets reported by the interviewees as those that distinguish them from the competitors, and also evaluates the dialectical effects of the early investment made by the parents in the later job search.

Hobby cultivation

Nearly all of the 30 middle-class interviewees reported mastery of one or two hobbies from childhood. One of the students, whose father is the owner of a private bank and whose mother is a local university professor, stated:

> You know in the 1990s China witnessed a national incredible hot flash on piano in cities. Parents are keen on sending their children to learn piano playing at a quite early age. When, at 4, I was taken to a renowned private piano tutor who lives in another city twice a week. Each course lasted for 90 minutes, and cost 20 Yuan as the tuition fee, which was quite a lot of money at the time, because the monthly salary of my parents was around only 120 Yuan then. The childhood nightmare began from then on. I was forced to practise for at least two hours every day, and the observed half-heartedness brought me even longer practice. That continued until I entered middle school when being an academic top student became the No. 1 focus and much of the spare time had to be spent on private tutoring, but that is another story.

> (Interview No. 6)

This is a typical middle-class childhood description of the Chinese youngsters born in the late 1980s and early 1990s. It is very subtle to explore the reason why the 1960s-born parents are so enthusiastic in introducing Western musical instruments and arts into the lives of their offspring. One possibility is that, as a generation which witnessed the Cultural Revolution, they experienced a time when Western music and arts were considered to be an imperialist intrusion, in direct conflict with the native aesthetic. A response from a student may explain this complex situation:

> I believe they start to suspect many of the acts prior to the 1978 reform when the whole country began to reflect what happened during the past decade. They realised they had lost the best chance of learning and projected their lost desire on their children. Even though I suffered a lot during the childhood 'training', I really understand them now and appreciate the chance they tried hard to create for me.

> (Interview No. 2)

Such specialties are stated succinctly in the résumés when students look for jobs. In most cases students' résumés also recorded the performances with the specialty and awards won from the competitions they attended. These special lines 'express their difference from students with the same majors'. Students at the two universities 'who passed the national college entrance exam, do not feel much difficulty in passing exams or getting decent scores. Thus it is factors such as the ability to play piano or being awarded a prize in a painting competition that really matters' (Interview No. 12) in showing whether you are excellent or not.

Language training

Second-language learning has also been greatly emphasised by middle-class parents. Parents act differently in terms of how to make their children learn foreign languages. Some middle-class parents know or studied foreign languages when they were young, and want their children to learn the language and its culture at an early age. As some students reported, their mothers were their first English-language teachers. Furthermore, middle-class parents turn to private tutoring, language training centres or even travel to English-speaking countries to equip their children with more skills and a better language learning environment.

> When I was at my second year in junior middle school, my parents registered a summer school for me in Australia. It was a four-week summer camp for international students and I was the only student from Mainland China. This is a great opportunity. For the first time of my life, I have to abandon my mother tongue and use independently a second language. My English speaking improved dramatically during these four weeks. My parents felt so pleased with the progress and happily sent me to more exchange programmes later on.
>
> (Interview No. 15)

Many middle-class parents had long determined to send their children abroad to study; thus proficiency in a second language was seen not only as an excellent skill but also as a basic requirement that needed to be fulfilled.

> To continue the postgraduate study in America is common perspective we have made since high school. My parents do not trust the higher education quality [in China] so much, and planned to send me abroad if I failed the college entrance exam. Since I was admitted in this university, they postponed the studying abroad schedule. I began the preparation since sophomore study, mostly on passing GRE and TOFEL. I was in New Oriental School for two summers. My TOFEL score is satisfactory, but will have another try on GRE.
>
> (Interview No. 20)

In both universities, the English language is a required course for the first two years. In University A, students were required to take an English-language ability test upon their enrolment. Based on the test results, students were classified into two groups: the advanced English class and the average class. For the following two years, they attend English classes with students from the same group under university arrangement. It is very interesting to observe that the advanced English classes with an average number of 20 students are dominated by students from urban middle-class families, given that all 15 students from University A are located in the advanced English class.

Such language ability has been identified as vital both from the students' responses and from the employers' survey (MyCOS, 2009, 2011). During the job search, language proficiency is an 'absolute item to be examined by employers'. In some English-conducted job interviews, the interviewees report that they can comfortably demonstrate their language ability in the circumstances they are familiar with, and naturally received satisfactory feedback from the employers.

Parental involvement and practices during the job search

While middle-class expectations and awareness of future uncertainties and competition influence the cultivation of children from an early age, they also shaped the parenting styles and practices in the job search process of the students. This section examines the distinctive combination of effective support and 'pushing' that characterised middle-class parenting styles. It describes parents' skilful abilities in intervening in job search behaviour, drawing upon their cultural knowledge and professional networks to appropriate special resources for the benefit of their children.

As mentioned in earlier sections, much of the most compelling research on job search and socio-economic linkage in transitional China has used the social capital approach represented by Bian Yanjie and his colleagues (Bian, 1994b, 1997; Bian and Huang, 2009). Based on survey findings, Bian (1997) concluded that with the unstable legal enforcement in binding contracts and the lack of procedure neutrality in management, many turn to informal mechanisms such as personal relationships and family ties, also known as an important part of *guanxi* (Yan, 1996; Xie, 2011), to improve their job prospects. They claim that both information and influence are distinct resources, embedded in and mobilised from networks of personal contacts. Thus individuals with higher social status rely on strong ties of trust and obligation to obtain higher status jobs, contributing to an unequal social pattern in contemporary China. As valuable as this line of study is, it fails to provide a reasonable explanation of the negotiation between the gradually formalised selection procedure forced by marketisation, the agency of the job-seekers, and the sphere of influence based on socio-economic status. This section examines how the 'class practices' of middle-class parents influence the job search. The findings imply that middle-class parents align themselves with the standard of gatekeeping institutions responsible for 'social selection', and such explicit actions conferred important advantages upon their offspring.

Economic support

The enhanced level of economic support is probably one of the most apparent disparities that distinguishes middle-class students from their socio-economically disadvantaged classmates, since job searching is not only time-consuming but also rather costly. According to MyCOS (2009), students who graduated in 2008 in Middle China spent an average of 1,337 Yuan on the job search. Again, in a recent report on graduate job search costs in Hubei province, it was found that graduates spent three months and more than 2,000 Yuan on average in 2009, while a majority of students (81%) depended on family financial support for job hunting (Zou *et al.*, 2010). Money is spent chiefly on clothes in preparation for interview, on preparing a CV professionally, and on travelling and other communication expenses. Even though there is no causal link between cost and occupational attainment, students are spending more money on job searches year by year. One reason for the increased economic investment is probably the 'stagflation which makes people spend more money now', as many students claimed. The other reason is that some students' costly and thorough preparation naturally forced up the expense of job search for the class as a whole. This phenomenon is found widely and it is usually the middle-class students who spend more.

> I began the job search from last October. The first thing to do is to invite a consultant firm help me prepare a résumé. The school career office did hold several seminars on CV preparation, but I do not think the presenters are professional enough, nor are the courses they supplied. The résumé packing costs me 200 Yuan, which is okay. After I received interview invitation I bought myself two suits since most of my clothes are sports style which is too casual for job interviews. The suits and shoes altogether took around 3,000 Yuan. [This student probably sensed my surprise when I heard how much they cost, and he further explained in the following.] This is actually okay. This is the average cost of my clothes. The living cost is rising year by year, and if you go to Wuhan Plaza [the biggest shopping mall in Wuhan], you will find most of the clothes cost over 1,000 Yuan. I did not try chances in other cities, so basically these are all the costs.
>
> (Interview No. 21)

Again, some students seek jobs in other cities due to the fierce competition with so many higher education institution graduates in Wuhan and the relatively low salary levels available. The reports noted below are interesting examples. Ding Wei made a deal with his parents that he would like to try his chances in Beijing for one month. If he could not find a satisfactory job he would return to Wuhan and follow his parents' arrangements. His parents gave him 10,000 Yuan and told him not to disturb other family members who live in Beijing. He bought clothes and a laptop, paid 6,000 Yuan for a nice apartment in the central part of the city, and set out to be 'independent'. After several days he found that even though he happily reported his progress to his parents, he continued to receive money transferred from home and packages of new clothes which his mother prepared for him. His relatives, on the other hand, invited him to meals nearly every day and he was embarrassed to discover that he had spent just 2,000 Yuan other than the rent on his apartment.

Parental suggestions

It is clear that, first, students from higher socio-economic backgrounds are eager to communicate with their parents. Second, parents from more affluent socio-economic backgrounds are eager to offer suggestions to their children. And, third, students from more affluent socio-economic backgrounds are likely to accept the suggestions from their parents.

Several middle-class students commented on the importance of their parents' support in their job search. For example, Xuxu's mother edited her résumé and proofread her application letters before she sent them to prospective employers. When she received interview invitations, her mother rehearsed with her, acting as the company interviewer, challenging her with all the possible questions. She thought this was really useful and beneficial. The whole process was 'much easier with her involved' and she attributed 90 per cent of her success to the support of her parents.

Again, Tian Liang received several job offers after two months of job hunting. The job categories were very distinctive from each other. Three seemed very satisfactory and he could not make up his mind. He turned to his father for suggestions. His father suspected that one of the private companies was conducting illegal sales and stopped him communicating further with the company. It turned out that his father was right, while some students from other majors were deceived by such frauds.

Parental intervention

As mentioned above, the reforming structure, educational change and increasing unemployment make many middle-class parents aware of the uncertainties of the future and about losing their socio-economic status. Many adopt a supervisory view of the job search behaviour of their children, offering suggestions and 'corrections' persistently. When major differences with their children occurred parents identified the disagreement as a significant negative and exploited it in their efforts to drag their children back on to the right track.

For example, a closer look at Yin Zhiluo's parents' intervention in their son's career choice is telling. Yin expressed his wish to be a singer following graduation. He was proficient in the guitar and composing, organised his own band with two of his friends, and performed at campus activities and in nearby pubs around the school. He planned to tell his parents about his dream of singing professionally. However, his family ran a law firm in another city not far from Wuhan, which was identified as one of the best ten law firms in China the previous year. In his interview he expressed his anxieties about his parents objecting to his career plan, since they wanted him, their only son, to join the family firm. This was why he was a law major at university, and his parents planned to send him abroad to obtain further legal qualifications and then for him to return home to practise law in China.

During Yin's first interview, he was struggling with his parents over his dream career. This made his responses somewhat emotional.

I: What kinds of concerns and anxieties do your parents have about your plan? Can you talk about that?

Y: They strongly disagree with my idea, as I anticipated months ago. They say it is quite an unrealistic and improper plan, so let the dream just be the dream, and come back to earth. Basically they have three concerns. First, how can I feed myself with such an unstable job? Every year there are so many dream carriers who train themselves as singers or actors, but very few of them succeed at the last. Second, this is not a decent job. They say singers, actors and the so-called entertainers are lower occupations in traditional opinions. Even today the entertainment business is not a bright industry. People will look down upon me and the family if I undertake it. And lastly, I should take responsibility to the family business as the only son. They work hard for years to earn this decent and venerable life, and I am obliged to maintain it.

I: Did you have any negotiations with each other on how to deal with this disagreement? Any compromise or discussion?

Y: Both my parents and I have strong ideas right now. The whole thing has made this spring festival very unpleasant. They force me to abandon the unrealistic idea and I do not think I can make it. They signed a contract with an overseas education agency and try to persuade me abroad. I have not sent any required document to the agency by now. I just do not want to follow it. Even though I do understand the concerns they have, and my duty to the family firm. I just really do not want to abandon the dream like this. This makes my dream so cheap.

However, during the follow-up interview Yin admitted that he had finally achieved a compromise with his parents. His parents respected his dream to be a singer and allowed him to study music as a minor. He will not become a singer as a full-time career but will continue it as a lifelong hobby. He will go abroad to study finance and will join the family firm after graduation.

Conclusion

The family plays a vital role both at the early stage and during the job search process of junior secondary class students. In this study the early stage refers specifically to the years prior to senior secondary school when the core task for students is the aim of entering a good university. However, these early stage family influences enhance the campus experience and allow middle-class students to outpace the rest (Gaddis and Payton, 2011; Roksa and Potter, 2011; Wu, 2011). They also enhance the job search in that such influences function as extra credits towards students' employability. In the early stage, middle-class parents place a high premium on 'personal qualities' such as language training, hobby cultivation and communication skills, and these cultural assets mark out middle-class students from others both at school and during the job search.

The literature (Bian, 1997; Lin and Dumin, 1986; Obukhova, 2011; Yong and Yu, 2011) consistently confirms the pattern that middle-class students, with more job information, higher status contacts and wider social networks, are more likely to obtain better jobs than their underprivileged counterparts. However, we claim that the discrepancy in job search is not merely attributed to network differences, but also to the joint work of the delicately constructed 'excellence' (the capitalised cultural assets), family socio-economic support, and the strong intervention of parental encouragement and direction. This chapter has also described the negotiation between students' aspirations and choice and parental willingness and support during the job search process. When students and parents look in the same direction for a future career, all available resources are activated to make it happen. When disagreements occur parents tend to take a stronger role to 'correct' the inclination of their children and to bring them back to the 'standard middle-class career path'. These parental practices devoted to negotiating special circumstances for their own offspring certainly form a central component of the middle-class code: they make up a key link that binds together this urban Chinese middle-class cultural system oriented towards personal advancement. All of these strategies adopted by middle-class families are rarely available to poor families from both urban and rural China, although such groups are not the focal point of this chapter.

As one of the three pivotal equal education processes, the equity of educational outcomes – in other words, the application of educational credentials – plays a critical role in maintaining social justice (Coleman, 1975). This chapter suggests that social reproduction takes place more subtly nowadays. For most middle-class families, the passing on of privileges to their children happens more obliquely. This study explains how advances in job search are delicately constructed with parental cultivation at the early stage and parental intervention at a later stage, in order to construct a new cultural capital explanatory framework to supplement the social ties approach. This chapter calls also for more empirical studies with richer data and a wider field to examine this argument, especially from a comparative perspective, and to analyse the different educational practices in middle-class and lower class families

Notes

1 Dian Liu is lead author, and contributes to a literature review of the analytical framework, data and data analysis in this chapter. Hong Yanbi contributes to the literature review of cultural capital theory.
2 Available online at: www.cnr.cn/jyxw/201305/t20130521_512631190.shtml (accessed on 12 September 2014).

3 However, in a 2003 survey, Li and colleagues (2009) found that graduates' family class backgrounds had no significant effects on their starting wages. Thus they support the signal model of higher education graduates' job search processes.
4 Lu Xueyi's view on the Chinese middle class is adopted in this chapter (Lu, 2004). This combines the ownership concept of neo-Marxism, Weber's ideas on authority and Bourdieu's concept of expertise. He argues that the classification of Chinese social classes is based on industrialisation and marketisation with the dynamic mechanisms of division of labour and dominance hierarchy.
5 Basil Bernstein also carried out studies within the cultural capital framework, while focusing more on the pedagogy and differentiated codes between the middle and working classes (Bernstein, 2000).
6 The Wisconsin Model of educational and occupational attainment emphasises the importance of significant others and expectations. This is different from Blau and Duncan's Social Status Attainment Model which primarily examines the effects of fathers' education and occupations and respondents' education and first job on respondents' current occupation. For details of the Wisconsin Model, see Sewell and Hauser (1993).

References

Bernstein, B.B. (2000), *Pedagogy, Symbolic Control and Identity: Theory, research, critique*, Lanham, MD: Rowman & Littlefield.

Bian, Y. (1994a), *Work and Inequality in Urban China*, New York: State University of New York Press.

Bian, Y. (1994b), Guanxi and the allocation of urban jobs in China, *The China Quarterly*, 140: 971–999.

Bian, Y. (1997), Bringing strong ties back in: Indirect ties, network bridges and job search in China, *American Sociological Review*, 62: 366–385.

Bian, Y. and Huang, X. (2009), Network resources and job mobility in China's transitional economy, in Keister, L. (ed.) *Work and Organizations in China After Thirty Years of Transition* (Research in the Sociology of Work, Vol. 19), Bingley: Emerald Group Publishing, pp. 255–282.

Bourdieu, P. (1977), Cultural reproduction and social reproduction in power and ideology in education, in Karabel, J. and Halsey, A.H. (eds) *Power and Ideology, Society and Culture*, New York: Oxford University Press, pp. 487–511.

Bourdieu, P. and Passeron, J.C. (1979), *The Inheritors: French students and their relation to culture*, Chicago, IL: University of Chicago Press.

Brown, P. (1995), Cultural capital and social exclusion: Some observations on recent trends in education, employment and the labour market, *Work, Employment and Society*, 9(1): 29–51.

Burgess, S. (1997), The role of shared reading in the development of phonological awareness: A longitudinal study of middle to upper class children, *Early Child Development and Care*, 127(1): 191–199.

Coleman, J.S. (1975), What is meant by 'an equal educational opportunity'?, *Oxford Review of Education*, 1(1):27–29.

Crozier, G., Reay, D. and James, D. (2011), Making it work for their children: White middle-class parents and working-class schools, *International Studies in Sociology of Education*, 21(3): 199–216.

Demerath, P. (2009), *Producing Success: The culture of personal advancement in an American high school*, Chicago, IL: University of Chicago Press.

Demerath, P., Lynch, J. and Davidson, M. (2008), Dimensions of psychological capital in a US suburb and high school: Identities for neoliberal times, *Anthropology and Education Quarterly*, 39(3):270–292.

Gaddis, S.M. and Payton, A.R. (2011), The influence of habitus in the relationship between socioeconomic status, cultural capital, and academic success, Working paper, Department of Sociology, University of North Carolina at Chapel Hill.

Graham, S. (1992), Most of the subjects were white and middle class: Trends in published research on African Americans in selected APA journals, 1970–1989, *American Psychologist*, 47(5): 629–639.

Granovetter, M. (1995), *Getting a Job: A study of contacts and careers*, Chicago, IL: University of Chicago Press.

Hardaway, C.R. and McLoyd, V.C. (2009), Escaping poverty and securing middle class status: How race and socioeconomic status shape mobility prospects for African Americans during the transition to adulthood, *Journal of Youth and Adolescence*, 38(2): 242–256.

Kraus, R.C. (1989), *Pianos and Politics in China: Middle-class ambitions and the struggle over Western music*, New York: Oxford University Press.

Lareau, A. (2003), *Unequal Childhoods: Class, race and family life*, Berkeley: University of California Press.

Lareau, A. and Horvat, E.M.N. (1999), Moments of social inclusion and exclusion race, class, and cultural capital in family–school relationships, *Sociology of Education*, 72(1): 37–53.

Lareau, A. and Weininger, E.B. (2003), Cultural capital in educational research: A critical assessment, *Theory and Society*, 32(5–6): 567–606.

Li, C. (ed.) (2010), *China's Emerging Middle Class: Beyond economic transformation*, Washington, DC: Brookings Institution Press.

Li, F., Ding, X. and Morgan, W.J. (2009), Higher education and the starting wages of graduates in China, *International Journal of Educational Development*, 29: 374–381.

Li, F., Morgan, W.J., Ding, X. and Hou, L. (2012), The choices and effects of institutional embeddedness: Evidence from China's highly transitional graduate labour market, *China: An International Journal*, 10(3): 42–62.

Lin, J. and Sun, X. (2010), Higher education expansion and China's middle class, in Li, C. (ed.) *China's Emerging Middle Class: Beyond economic transformation*, Washington, DC: Brookings Institution Press, pp. 217–242.

Lin, N. and Dumin, M. (1986), Access to occupations through social ties, *Social Networks*, 8: 365–385.

Lu, X. (2003), The divisions and changes of the contemporary Chinese social classes (in Chinese), *Jiangsu Social Sciences*: 4.

Lu, X. (2004), *Social Mobility in Contemporary China* (in Chinese), Beijing: Social Sciences Academic Press.

Lu, X. (ed) (2012), *Social Structure of Contemporary China*, Singapore: World Scientific.

Marshall, A. (1920). *Principles of Economics*, London: The Macmillan Press.

Meng, D., Su, L. and Shi, L. (2012), Review of studies on human capital, social capital, and graduates' employment (in Chinese), *Economic Perspectives*, 1: 86–90.

Min, W., Ding, X., Wen, D. and Yue, C. (2006), An empirical study on the employment of graduates in 2005 (in Chinese), *Journal of Higher Education*, 27(1): 31–38.

Ministry of Education (MoE) (1998–2007), *Statistical Bulletin for Chinese Educational Development:* 1998–2007. Available online at: www.moe.edu.cn/edoas/website18/level2.jsp?tablename=1068.

87

Ministry of Education (MoE) (2003–2009), *Statistical Bulletin for Chinese Educational Development:* 2003–2009. Available online at: www.moe.edu.cn/publicfiles/business/htmlfiles/moe/moe_335/index.html.

Modood, T. (2004), Capital ethnic identity and educational qualifications, *Cultural Trends*, 13(2): 87–105.

MyCOS (2009), *Chinese College Graduates' Employment Annual Report* (in Chinese), Beijing: Social Science Academic Press.

MyCOS (2011), *Chinese College Graduates' Employment Annual Report*, Beijing: Social Science Academic Press (in Chinese).

Obukhova, E. (2011), Motivation vs. relevance: Using strong ties to find a job in urban China, *Social Science Research*, 41(3): 570–580.

Roksa, J. and Potter, D. (2011), Parenting and academic achievement, *Sociology of Education*, 84(4): 299–321.

Rothstein, R. (2004), *Class and Schools: Using social, economic, and educational reform to close the achievement gap*, Washington, DC: Economic Policy Institute.

Sewell, W.H. and Hauser, R.M. (1993), *A Review of the Wisconsin Longitudinal Study of Social and Psychological Factors in Aspirations and Achievements 1963–1992*, Madison, WI: Centre for Demography and Ecology.

Sewell, W.H., Haller, A.O. and Portes, A. (1969), The educational and early occupational attainment process, *American Sociological Review*, 34(1): 82–92.

Ujiie, J. and Krashen, S.D. (1996), Comic book reading, reading enjoyment, and pleasure reading among middle class and chapter I middle school students, *Reading Improvement*, 33: 51–54.

Weber, M. (1978), *Economy and Society: An outline of interpretive sociology*, Berkeley: University of California Press.

Wen, D. (2005), The impacts of SES on higher education opportunity and graduate employment in China (in Chinese), *Peking University Education Review*, 3: 58–63.

Wu, S. (2011), A study on the correlation between the cultural capital and the academic achievement of the fifth grade students in Penghu, A Master's thesis, Tainan: National Tainan University.

Wu, X. (2002), Work units and income inequality: The effect of market transition in urban China, *Social Forces*, 80(3): 1069–1099.

Xie, A. (2011), Guanxi exclusion in rural China: Parental involvement and students' college access, PhD thesis in Faculty of Education, Hong Kong: The University of Hong Kong.

Xue, Z. (2009), A review on social capital and employment of graduates (in Chinese), *Chinese Youth Studies*, 11: 76–81.

Yan, Y. (1996), The culture of guanxi in a north Chinese village, *The China Journal*, 35: 1–25.

Yong, Q. and Yu, P. (2011), The employment probability difference of college graduates between urban and rural background in China: Based on social capital theory (in Chinese), *Economic Review*, 2: 113–118.

Zou, Z., Han, Q., Zhou, C. and Gong, Y. (2010), Report on graduate job search costs in Wuhan (in Chinese), *Modern Business Trade Industry*, 23: 323–324.

5   Moving to find a job

Chinese Masters' degree graduates and internal migration[1]

Fengliang Li, Yandong Zhao and W. John Morgan

Introduction

It is clear that graduates from Chinese higher education, like their counterparts elsewhere in the world, expect to find employment which provides a return on the investment they and their families have made in their formal education and training. They aspire also to employment appropriate to the level of education they have achieved and which provides opportunities for career progress, and which is preferably located somewhere congenial to their personal circumstances. Such expectations are based on an understanding and acceptance, simple or sophisticated, of the basic principles of human capital theory (Schultz, 1961; Becker, 1993a). These are very well known and are summarised here only briefly. The argument is that individuals who consciously invest in education and training with the aim of enhancing their employability, productivity capacity and lifetime earnings acquire human capital.[2] The investment itself comprises both time and money, which includes fees and associated expenditure, living expenses, and earnings forgone during the process of *education*. There is, as with other investments, an expectation of a return. In the same way, state and society invest in the education of citizens and members through the provision of educational facilities and subsidies. In China the state provision of education predominates, although there is a growing private sector, especially in higher education (Li *et al.*, 2011; Li and Morgan, 2013). This constitutes a major stake in the education of Chinese graduates which expects a social return on the investment made (Li *et al.*, 2011).

It is also a key aspect of labour mobility or the capacity of workers, including highly qualified ones, to move freely, in our case physically, from one geographical location to another. This remains problematic in China, chiefly because of the continued, if moderated, application of the household registration system or *hukou* and of the work unit system.[3] Yet such mobility is a fundamental aspect of the effective functioning of an open labour market. These may be seen as relatively neglected aspects of economic and social justice in contemporary China. The theory suggests that, through the process of migration, employment is created that benefits both individuals and society. The former benefit through acquiring employment with its guarantee of income; the latter from the increase in labour capacity as a result of the more effective matching of qualified and skilled individuals to the employment dimension of human capital as education. It can not only achieve economic opportunities through free migration.

The contemporary importance of human capital development for China's sustained economic growth is noted in a significant and relatively recent book, *Investing in Human Capital for Economic Development in China* (Liu *et al.*, 2010). This is an excellent example of contemporary economic and social research on China. It reports on the impact of human capital on economic development and social welfare in contemporary China, drawing upon substantial and recent empirical evidence. In almost 400 pages of closely argued text, often using sophisticated yet accessible econometrics, it provides a major contribution to our knowledge and understanding of this crucially important topic. It teaches us several important things about investing in human capital for economic development in China. The substantial evidence it details provides grounds for optimism while, at the same time, it identifies potential problems, notably socio-economic inequalities which will need to be addressed if the state's objectives of economic growth and a *harmonious society* are to be achieved.

According to human capital theory, migration is as important a dimension of human capital as education. It can not only achieve economic benefits for individual employees, but it also improves the matching quality *between* knowledge and skills and their physical location so that both individual economic and indeed social benefits can be achieved, together with the development of the economy and society generally (Greenwood, 1981; Borjas, 1994).

Over 50 years ago, Sjaastad (1962) initiated the analysis of the possible benefits of migration on individual workers by means of the cost–benefit analytical framework in human capital theories. The benefits identified include increases in income, decreases in living and working costs, as well as growing personal satisfaction towards both life and work. In the wake of this innovative research, many researchers, including Sjaastad himself, hoped to show empirically, using reliable statistics, the income benefits to individual workers of their labour migration. Although some attempts did confirm such a substantial economic benefit (Wertheimer, 1970; Borjas, 1994), others were not able to justify a similar conclusion. For example, research in Canada carried out by Grant and Vanderkamp (1980) found that migration brought negative income effects for individual workers at first, while over the following five years the benefits still remained slight. Even though more evident benefits could be seen beyond the first five years, they still seemed to be rather mediocre. It should be noted that the motivations, processes and outcomes of labour migration are very complex and the identification of economic and other benefits empirically is very difficult. The benefits or otherwise over the short, medium and long term also need to be taken into consideration.

The graduate labour market in China

What is a labour market and how does it operate in China? It is important to note that, other than in a slave economy, labour's services can only be rented, as individual workers cannot be bought and sold. There is also the question of the conditions under which labour is rented: the so-called unpaid or supplementary factors. These include, for instance, the conditions of the work environment, the possible risk of injury, the hours worked and when, and the length of the employment contract. The place of employment should be counted among these factors which affect the labour market in ways which are quite different to the market for commodities such as oil, food, timber and so on. As we have shown above, during the process of turning from a planned to a market economy, China has also liberalised the restrictions on labour migration which is a key to the effective mobility of labour. The moderation of the household registration system or *hukou* and of the work unit system or *danwei* is part of this. Such changes have particularly important consequences for graduates from higher education (Li *et al.*, 2011 and 2013). The Chinese state no longer allocates graduates to jobs according to a system of socialist conscription, but rather encourages a free choice of careers according to labour market demand and individual preferences. This includes the option to migrate in search of employment. As we have seen, this may include emigration from the country of origin, as well as forced migration. In this chapter we are concerned only with voluntary internal migration of Masters' graduates within China as part of an emerging open labour market.

However, such opportunities are now possible in China because of a fundamental policy change based on acceptance of the human capital theories described above. Indeed, it has been pointed out that the relationship between higher education and the general labour market in China is becoming ever closer. As the Chinese economy continues to grow, so the demand for highly qualified workers continues to grow also. As we have pointed out, as individual living standards have grown, they have brought with them an increase in expectations. This has led to twin pressures from the employer demand for highly qualified workers and from individual and family aspirations which, in turn, has led to an expansion of Chinese higher education provision (Li *et al.*, 2013). At the same time, the autonomy of universities and colleges and their institutional ability to provide employment advice and direction to their graduates is also expanding. It is also important to note that a record of success in graduate employment is becoming an essential recruitment factor for many Chinese universities, as is the case elsewhere in the world.

Graduates and internal labour migration

The question here is whether such internal migration in search of employment actually brings significant economic benefits for Chinese higher education graduates. There are in fact many studies of the economic benefits of internal labour migration, both for the individual and for the economy generally; however, most focus on already employed sample groups, notably the migration employment of peasant workers (Zhao, 1999). The migration employment of higher education graduates is under-researched, with only one significant empirical study available

(Yue and Zhou, 2005). This is based on data from a 2003 national investigation of the employment destinations of college and vocational school graduates. It showed that the starting salaries of higher education graduates who moved to another province to find employment were substantially higher than those of their counterparts who remained in their home province. Yue and Zhou concluded that the empirical data they had analysed supported the human capital theory that migration provided the opportunity for talented graduates to find employment with an enhanced starting salary; and that labour market segmentation would restrict the efficiency of the economy as a whole.

In this chapter we continue to use empirical methods, together with a number of innovations and, we hope, improvements. First, we not only investigate the purely monetary benefits of internal migration employment, but also job matching and over-education. We do this because the acquisition of a higher starting salary can only be seen as a private benefit instead of contributing also to the common economic welfare of society, which should be seen as an aspect of social justice; and, according to human capital theories, the value of migration employment lies in optimising the matching qualities of the labour market so as to promote labour capacity and economic efficiency generally. Second, the data used by Yue and Zhou (2005) were from 2003. This was the graduation year of the first class of college students since China started to increase higher education enrolments in 1999. The state policy of expanding higher education enrolments has been maintained vigorously since then. Therefore, it is necessary to analyse the possible economic benefits of higher education graduates' migration employment in the context of this continuing expansion of higher education, and the findings reported in this chapter are based on data obtained in 2007. The sample cases reported in Yue and Zhou's (2005) study are those of college and university graduates, while the sample cases used here are those of postgraduate students at the Master's degree level. The rest of this chapter is organised as follows. The first section covers the research hypotheses. The second section presents the data and explains the design of the research. In the third section we discuss the findings of the research and, finally, offer a set of conclusions and policy implications, including those affecting social justice issues, together with possible directions for further research.

Our research hypotheses

As we have said, according to human capital theory, voluntary migration serves the same purpose as education: to enhance individual capacity to maximise economic income (Becker, 1993b). The qualified and skilled worker invests in a move to a location where job and salary opportunities are greater. Recent empirical studies focusing on China show that when other factors are controlled, moving to another province to find employment can provide a substantial starting salary for graduates of colleges and vocational schools. Hence, in this chapter we hypothesise that this applies also to postgraduates, and specifically to Masters' degree graduates, against an historical background of expanded higher education enrolment. Thus our first hypothesis is that when other factors are controlled, migration in search of employment will bring postgraduates a substantially higher starting salary.

We said above that the economic and social benefits of employment through migration mean not only monetary benefits to individuals but also, more importantly, improvements in the integration of individuals and the contribution of their employment to the economy and to society generally. Even if a higher starting salary is realised, there will be a seriously negative impact on general society if graduates are working outside their qualification range or below the level of their qualifications and abilities. This is, perhaps, another way of describing over-education.[4] For example, if migration employment should render what the graduate has learned in college of little or no value in job terms then this would be a significant waste of specific human capital (Becker, 1993a).

In socio-economic terms, over-education experienced through migration employment would result in a significant waste of higher educational investment by the state or the region, in addition to its potentially limiting career consequences for the individual. Either way, substantial negative effects would be experienced by the general society. A typical example is that many female college graduates from the Philippines migrate to Hong Kong to work as domestic helpers despite the investment in advanced knowledge and formal qualifications through higher education that they and their country have made. Although it may be rewarded generously, such migration has long-term negative effects on the country of origin. Therefore, the research reported here considers empirically the quality of migration employment based on the above two criteria. The second and third hypotheses can be stated more succinctly. They are that: (2) When other factors are controlled, the employment of postgraduates through migration would give them a greater probability of finding a job in which they could apply what they have learned; and (3) When other factors are controlled, the employment of postgraduates through migration would allow much less probability for over-education to occur.

Presentation of data and design of research

The data used are derived from a study of fresh postgraduates' employment conducted in 2007 by the National Research Centre for Science and Technology for Development (now the Chinese Academy of Science and Technology for Development). The survey, employing a stratified random sampling method, focused on 14 higher education institutions and research institutes that offered postgraduate programmes in the cities of Beijing, Shanghai, Wuhan and Lanzhou. A sample allocation was based on the overall number of postgraduate students from each institution and a total of 4,200 samples was collected using random sampling. Self-administered questionnaires were completed between May and July 2007 and, altogether, 3,104 effective questionnaires were collected, with a response rate of 73.9 per cent.

The aim of this chapter is to consider empirically the economic benefits of postgraduates' employment through internal migration. We referenced Yue and

Zhou's (2005) research to provide a general definition of such employment. Here we have divided the graduates surveyed into three separate categories: Type I, non-hometown employment, which means that the province where the graduate student found a job is different from the province from which the graduate student originates; Type II, non-degree-seeking location employment, which means that the province where the student found a job is different from the province where the student earned the postgraduate degree; Type III, a combination of Types I and II. One thing which needs to be made clear in the Chinese cultural context is that the province where the sample students' parents were living at the time of the investigation determined the hometown factor, not the province of their ancestral place. The information gathered showed that some graduate students did not plan to find employment immediately on graduation, but intended to pursue a doctoral degree or to study abroad; others had not found a job when the investigation closed; yet others did not state where their employment was located. After eliminating these unqualified samples, there remained 763 samples in which the student had found a job after graduation and had provided information about the location of employment.

Table 5.1 provides the simple descriptive statistics of the three categories of migration employment. It may be seen that Type I graduates amount to 69.7 per cent of the entire sample, indicating that almost 70 per cent of the postgraduate students work outside their hometown provinces. Type II amounts to 56.5 per cent, indicating that more than half of the postgraduate students work outside the province in which their place of study is located. Type III amounts to 40.8 per cent, which indicates that a substantial proportion choose internal migration in order to find a job. Moreover, other research shows that migration employment is focused on provincial regions containing major cities such as Beijing, Shanghai, Guangdong and Zhejiang, with job migrations to the other provinces being rather fewer (Li *et al.*, 2009).

In order to test Hypothesis I we used a multivariate linear model, with starting salary being the dependent variable. The crucial independent variables on which we focused were the three types of migration employment. In addition to adding the above three necessary independent variables into the regression equation of the multivariate linear model, we aimed also to control the following variables:

- The sex, age and major of the postgraduate students, among which there were 18 dummy variables of majors with the basic standard being science majors.

Table 5.1 Descriptive statistics on the migration employment of postgraduate students

	Frequency	Percentage (%)	Total Number
Type I	532	69.7	763
Type II	431	56.5	763
Type III	311	40.8	763

- The property of the high school of each postgraduate student, two dummy variables 'provincial key school' and 'city key school', based on 'non-key school'. The, reason for this was to control for the initial capacities of the postgraduate students.
- The category of '985 university' indicates the property of the higher education institution in which each postgraduate student had studied, with a dummy variable set against the base of a 'non-985 university'. The reason for this was to control for the quality of the Masters' programme or the strength of the signal.

In order to test Hypotheses II and III, we used a bivariate logistic model. For Hypothesis II, the dependent variable was the bivariate dummy variable of the matching quality between learning and application (the first criterion) at work. The required information came from the answers to the following question:

Does your job match well with what you learned in your major?

a   Very much
b   to some extent
c   Not very much
d   Not at all.

If the postgraduate student answered 'very much' or 'to some extent', the answers were represented as 1; if the respondent chose one of the two latter choices, the answers were represented as 0.

In order to test Hypothesis III, the dependent variable used was the bivariate dummy variable of whether over-education is apparent. The required information came from the answers to the question: 'What is the requirement of this job compared with the education level of the job applicants?' However, the highest level of education provided in this question was 'postgraduate or above' which did not differentiate between Masters' degree students and Doctoral degree candidates. On the other hand, the sample used comprised the former. Therefore, the sample could only come within one of two categories: the job requirement was either higher than Masters' degree level or equal to it, or to a similar level of education. The independent variables of the bivariate logistic models of Hypotheses II and III were the same as those of the multivariate linear regression model. The focus of this research was on the coefficients and level of significance in the results in each of the three regression models from Type I to Type III. If the empirical research results supported the three hypotheses (i.e. migration employment would bring postgraduate students a substantially higher starting salary and a better match between *education* and its application in employment), then in the three regression models the coefficients of the crucial independent variants should all be significantly positive.

What do our findings show?

Table 5.2 presents the results of using the three regression models. However, we should note that most of the coefficients of the three crucial independent variants were non-significant. Only in the multivariate linear regression model (i.e. the starting salary model) was the coefficient of Type I substantially positive, while the rest were non-significant with a further few even being negative. This means that while Hypothesis I has been partially tested, the empirical results have denied Hypotheses II and III. Moreover, considering the fact that none of the coefficients of the variants in Type III was significant, this indicates that finding employment through migration is actually not so effective in increasing the economic benefits to postgraduate students, including both the starting salary and the match between education and its application in employment. Furthermore, in order to ensure the stability of the regression conclusions, we applied the method of logistic regression so as to bring the three crucial variables with the other controlled variables into the model; and yet we achieved almost identical results as those shown in Table 5.2.

We mentioned above that, using the same set of data, preliminary research found that postgraduate migration employment is concentrated in the four provincial regions of Beijing, Shanghai, Guangdong and Zhejiang (Li *et al.*, 2009). This means that although migration has gathered in the most economically developed 'first-tier world' of China, in general migration employment cannot bring postgraduate students the expected significantly positive returns, especially when the costs of moving to and living in such provinces are taken into account; rather, it sometimes results in negative results, although statistically much less significant. Our empirical research indicates that there is a gap between the highly developed migration destinations and the non-significance of the returns to individual migration. Why does this happen? Basing our analysis on existing international research conclusions about migration employment, we will consider the issue from the following two aspects.

First, Todaro (1969) developed a model of an expected income gap when analysing the coexistence of the conflicting phenomena of major urban unemployment and the yet continuous flow of rural workers into urban areas. This suggested that there were two reasons for such workers to migrate to cities in developing countries: one is the actual gap of average income between rural and urban workers; the other is the probability of rural workers finding a job in urban areas and the associated prospects for the future. According to the logic of Todaro's model of an expected income gap, those postgraduate students who chose to migrate were not aiming at either a higher starting salary or a better match between their educational qualifications and the requirements of the job. Instead, they hoped, instead, to settle down in a place with greater expected economic returns over time and more opportunities for future personal development. Especially given the restriction of the household registration policy mentioned above, migration for new graduates is much easier than when they have already started working. Therefore such graduates may not be too demanding about the

Table 5.2 Regression conclusions of the three models

	Beginning salary		Learning–application Match = 1			Over-education = 1		
	Coefficient	Value (T)	Coefficient	Wald value	Likelihood ratio	Coefficient	Wald value	Likelihood ratio
Constants	3,927.31***	4.38	1.21	0.85	3.34	-2.94***	7.61	0.05
Male	450.29***	3.08	0.09	0.20	1.10	-0.45***	6.74	0.64
Age	-68.40**	-2.15	-0.03	0.31	0.97	0.07*	3.64	1.07
Province key	245.52*	1.70	0.94***	11.55	2.56	0.12	0.25	1.13
City key	-77.81	-0.42	0.83***	11.47	2.29	-0.09	0.17	0.91
985 university	646.47***	3.95	-0.60***	5.61	0.55	-0.23*	3.35	0.80
Type I	-140.83	-0.55	0.67	2.06	1.95	-0.20	0.44	0.82
Type II	719.68***	3.09	0.30	0.79	1.35	-0.18	0.44	0.83
Type III	127.16	0.41	-0.61	1.85	0.54	0.42	1.28	1.52
Adjusted R²	0.252							
Value (F)	10.810***							
Chi Square			59.960***			48.061***		
Value (-2 LL)			671.260			936.769		
Sample No.	763		763			763		

Notes
The coefficients of the dummy variables of majors have been omitted; Significance level: ***= 1%, **= 5%, *= 10%.

conditions of their initial job, but look to find employment in a more economically developed metropolitan area to obtain a local household registration; as for salary, welfare and working conditions, considering the vast opportunities such a metropolitan area can offer, they have plenty of time to adjust to their initial employment or to switch to another position once they have settled down.

It should be noted that other research on job hunting by college graduates in China supports these arguments. For instance, Meng (2005) has observed that the priority sequence of college graduates in looking for a job is, first, location, second, industry, and third, the specific employer. In other words, the geographical location of employment is given the greatest importance while the target industries and the specific company are later considerations. Again, although basic economic models are applicable to all migration activities (Lei and Li, 2008), the factors affecting the migration of quality groups such as those in our sample are more complicated. In addition to taking into account direct economic gains and profits, quality groups also pay attention to the cultural and natural environments of their employment location (Grubel, 1995). Furthermore, some research has found that non-economic factors are on occasion no less attractive than economic factors for college graduates (Kodrzycki, 2001). The cultural and social attractions of life in big cities, especially for young people, should clearly be taken into account (Grubel, 1995).

For example, the reason why many students choose to work in economically developed large cities may often be attributed to a personal desire to be with a partner or a wish to escape what is perceived to be an inferior educational and cultural environment and the more staid and conservative atmosphere commonly found in small and medium-sized cities. Consequently many graduates and postgraduates prefer to migrate to a metropolitan area, even though they may earn only a relatively small salary and probably live in a tiny apartment, rather than find a job in their hometown or at the place where they studied. Moreover, compared with college and vocational school graduates, such non-economic factors weigh even more heavily with postgraduate students (Gottlieb and Joseph, 2006; Li *et al.*, 2011). Therefore we can see that although lacking in immediate positive effects at work for the postgraduate students (including the starting salary and the quality of the match between the education received and the job requirements), other perceived benefits may nevertheless be obtained in the process.

It should be noted that this tendency whereby quality talents including postgraduate students show limited concern for short-term benefits when choosing to migrate to economically more developed metropolitan areas accords, to some extent, with China's current economic development of still rapid industrialisation and urbanisation. According to standard economic theory, when a society has reached such a stage, the concentration of industries and talents is the important means by which to facilitate the division of labour, encourage knowledge sharing and development, achieve economies of scale and reduce the economy's trading costs (Marshall, 1920: 271; Krugman and Venabals, 1996).

However, we should also be aware that postgraduate students who migrate in search of employment can neither substantially raise the probability of finding a better match between education and job and reduce the prospects of over-education; nor can they prevent, under certain conditions, the reverse from happening, even though such deficiencies are statistically non-significant. In a market economy, we should expect both employers and employees to make employment decisions within a labour market framework. However, the state and the higher education institutions should still, in order to raise social benefits, encourage ambitious graduates to locate and thrive in less developed areas of the country; and to provide incentives and opportunities which encourage them to settle in small and medium-sized cities or county towns and rural areas; and to look for jobs that match more closely their qualifications and skills.

Three aspects of benefits could follow on from such policies which would, first, still satisfy the need to bring talented people to the metropolitan areas; second, satisfy the pressing social and economic need for talented people in less developed regions of the country; and third, support the careers of those graduates who show a sense of social justice and responsibility through contributing to the development of disadvantaged areas. In fact, many prestigious universities, such as Tsinghua University in Beijing, have encouraged graduate students from various disciplines to broaden their employment in this way. This encourages a sense of social justice, of social responsibility and of citizenship among relatively privileged university students: important if China is to build an 'harmonious society' (Wang and Morgan, 2012).

Although the university realises that such a practice may be seen as going 'against the market', it also believes that a university education should mean more than simply job training, while the broader experience gained enhance individual character and capabilities, which is in fact attractive to potential employers. It realises also that if its graduates cluster in metropolitan areas they can only 'gain small instead of large; contribute little instead of much'. This confirms the university in its belief that another employment route should be offered to students (Du, 2010). However, there is a continuing phenomenon that 'the strong takes all' (Li *et al.*, 2009) exemplified by the various promotional attempts by different provinces to persuade outstanding postgraduates to migrate.

In the face of this, students, the state and the universities should be aware of the economic and social implications and take the initiative when appropriate. This is because the migration of postgraduate students to metropolitan areas does not necessarily bring a higher starting salary, a better match between skills and their application, or between their formal educational level and the actual job requirements. Moreover, the clustering of graduates in a relatively few metropolitan areas can bring negative social effects. For example, less economically developed areas have been obliged to invest heavily in higher education in order to produce high-quality talented people to assist them in regional and local development.

However, the prospect of such graduates migrating to Beijing, Shanghai or other metropolitan areas undermines the effectiveness of such a policy and discourages further local educational investment, especially in higher education.

This carries with it the danger of these areas falling into a downward spiral in which they lose talented people, and therefore underachieve economically and culturally, and thus become even less attractive to well-educated and talented individuals. This is a neglected aspect of the relationship between higher education and social justice in Chinese higher education. The research which we have reported here has analysed empirically the effect of the migration employment of postgraduate students on their starting salary, learning and application matching quality and education level and job requirement matching quality. According to the empirical study, except for Type I, migration can bring about significant profits on starting salary, but none of the three types of migration, in general, can achieve the same effects. On the contrary, migration can to a certain extent result in a lower starting salary, a mismatch between skills learned and their application and, more broadly, between education level and job requirements, although these trends are statistically not significant.

Given this conclusion, the state and universities should offer guidance about graduate employment, together with appropriate inducements in certain circumstances. The universities should help those students who do not want to move to metropolitan areas, those who prefer to settle in small and medium-sized cities, and those who expect to go to the far west of China, to the boundary areas and other disadvantaged regions. This would diversify employment opportunities so that graduates can develop more effectively both their general and specific human capital, to thrive in their own careers, as well as contributing to local economic and social development across the country. This type of migration employment could bring about both abundant individual gains and social benefits.

The priority of future research is to systematically and empirically analyse the factors which affect the employment of higher education graduates. Only by getting to know which factors are pulling or pushing higher education graduates to migrate can a firmly based empirical policy foundation be laid, enabling the state and the universities to regulate and support graduate employment. Second, it is necessary to learn from international research experience and longitudinal data. This would enable analysis of the medium- and long-term careers of graduates who have migrated to either metropolitan or to less developed areas, facilitating medium- and long-term comparison with the view to both economic and social benefit. Finally, Todaro (1969) believed the expected wage to be a major variant in migration models with the reservation wage a closely related factor. This can also affect the outcome of job hunting significantly (Montgomery, 1991, 1992). The availability of graduate employment benefits both the individual and society and is an important aspect of social justice in contemporary China.

Notes

1 This chapter is developed from a much shorter earlier version in Chinese published in *Research in Higher Education of Engineering*, 2010(3): 60–65.

2 It is assumed that employers behave rationally, paying employees according to their productivity. However, the difficulty of measuring productivity and the use of formal qualification as a proxy is an objection to human capital theory.
3 According to this system all households have to be registered in the locality in which they were resident, and are categorised as either rural or urban households.
4 Over-education is commonly believed to be an imbalance between the supply of labour and the demand for skills in the labour market (Rumberger, 1981). Moreover, many empirical studies have found that over-education could also reduce the return on education. Based on research in the UK graduate labour market, Dolton and Vignoles (2000) found that the economic return on over-education was less than the return on required education.

References

Becker, G.S. (1993a), *Human Capital: A theoretical and empirical analysis, with reference to education*, Chicago and London: The University of Chicago Press.

Becker, G.S. (1993b), Nobel Prize Lecture: The economic way of looking at behaviour, *Journal of Political Economy*, 101(3): 385–409.

Borjas, G.J. (1994), The economics of immigration, *Journal of Economic Literature*, 32(4): 1667–1717.

Dolton, P. and Vignoles, A. (2000), The incidence and effects of over education in the UK's graduate labour market, *Economics of Education Review*, 19(2): 179–198.

Du, H.L. (2010), Student management work at Tsinghua University, a presentation at Tsinghua University (in Chinese), 19 April.

Gottlieb, P.D. and Joseph, G. (2006), College-to-work migration of technology graduates and holders of doctorates within the United States, *Journal of Regional Science*, 46(4): 627–659.

Grant, E.K. and Vanderkamp, J. (1980), The effects of migration on income: A micro study with Canadian data 1965–71, *Canadian Journal of Economics*, 31(1): 47–62.

Greenwood, M.J. (1981), *Migration and Economic Growth in the United States: National, regional, and metropolitan perspectives*, New York: Academic Press.

Grubel, H.G. (1995), Economics of the brain drain, in Carnoy, M. (ed.) *International Encyclopaedia of Economics of Education*, Oxford: Pergamon Press.

Kodrzycki, Y. (2001), Migration of recent college graduates: Evidence from the national longitudinal survey of youth, *New England Economic Review*, January/February: 13–34.

Krugman, P. and Venabals, A.J. (1996), Integration specialization and adjustment, *European Economic Review*, 40(9): 59–67.

Lei, H. and Li, F.L. (2008), Economics of international migration of educated workers (in Chinese), *Tsinghua Journal of Education*, 3: 14–19.

Li, F. and Morgan, W.J. (2013), Private higher education in China: Problems and possibilities, in Morgan, W.J. and Wu, B. (eds) *Higher Education Reform in China: Beyond the expansion*, London and New York: Routledge, pp. 66–78.

Li, F.L., Chen, X.L. and He, G.X. (2011), Post-graduates' migration employment and their job satisfaction (in Chinese), *Population and Economics*, 6: 34–40.

Li, F.L., Liu, F. and Guo, Z.M. (2009), An empirical study of migration in postgraduate employment (in Chinese), *Tsinghua Journal of Education*, 4: 67–71.

Li, F., Morgan, W. J. and Ding, X. (2013), The labour market for graduates in China, in Morgan, W.J. and Wu, B. (eds) *Higher Education Reform in China: Beyond the expansion*, London and New York: Routledge, pp. 93–108.

Li, F., Zhao, Y. and Morgan, W.J. (2011), The rate of return to educational investment in China: A comparative commentary, *Education, Knowledge and Economy*, 5(1–2): 45–52.

Liu, G.G., Zhang, Z. and Zhan, Z. (eds) (2010), *Investing in Human Capital for Economic Development in China*, New Jersey: World Scientific Books.

Marshall, A. (1920), *Principles of Economics* (8th edn), London: Macmillan.

Meng, D.H. (2005), Individual choice and graduate employment under the circumstance of risk (in Chinese), *Fudan Education Forum*, 1: 70–73.

Montgomery, J.D. (1991), Social networks and labour market outcomes: Toward an economic analysis, *American Economic Review*, 81(5): 1408–1418.

Montgomery, J.D. (1992), Job search and network composition: Implications of the strength of the weak ties hypothesis, *American Sociological Review*, 57: 586–596.

Rumberger, R. (1981), The rising incidence of over education in the U.S. labor market, *Economics of Education Review*, 1(3): 293–314.

Schultz, T.W. (1961), Investment in human capital, *American Economic Review*, 51: 1–17.

Sjaastad, L A. (1962), The costs and returns of human migration, *Journal of Political Economy*, 70: 80–93.

Todaro, M.P. (1969), A model of labor migration and urban unemployment in less developed countries, *American Economic Review*, 69: 486–499.

Wang, N. and Morgan, W.J. (2012), The harmonious society, social capital and lifelong learning in China: Emerging policies and practice, *International Journal of Continuing Education and Lifelong Learning*, 4(2): 1–15.

Wertheimer, R.F. (1970), *The Monetary Rewards of Migration within the United States*, Washington, DC: Urban Institute.

Yue, C.J. and Zhou, J.B. (2005), Why do college graduates choose inter-province employment? (in Chinese), *Tsinghua Journal of Education*, 2: 34–41.

Zhao, Y.H. (1999), Labour migration and earnings differences: The case of rural China, *Economic Development and Cultural Change*, 47(4): 767–782.

6   Residential colleges as living-learning communities in China

Some recent developments[1]

Kai-yan Choi

Introduction

Chinese universities in particular are adopting the idea of residential college (RC) education in innovative ways. This chapter reports recent developments and envisages the possible impact on higher education outcomes at four universities in Greater China. These universities are located in major cities and have built their RC systems in quite different ways over the past eight years. There are significant differences found in the education contexts of their respective jurisdictions, which has affected their missions, goals and educational practices.

In the following sections, I first outline the specific contexts in which the residential college systems presented have been developed. The launch of residential colleges at these universities is an experiment in reforming the curriculum for general education; enhancing the effectiveness of undergraduate education; and improving the quality of university education generally. In a Chinese context, they provide a different agenda for higher education reform compared with their Western counterparts. Second, I give an account of institutional design and organisational structure. This shows variations in the strategic roles of RC systems in respect of general undergraduate education. The discussion focuses on the coordination with other academic units, on institutional autonomy, and on the resources given to RC education. In the third section, selected activities within RCs at each of the four universities, such as the formation of student organisations and service-learning programmes, are cited as examples of variations in education processes and outcomes. The development of a sense of citizenship, in a fair and socially just environment, is an essential goal of both liberal education and of student-centred learning. However, the RC systems considered in this chapter show different outcomes which were, in some cases, found to be counter-productive to a liberal arts education.

The concept of 'Greater China' refers to mainland China, Hong Kong, Macau and Taiwan, but the findings reported in this chapter come from an extensive literature review, field studies, and interviews with staff and students at the selected universities in three educational jurisdictions other than Taiwan.

Return of liberal education

It is necessary to begin with a short account of liberal education in relation to residential college education in general and particularly in Occidental societies. The residential college system has a history dating from the medieval European universities. At that time, liberal university education took place in what we today consider a 'living-learning community', where mentors and mentees lived and worked in close, intimate relationships. 'Education' was not limited to the exchange of professional knowledge and experience, but included a focus on intrinsic values and beliefs as well – in other words, on personal character building. Such 'liberal education' stresses a foundation of broad-based knowledge, generic knowledge and skills across various domains, including the development of social competences. This may echo what Cardinal John Henry Newman claimed about the goal of university education in his time. Newman considered the university as a place to provide liberal education; that is, to nurture personal character and to disseminate knowledge and wisdom rather than knowledge invention. In contrast to the notion of liberal education, Wilhelm von Humboldt emphasised the role of research and knowledge innovation as the centre of the university mission. These two different notions of university education have been influencing university positioning and the practice of university education, as well as the discourses of university education today (Newman, 1959; Hersh, 1999; Markwell, 2010; Huang, 2010; Kerr and Tweedy, 2006).

As it has moved along with the rationalisation process, the university system has become more differentiated and professionalised in terms of disciplinary knowledge and their demarcations, of university management and of course offerings, which now emphasise the importance of professional education over the cultivation of personality. Meanwhile, numerous problems are identifiable in this type of highly differentiated and professionalised knowledge community. They may lead to feelings of anonymity among students lost in a sizeable organisation, to low retention rates, to an unfavourable context for first-generation college students, and so on. In response to this trend, some Western universities, with a mission to foster liberal education, started to reform these structures and curricula. Reintroducing residential colleges is an attempt, in this fashion, to reclaim the importance of liberal education in the Occidental educational tradition. It has become a new, developing trend in higher education over the past 30 years, and many universities around the world are introducing both formal and non-formal residential learning programmes.

In the early twenty-first century, some Western educators have found the provision of liberal education problematic in a highly differentiated and specialised knowledge organisation like the modern university. For example, teaching and character building have become less important than doing research and publishing in academic journals. Derek Bok argues, in his book on the commercialisation of higher education, that profit generating has become the leading principle of university management. Seeking research grants, doing research, producing research outputs, and introducing various forms of new educational practices (such as online teaching) are driven by the desire for profit generation. Money making becomes a higher goal leading the innovation of knowledge (Bok, 2003). College students, meanwhile, enter a sizeable organisation and often learn very little other than what is on offer in their professional areas. The feeling of anonymity among students is a result of studying in a large organisation; meanwhile, university professors are occupied with university administration and research projects. Some educators have recognised the benefits brought about by the highly specialised differentiation of disciplinary knowledge in the modern form of knowledge organisation, while advocating the concept of a 'small and intimate living-learning community' that involves students and professors. These new living-learning communities are less concerned about education in professional knowledge, but act as springboards for developing generic skills, helping the transition of freshmen, encouraging cross-disciplinary learning, forming close friendships, and developing service partnerships with the wider social community (Hersh, 1999; ACER, 2009).

Beginning in the 1960s, there was an increasing trend of launching residential college programmes at universities in the United States, serving various educational purposes. For example, resident freshmen induction groups were introduced at universities such as Oregon and Missouri-Columbia, and a two-year college programme was introduced at Yale, while other residential living-learning programmes came into operation and met with success (Jacobson, 2007). As a consequence, a considerable number of research and evaluation assessments of different models of residential college programmes have been made: evidence of growing interest in the practical delivery of the concept. However, as some critics have commented, this has brought to universities the idea of liberal education as being merely complementary to professional education (Longerbeam et al., 2007; Inkelas et al., 2008; Smith and Bath, 2006; Badcock et al., 2010).

At the same time, in the 1960s, higher education in China was undergoing a difficult period in its history. Due to the close connection between the Chinese and Soviet Communist Parties the university model in Mainland China was copied from the former Soviet Union, with professional education taking precedence over liberal education, which was looked upon with ideological suspicion. Some of the technical disciplines of the resulting mono-technic universities, such as the normal universities (for teacher training), marine universities and police universities, may still be found. Again, during the Cultural Revolution of 1967, university education in the mainland was effectively suspended until the late 1970s. Indeed, the formal education system of Mainland China was seriously damaged for a generation. In 1978, the restoration of social and political order revitalised the whole formal education system, including the restoration of university education, but the university model still followed the former Soviet model, where professional education prevailed (Zhang, 2012; Qiu et al., 2010).

In the Soviet model all universities were under the strict control of the Chinese Communist Party (CCP). The party organs and leadership were essential, visible to the university management, and took a leading position in ideological education (political thought) for students and staff. This model has remained at contemporary universities in China. In a field interview, a participant commented on the role and influence of the CCP Secretary in university management: 'the level and style of influence are various. It depends how an individual Secretary understands their work and what they want to do with the management team.' He gave an example of a former Secretary in his university, a very proactive and 'visible' leadership in university management, while the President became an ordinary member of the management team (field interview). In a research report sponsored by the Ministry of Education, for example, the leadership of the CCP in ideological education was considered indispensable, and required strengthening amid the rapid changes of global social politics. The authors of that report admitted that old-school ideological education has lost its influence among university students, making ideological education problematic.[2] The call for a new model of ideological/political education takes priority over other educational issues, the report argues. Seen as one of the plausible new models for ideological/political education to the university students of this era, residential college system pilot projects at universities located in Shanghai and Xian were approved by the central government in 2005 (Qiu *et al.*, 2010).

University education on the mainland is still under strict control by the CCP, and is seen as ideological/political education for all university students. It is also seen as an important seedbed for developing prospective core members and prospective leaders of the party, and proper political education tends to uphold the CCP's ideology. Loyalty to the party, patriotic passion, nationalism and traditional Chinese virtues are highlighted as core missions of residential college education. Insofar as the mission of the residential college system on the mainland is politicised, it creates a new form of management and new forms of scrutiny over students' political thought and behaviour. We consider next the situation in the Special Administrative Regions of Hong Kong and Macau.

In Hong Kong, there were demands for another university in the territories, in addition to the University of Hong Kong, to satisfy social and economic needs. The British Hong Kong colonial government responded by sponsoring three independent colleges – New Asia, United and Chung Chi – to unite as the founding members of the Chinese University of Hong Kong (CUHK). Unlike the colonial university, CUHK adopted a federal system of university management, in which each of the three member colleges could maintain relative independence and autonomy. The three colleges have their own education philosophies and missions, and they independently carry out academic and residential education programmes. Their four-year undergraduate programmes were very different from the English university model used by the University of Hong Kong, and left room for the implementation of general education components (Committee on Bilingualism, 2007; Sweeting, 2004: 150–155). The CUHK may be viewed as the first university in Greater China to provide residential college education to undergraduate students, whereas there was no such university in Macau until 1980.

The three founding colleges of the CUHK had all originated in Mainland China before 1949. Two were originally founded and supported by Christian churches and missionaries from the West, with New Asia College the only one placing emphasis on promoting Chinese culture. Chung Chi College positioned itself as a bridge between Chinese and Western civilisations. The United College is a former Christian university which operated in the mainland before being taken over by the CCP. In other words, these founding member colleges of the CUHK were under Western influence in all their early stages of development before accepting financial support from the colonial government of Hong Kong. The influence of this on their understanding of modern Western higher education, and its philosophy and operation, was relatively profound. The CUHK was also the first and only university to adopt liberal education as a mandatory part of all undergraduate programmes. As Chung Chi College said in its mission statement,

> The College aims to provide higher education in accordance with Christian traditions, using the Chinese language as the primary medium of instruction. It seeks to promote Christian faith, learning and research.
>
> (Chung Chi College website)

As this shows, the objective of education at Chung Chi College was that of whole-person education in the light of Christianity. The general education components remain an essential part of the university and college requirements for undergraduate programmes.

Modern university education in Macau was developed very late, although, historically, Macau can claim to be a forerunner for Asian universities.[3] The first modern university, East Asia University, was planned and financed by three professionals from Hong Kong in 1980, with reference to the three-year English university model and adopting English as the medium of instruction. The mission of this privately funded university was, until 1988, to provide professional education and training. However, the prospect of the handover of Macau to the Chinese government in 1999, and the need for a highly qualified local labour supply, saw the Portuguese Macau government, through the Macau Foundation, turn this university into a publicly funded institute in 1988. This became the University of Macau, which gradually developed graduate programmes up to doctoral level.[4] Given the scarce land resources of the Taipa campus, the university management and the Macau government successfully secured a piece of land from neighbouring Zhuhai city, with the permission of the Chinese government, to build the new campus on Hengqin Island in 2008. The university management has also planned a large residential college project on the new campus. The first two pilot residential colleges were launched in September 2010 and moved to the new campus in autumn 2014. Eventually there will be 12 residential colleges at the University of Macau, each accommodating up to 500 students.

The university management visited a couple of world-renowned universities with a good reputation for residential college education such as Cambridge, Yale, Princeton, Harvard, the University of Melbourne, the Australian National

University, the National Tsinghua University in Taiwan and the CUHK. The university management then announced a new education blueprint: a 'four-in-one' education model, in which social and peer education is implemented in the residential college system in parallel with professional education, general education and research/internship education. This ambitious plan to build so many residential colleges in Macau was driven by the Macau government and supported by the central government of China, which is pushing to make the university a world-class institution in 20 years' time. Each of the first-year students admitted to the University of Macau will have a one-year mandatory stay in a residential college, and will receive a credit-bearing general education module in the same year. This mandatory stay is also specified in the graduation requirements.

In contrast with Mainland China, the SARs of Hong Kong and Macau have been enjoying a relatively less politicised environment than their mainland counterparts; and university education in these cities takes little account of communist ideology and control in terms of the design of the curriculum and of university management. Instead, residential college education in Hong Kong and Macau is pluralistic, embracing liberal education, religious tradition and economic-utilitarian factors. Such a significant difference has a remarkable influence on the institutional design and organisational structures of residential colleges, as well as on educational processes and outcomes.

Institutional design and organisational structure

The reasons for the founding of the RC systems in Greater China are complex. In Mainland China, the purpose of ideological/political education and control is primary, together with related educational purposes, such as talent development, the strengthening of moral and ethical education, and the management of student life. The institutional design and organisational structure of RCs, therefore, reflect political and other educational functions, as may be seen in the selected universities of Xian and Shanghai. In comparison with their mainland counterparts, RCs in Hong Kong and Macau are found to work for other civil purposes (e.g. religious missionary, inter-cultural exchange or whole-person education in a liberal sense). These characteristics are also reflected in the institutional designs and organisational structures discussed in this section.

Mainland China

Fudan University in Shanghai was the first university on the mainland to officially introduce an RC system into its undergraduate programmes. In reference to some well-known American universities, such as Yale and Harvard, Fudan University institutionally split Fudan College and Fudan Graduate School to manage their undergraduate and postgraduate programmes respectively in 2005. Fudan College initially took up the admission management of undergraduate programmes, residential college education for first-year students, and university-wide general education management for these and for second years. In order to increase educational opportunities for undergraduate students, the university management decided to empower Fudan College by merging the Registry, Admission Office, General Education Office and the residential college system under the administrative capacity of the College. The reformed Fudan College became the administrative unit which linked residential colleges and the academic faculties. In other words, academic and non-academic affairs regarding student management are all under the administrative control of Fudan College. The provision of professional education, supervision of research projects, general education programmes and academic administration are under the control of the academic faculties; while residential colleges are also responsible for non-formal forms of learning out-of-class.

The system in Fudan was thus first introduced in 2005, and living in RCs throughout the four-year study period has become mandatory since 2011. In 2009 students in all five RCs were reallocated in accordance with their faculties. Each of Fudan's RCs can house more than 2,000 students from a designated group of faculties. This number is not ideal for developing close community as in its Western counterpart. All the residential colleges were built over the former on-campus student dormitories, with remodelling work for student activities, such as a TV room, an in-house library and a café managed by the students. However, there are no separate dining facilities in the RC building; students from different RCs take meals in university canteens together. This arrangement of dining facilities is not beneficial to the development of sense of college identity. The administrative status of the RCs is defined at the same level of the academic faculties.

The heads and fellows of RCs are jointly appointed by academic faculties so that the same group of academics can take care of students in both academic and social settings. Members of this group have an office in the RC buildings. The heads of the RCs are senior academics in Fudan, who take up both academic and administrative leadership, and among them is the Chair of the College Management Committee. The heads of the RC decide the appointment of the Committee members, allocate resources, and set up the programmes and activities in the RC. The heads of the RCs also report to the Dean of Fudan College.

Each RC appoints a certain number of fellows, including full-time and joint appointment academics, to mentor students. The full-time fellows are usually retired professors. The duty of these full-time fellows, as stated in the *Residential College Handbook*, is to mentor their students with respect to life and study planning, to advise on personal and emotional issues, social and financial difficulties, and so on. Each full-time fellow is assigned to take care of a designated group of students and to meet them at least once a month. When fellows find that students' problems cannot be handled in their capacity (e.g. in the case of emotional disturbance), they are responsible for reporting these cases to the respective faculties, or to the student counselling centre, as necessary. There are some college tutors and counsellors who assist in the coordination of work between students and fellows, as well as administrative routines for student organisations in the RC. The college tutors and counsellors are usually postgraduate students or fresh graduates, who are appointed to work for the CCP or the Youth League in out-of-class ideological and political education work through RC student organisations. For ideological/political education, all undergraduate students are required to attend courses of the 'public education group' as part of their graduation requirements. The administrative work of all the RCs is handled by centralised office and administrative staff, who do not live in the RC building with students.[5]

The signature of RC education in Fudan is its provision of an environment conducive to encouraging interaction between faculties and students and among students from different backgrounds. Students living in RCs can initiate their own projects, such as running a self-financed café in the RC building or social and community service projects, with the aid of additional resources. There is a student union in each RC, called the Students' Self-Management Committee. This serves as a coordinating unit for RC life and student activities, and as a contact point with other university-wide student organisations. The executive members of the Committee are nominated by class representatives instead of through the universal suffrage of all RC students. Executive members of the Committee are usually prominent members of the Youth League or preparatory members of the CCP.[6]

Xian Jiaotong University ran its first pilot RC in 2006 to accommodate a cohort of 697 male students in their second year from seven faculties. A total of eight residential colleges have been launched since 2008 following the success of the pilot programmes. All undergraduates now live in these eight RCs until graduation. Unlike Fudan, Xian Jiaotong University operates a single line vertical student management system, in which all undergraduate and postgraduate students are educated in the academic faculties, departments and research institutes, while the non-academic life spheres of students are addressed by the RCs. According to the former Executive Vice-President (Provost): 'It operates like people going to their workplaces every day, and returning home for social and family life.' The 'workplaces' are comparable to academic units, while the RCs are comparable to 'home' (Qiu *et al.*, 2010).

Each RC at Xian Jiaotong comprises students from all four years in a cluster of academic faculties. The original management unit, class teachers, class representatives and counsellors serving the Party and the Youth League are all migrated to their respective RCs. In other words, some of the resources and administrative structures are taken from academic faculties and become a part of the new RCs. The ideological/political education mission is more or less moved into the RC system at the same time. This is one of the major differences between Xian Jiaotong University and Fudan University. The RC Management Committee is the decision-making body comprising RC staff and representatives from academic faculties. An RC Management Committee coordinates relations between academic faculties and the RCs. The university management appoints heads, executive associate heads, academic fellows, full-time fellows, class teachers and adjunct fellows as the college management team. The Executive Associate Head of each RC is also the Party Secretary, taking care of party members and prospective members, as well as ideological/political education.

Academic fellows in RCs are adjunct appointees who mentor students on general academic questions. Teaching and research supervision are still major duties for the academic faculties.[7]

Each RC has two full-time fellows, originally 'counsellors', living in and working with the students. These full-time fellows take charge of instructing student unions and the recommendations of new Party members. The student unions, meanwhile, organise students' social, cultural and political education, and social services activities. RC students follow a fixed daily schedule set out by the RC management team. The structured management of student life in RCs was highlighted in the annual report and is considered a signature of the RC system in Xian's case. It constitutes another difference between Xian and Shanghai.

In summary, it is apparent that the RC systems in Mainland China are vehicles for solving a variety of educational problems, while ideological/political control is also fundamental. RC residency has become mandatory at the two universities, with political education implemented in both formal and informal ways. Misbehaviour among students is expected to be effectively removed by the new institutional scrutiny. The encouragement of student participation in social and community services, and the interaction of faculty and students from different disciplines in diverse types of cultural activities are all goals of RC education at the two universities. The identification of prospective CCP members and the development of leadership skills are also among the objectives.

Notwithstanding, the organisational structures and the styles of management are different between Shanghai and Xian. Student management in the Xian RC system seems to be more rigorous than the one in Shanghai. Regular meetings with fellows for mentoring purposes are required in both universities; but, in the case of Fudan, the university management stresses student-directed learning and provides substantial support in terms of academic advice and resources to the endorsed projects. Fudan students are eligible to initiate student projects and to seek endorsement by their respective college management. Students in Xian Jiaotong are required to sign up for one hobby group or more to fulfil part of their RC education. The approach to RC education in Xian seems to place less emphasis on student initiative but to fully utilise opportunities inside and outside the classroom to educate students.

Hong Kong and Macau

As stated above, Chung Chi College is one of the founding colleges of the CUHK. Before it merged into the federal system, Chung Chi was an independent liberal arts college and still maintains a certain level of independence in its college management and structure. Chung Chi and other member colleges have their own Boards of Trustees (Governors), deans and fellows who endorse the educational philosophy and ethos of their respective colleges. Each of the faculty members of CUHK must affiliate with one of these colleges and contribute to the college community, while Chung Chi students include both residential and non-residential members. In this case, Chung Chi College's relation to CUHK is characterised by devolution of power which illustrates a remarkable difference from the other RC systems in our study.

It should be noted that Chung Chi College has a strong Christian ethos in comparison with other member colleges of CUHK. For instance, it offers publicly funded academic programmes at both the undergraduate and postgraduate levels (e.g. Religious Studies), and also some self-financed theology programmes through the School of Divinity which lead to higher degrees. These programmes are not funded and accredited by the University Grant Committee (the statutory organisation appointed by the Education Bureau of Hong Kong). There is also a small chapel and chaplaincy under the management of Chung Chi College which serves all students and staff of CUHK.

The Board of Trustees comprises both academics of CUHK and representatives from the sponsoring Christian denominations (the Protestant Churches) in Hong Kong, from the United Board for Christian Higher Education in Asia, together with representatives of alumni and fellows. The Head of Chung Chi College is supported by a team of fellows and staff. In addition to the university-wide general education programmes, Chung Chi has its own general education programmes for undergraduates which are credit-bearing college requirements according to the Christian faith. The objectives are: rational thinking, critical awareness, and appreciation of Chinese and Occidental cultures, the contributions of sciences to society and culture, and personal commitment to both contemporary and perennial issues of life and its challenges. Such education takes place in both formal and non-formal settings, with some academic credits contributing to degree programmes. In comparison with non-formal education in the RCs of the mainland, Chung Chi seems to have much more autonomy, flexibility and power to pursue its educational vision.

The University of Macau, by contrast, is a publicly funded institution. It aims to provide whole-person education in a liberal sense, to foster multiple talents and competitive personnel to meet the needs of the development of Macau and the region.[8] To promote this higher education vision, the University of Macau has conducted educational reforms with respect to academic, administrative and student management since 2009. A review of all undergraduate programmes was completed in 2008, with the resulting report suggesting a restructuring of the programmes by reducing the proportion of professional education to make room for general education components. A General Education Office was launched to coordinate and support the implementation of the new general education courses. The original functions of the Student Affairs Office, under the Director of Student Affairs, included managing the dormitory, the student union and organisations, and student life. University management has created two new positions, including the Vice-Rector for Student Affairs (VRSA), to take charge of counselling, student organisations, residential colleges and sports management. The Dean of Students, meanwhile, supports the VRSA in coordinating various units of student management. The heads of the residential colleges ('College Masters') report directly to the VRSA and champion the administration of each residential college in the university.

Following these reforms, the first two pilot residential colleges in Macau were set up in 2010. They accommodated 200 and 150 students, respectively, in their early stages, and increased this number to 250 and 180 students in subsequent years. Each of these colleges has a College Master, an Associate Master and Chief of Students, Resident Fellows, and a team of administrative staff. The College Masters, who work solely for the RCs, are senior academics with substantial experience in residential college education and management, and are mostly appointed through international recruitment. The Associate Masters and Chiefs of Students at these colleges are usually academics who originally worked as university faculty, and include both joint appointments with academic faculties and those who work solely for the RCs. Resident fellows are all fresh doctoral graduates with some university teaching experience. These staff members are responsible for planning and implementing college life education in coordination with other academic units, such as academic departments and the General Education Office. By autumn 2014, eight residential colleges were fully operating and accommodated all undergraduate freshmen; each college can house about 500 students. Since the beginning of 2014 all newly admitted undergraduates have been required to fulfil a mandatory resident credit-bearing experiential learning programme in RCs in their first year. The major contents of the curriculum for this experiential learning module are standardised across all colleges but some flexibility is left in the pedagogy and class schedules for individual topics.

Regarding the flexibility of college life education, the RC systems in Hong Kong and Macau appear more structured than the RC systems operating on the mainland. Chung Chi College, for example, has implemented college requirements for residential learning, while the University of Macau requires a one-credit residency module in the RC for all first-year students. The RC systems on the mainland do not have similarly stringent requirements, though all undergraduate students are required to stay in RCs at some time over their four-year education. However, the RCs in the mainland seem to have the least autonomy or diversity among the three jurisdictions. Students from the same programme or class, for example, are designated to live in the same college; there is no choice according to individual students' preferences. This is for the convenience of administration, especially the Party organs in the colleges. This is not the case in Hong Kong, where students can choose to affiliate with any college in the CUHK, or at Macau, where students are allocated to RCs at random. In the latter case, students can choose not to live in RCs on completion of their first year.

Indeed, control of resources and ownership of student management are major problems for the implementation of RC systems on the mainland. RC staff in Xian and Shanghai, in particular, mentioned disputes over resource allocation and responsibility for student management when their universities planned to introduce RC systems. As a result of compromises between academic faculties and RCs, general education in the mainland RC systems is mainly informal, with academic faculty still controlling formal teaching, research and internship supervision. Mainland RCs are not granted resources to launch credit-bearing courses, nor do they play a role in general education programmes. By contrast, in Hong Kong and Macau, RC systems provide both formal general education pro-grammes and informal education activities. The compromised role of mainland RCs may foreshadow the effectiveness of education in these living-learning communities. For example, students from the same programme do not have the chance to choose different RCs. They meet in the same faculty for attending class, while going to the same residential college for informal education. This arrangement is considered counter-productive to peers' education. This will be further discussed in the following section regarding educational activities and student organisation in RCs.

Learning activities and student organisations in RCs

The mission statement of an educational institution should describe what its stakeholders say they believe about education. However, an academic study must examine how they realise the mission in practice. It should consider, for instance, types of learning activity and how student organisations in RCs actu-ally reflect the institution's approach to college life education and its possible outcomes.

The RCs in Fudan and Xian Jiaotong are supplementary in educational terms, since they do not provide credit-bearing courses. Instead, they offer a variety of supplemental learning activities, such as cultural salons, seminars by distin-guished guest speakers, sports and athletic tournaments, reading clubs, college cleaning days, business projects, high-table dinners, and social and community services. Many of these activities are arranged and coordinated by 'counsellors' and full-time staff, while a few are organised by the college student unions. Fudan places a special emphasis on student self-management and self-directed learning projects in the RCs; and this may be seen as one of the major differ-ences distinguishing Fudan from other mainland RC systems.

In Xian the RCs run many clubs and societies based on student hobbies and interests, in addition to college sport teams. This encourages students to develop interests and talents through participation in one of the university's many soci-eties and clubs. In a way, this form of RC serves to scale down the mega-size university community by installing smaller forms of university-wide student organisation into the college. Some RCs in Xian arrange for students to take part in social service programmes that help selected primary and secondary schools in the 'national under-developed counties' (such as *Lantian* County), while some of these programmes have become favourite events among students. It is believed that through these activities a service mentality can be developed, encouraging students to care about and help others in need.[9]

In common, each residential college in Fudan and in Xian has a student union that represents student members of the college. In Fudan, the student union has one seat on the college management committee, which takes part in college decision-making, but this is not the case in Xian. This practice reflects the spirit of student self-management at Fudan and probably makes Fudan the mainland's forerunner in this respect. However, the level of student participation in RC management is still very limited on the mainland overall, where the executives of student unions are all nominated by class representatives, who usually have a preparatory party membership or outstanding student status in the Communist Youth League. Students without CCP support or approved backgrounds are not eligible for executive positions in the union. This confirms the orthodox and oligarchic nature of mainland RC student unions and, to some extent, reflects the maintenance of the status quo in society itself.

This may be compared with Chung Chi College, where there is a wide array of learning activities, including those that aim to meet specific educational objectives in line with the College's mission. These include a Visiting Fellows' Programme, Cross-Cultural Exposure, Language Enhancement, Information Technology and (College) General Education, Physical Education and Creativity Development, Social Services, Leadership Training, and a Mentor and Spiritual Growth Programme. These are all aimed at developing students intellectually, socially, culturally and physically, and spiritually, both personally and as a community. Full-time academics and other young college staff manage most of these activities. Affiliated academics can choose to become mentors, and they contribute to the College General Education Programme through the Assembly of Fellows.[10]

Chung Chi College has its own student union, which is elected annually by all student members. According to the constitution, interested students can form a cabinet to run for election. The election and operation of the cabinet affords students opportunities for intensive exchange, debate, collaboration and compromise between competing interests, and to learn skills like presentation, argumentation and debate, convening projects, and teamwork. Students coming from different disciplinary backgrounds and in different years of study can learn and teach together. The success of this arrangement has been proved by the success of Chung Chi's alumni in the social and political arenas of Hong Kong over the past 30 years. Unlike its mainland counterparts, no political mandate for any political organisation commands the operation and election of student unions, even though Hong Kong has already returned to the sovereignty of China.[11]

Both the structured academic programme contributing to degree credit and the flexible college life education at Chung Chi fulfil various aspects of the college's mission. Some of the programmes aim at raising students' intellectual and social sensitivity; others stress experiential learning that brings students into contact with actual social or cultural circumstances to advance their understanding. Flexible and self-initiated learning has been built into some of these programmes. This variety of learning experiences can enrich students' studies and learning outcomes. Moreover, the Christian ethos of Chung Chi College highlights the college's concern for the spiritual well-being of students, with the college also educating through its chaplaincy and spiritual growth programme. Chung Chi College, with the longest history of college life education among the RC systems in this study, represents the most positive intentions and outcomes for college life education in Greater China.

The RC system at the University of Macau, meanwhile, is relatively new, but it is probably the fastest growing in comparison with the other RC systems in Greater China and aims to develop 12 RCs. Two pilot colleges were built in 2010 in addition to six newly launched RCs; a total of eight RCs were in operation by autumn 2014. Mandatory residency for all first-year students helps students to learn and develop five generic competences: interpersonal relations, cultural engagement, leadership and service learning, global citizenship, and healthy living. The initial part of the programme includes six workshops conducted with the aid of e-portfolio software. After attending these workshops, students are required to sign up for or organise learning activities throughout the year which address the competency areas and to prepare reflection notes on completion of the activities. These requirements count towards one credit at the end of the first year. The university management encourages individual RCs to submit proposals for new general education programmes, such as a new physical education module offered jointly by the university and the Office of Sport Affairs. In addition, each RC has dining facilities exclusively for staff, fellows and students of the college, instilling the college with a spiritual and cooperative identity.

Apart from the structured curriculum, RCs at Macau organise a wide array of social and intellectual activities, and are empowered to conduct student-initiated activities such as regular high-table dinners, parties and cultural workshops celebrating Chinese and Occidental festivals, seminars on current local and international issues, reading clubs, and seminars given by distinguished speakers. The academic staff of the RCs, together with the resident fellows, arrange regular training workshops to develop student leadership and related skills. These can take different forms, such as leadership camps for office holders and prospective student leaders, workshops, small projects and so on. For example, a group of students first assisted in a business project convened by a resident fellow in the Chinese New Year of 2012, which has now become an annual event in the RC. It is led by students, who have learned how to initiate projects, manage resources, market, and keep a balance of costs and benefits. The discussion of business ethics and of social services is also encouraged in the preparation stage of the business project.

College life education in Macau stresses developing the self-discipline and self-management of students. A number of resident tutors, usually postgraduate students of the university, are appointed as student staff to help undergraduate students manage floor activities and to provide pastoral care and mentoring. They may also assist in the convening of first-year workshops. A further group of mature undergraduate students are appointed as resident assistants to assist with college management. Such appointees receive some financial contribution and undergo a job performance appraisal run by the college management. This is useful for their subsequent career development. There is also a student union, representing all student members of an RC and openly elected by all students in the college. Interested students may sign up for individual, not cabinet, election and present their election platforms on the occasion of the college assembly.

Similar to those in Hong Kong, the RCs in Macau do not account for the mandate of a political party and students can vote based on their own individual preferences.

Nevertheless, Macau, with the shortest history among RC systems in Greater China, is still in search of ways to provide college life education. Both its formal and informal learning programmes are still at the experimental stage and leave much room for improvement. One of many challenges to the university's management has been the reception of college life education among local students and their parents in Macau. It is a small city, within a territory of 110 square kilometres and, in the past, most local students lived at home during their four-year studies. Some local students and their parents remain hesitant about on-campus residential colleges, although the university and college management have attempted to explain the beneficial educational outcomes. Such hesitation may undermine the effectiveness of college life education and affect the success of the whole residential college project.

Conclusion

The investigation of residential college education in Greater China reported in this chapter sheds some new light on higher education reforms in the region. Research studies on the effects of educational equality on social reproduction are plentiful. However, little attention has been given to the processes and outcomes of specific types of higher education provision with regard to the promotion of social justice. The newly introduced residential college education in the different jurisdictions of Greater China, with their emphasis on liberal and service education, may answer some questions, insofar as student-centred and experiential learning may promote social justice.

RCs in Mainland China are supplementary to professional education and have a mission to develop talents other than those encouraged in students' disciplinary majors. The service of these talents to the ideology of the CCP and the state is central to RC education and this political mandate contributes to the social and political status quo. As a result, mainland RC education does very little to promote conceptual changes with regard to social justice, which is usually considered politically threatening. Consequently, RC educational activities are teacher-centred: students must fulfil the requirements and expectations set out by the university management and its CCP organs. While some learning projects, like social service projects, may engage students in small-scale social reform practices, in general, mainland RCs provide little freedom for growing student-centred learning experiences.

The strict ideological control over the curriculum and the activities offered in mainland RCs overshadows the importance of social justice and limits opportunities for innovative approaches, since economic development and the maintenance of an harmonious society are given priority, as they are in political discourse generally. A specific version of citizenship for Chinese students has resulted. It aims at developing a group of well-educated and patriotic professionals capable of maintaining social stability. This interpretation is congruent with other empirical findings on the political orientations of mainland university students (Li, 2009).

In contrast, the RC systems in Hong Kong and Macau are located in pluralistic societies in which diverse ideas and discourses in respect of education and social justice are open to competition and debate. Consequently, religious and liberal ideals of education can have equal status in the design of learning activities, while students are encouraged to choose and co-develop their learning experiences in these RC settings. In terms of student-centred learning, the RC systems in Hong Kong and Macau may have been better prepared to involve students by instilling a safe environment conducive to learning, providing substantial guidance, support and mentoring from experienced academics. It should be noted that concerns for social justice and social action are acknowledged in these social service programmes and in leadership development initiatives. The RC programmes have ways to mediate students' understanding of the practical and ethical uses of their professional know-ledge, to foster critical thinking in a substantial topic, and to promote innovative scholarship of practices. The version of socially responsible citizenship in such learning environments includes high tolerance for diversity and self-determination, which distinguishes them from the other RC systems in Greater China. This is a tension that will continue to affect relations between Mainland China and the Special Autonomous Regions of Hong Kong and Macau, to say nothing of Taiwan.

Notes

1 The investigation reported in this chapter was completed during my service in Henry Fok Pearl Jubilee College, University of Macau. I wish to express my gratitude to the College Master, Professor George Watt, for his support and encouragement in this project.

2 The loss of effective ideological education and control over university students is said to be a very serious problem in the report. The worst case is that it would endanger the legitimacy of the Communist Party's ruling status in Mainland China. The detailed diagnostic analysis of the problem attributes the lack of professional training and career prospects for the student affairs personnel (they are generally called 'counsellors' in China) to a loosely organised structure. The possible solutions suggested in the report are to develop a mechanism that provides more intensive and professional training, and to introduce professional credentials and recognition and clear career prospects to the student affairs personnel.

3 St Paul's College (Colégio de São Paulo), also known as College of Madre de Deus, was launched in 1594 and was the first higher education institute in Asia to prepare Catholic priests. The college was eventually burned down by an accidental fire in 1835 and the main entrance remains in Macau as its well-known legacy.

4 See www.umac.mo/about_UM_history.html.

5 According to a field visit to Fudan on 18 March 2013.

6 Interviews with RC students in Fudan, 18 March 2013.

7 Prospectus of Chongshi College in Xian Jiaotong, 2012.

8 See http://rc.umac.mo/mission.

9 Prospectus of Chongshi College in Xian Jiaotong 2012.

10 See www.ccc.cuhk.edu.hk/index.php?option=com_content&view=article&id=102 &Itemid=107&lang=en (accessed 30 September 2013).

11 Field visit to Chung Chi College on 15 June 2013.

References

Australian Council for Educational Research (ACER) (2009), *Engaging College Communities: The impact of residential colleges in Australian higher education*. Available online at: http://research.acer.edu.au/cgi/viewcontent.cgi?article=1007&context=ausse (accessed 25 September 2012).

Badcock, P.B.T., Pattison, P.E. and Harris, K.L. (2010), Developing generic skills through university study: A study of arts, science, and engineering in Australia, *Higher Education*, 60: 441–458.

Bok, D. (2003), *Universities in the Marketplace: The commercialization of higher education*, Princeton, NJ: Princeton University Press.

Committee on Bilingualism (2007), *Report of the Committee on Bilingualism*, Hong Kong: The Chinese University of Hong Kong. Available online at: www.cuhk.edu.hk/policy/english/bilingualism/downloads/cob-report-e.pdf.

Hersh, R.H. (1999), Generating ideals and transforming lives: A contemporary case of the residential liberal arts college, *Daedalus*, 128(1): 173–194.

Huang, H.M. (2010), A comparative study of the academy mode and the residential college mode of student management in university (in Chinese), *Advanced Study in Engineering Education*, 3: 108–113.

Inkelas, K.K., Soldner, M., Longerbeam, S.D. and Leonard, J.B. (2008), Differences in student outcomes by types of living-learning programmes: The development of an empirical typology, *Research in Higher Education*, 49: 495–512.

Jacobson, S.P. (2007), Initiating residential learning communities: Critical elements and practice, unpublished Ed.D thesis, University of the Pacific, Stockton, California.

Kerr, K. and Tweedy, J. (2006), Beyond seat time and student satisfaction: A curricular approach to residential education, *About Campus* (November/December): 9–15.

Li, J. (2009), Fostering citizenship in China's move from elite to mass higher education: An analysis of students' political socialization and civic participation, *International Journal of Educational Development*, 29: 382–398.

Longerbeam, S.D., Inkelas, K.K. and Brower, A.M. (2007), Second hand benefits: Student outcomes in residence hall with living-learning programmes, *Journal of College and University Student Housing*, 34(2): 20–30.

Markwell, D. (2010), The value of university residential colleges, a speech at the Ashley Lecture at Trent University, 2 February, Peterborough Ontario, Canada.

Newman, J.H.C. (1959), *The Idea of a University*, New York: Images Books.

Qiu, J., Luo, N.G., Xu, W.S. and Yep, M. (2010), A study of the reform of the role and career development of university counsellors, an internal report for the key research project commissioned by the Ministry of Education, P.R. China.

Smith, C. and Bath, D. (2006), The role of the learning community in the development of discipline knowledge and generic graduate outcomes, *Higher Education*, 51: 259–286.

Sweeting, A. (2004), *Education in Hong Kong, 1941 to 2001: Visions and revisions*, Hong Kong: Hong Kong University Press.

Xian Jiaotong University (2012), Prospectus of Chongshi College, promotion brochure, Xian: Xian Jiaotong University.

Zhang, Y. (2012), *A Study of the Developmental Path of China's Higher Education* (in Chinese), Beijing: People's Publishing House.

7 Adult higher and continuing education in Mainland China and in Hong Kong

Social justice or user pays?

Ning Rong Liu and John Cribbin

Introduction

The provision of adult, higher and continuing education in China and Hong Kong has both similarities and differences. For China itself there is the long Confucian tradition and history of the Imperial Examinations as well as Western influences introduced from the late nineteenth and early twentieth centuries (Li, 2011). Hong Kong, as part of China, shares this tradition but also had the more specifically British colonial influences in the period from 1841 to 1997 and, because of its geographical situation, it also developed its historical role as a bridge between East and West (Young and Zhang, 2008).

This chapter explores these different traditions and influences, their impact in terms of social justice and the extent to which this has been an aim or objective of policy, or whether what has developed was a reaction to market pressure. We commence with a brief survey of the social and economic purposes of adult higher education. We then proceed to review the historical perspective of Mainland China and current changes in scale and direction. This is followed by a historical perspective of adult and higher continuing education in Hong Kong, with particular reference to Hong Kong's efforts to serve the needs of Mainland China. Finally, our conclusion draws together the notions of social justice or marketisation (user pays) in adult higher and continuing education in both Hong Kong and China.

Social and economic purposes of adult higher education

There are historically two different theoretical and ideological views that argue for lifelong education and training (Gustavsson, 1997). One dominant trend in the Western world is the human capital school, which is supported by neo-liberal ideology and strengthened by the fashion of decentralisation and marketisation. This is more concerned with productive labour and economic competitiveness. The other trend is the humanistic school, which is concerned with democratic, social and holistic approaches to education. As a consequence of globalisation, a neo-Marxist or anarchistic-utopian template for reform (Faure *et al.*, 1972) has shifted to a neo-liberal, functionalist rendition (OECD, 1996) in a comparatively short time. A resurgence in 'human capital theory', which argues that there is a direct relationship between education and the economy, has also facilitated change in the field of adult and continuing education. Adult and continuing education is seen to have a more direct impact on human resource development.

It is evident that governments in both developed and developing countries are concerned about the role of education in improving the competitiveness of their citizens. 'Adult education serves global/local interests by the development of human capital as a means of gaining a competitive advantage in a global market-place' (Harris and Simons, 2004: 138). This focus on employability is criticised variously as merely 'learning to labour' (Martin, 2000) and as a form of social control (Coffield, 1999). This explains why the advocacy of lifelong learning has consequently been a high priority for policy-makers around the world. The OECD tends to focus on the strong connection between learning and work. It, therefore, suggests that the role of governments is 'to monitor the conditions under which markets for learning can lead to responsive and efficient provision' (OECD, 1996: 185). 'The notion of adult learning or lifelong learning tends to de-emphasise government responsibility for learning. It fits more closely with the market-driven approach to adult education and training, which is concerned mainly with developing the economy' (Walters, 2000: 201), a point that has also been emphasised in relation to China (Ge, 2008).

Lifelong learning frameworks clearly show a shift in responsibility from the state to the individual; and increasingly, individuals are required to engage in their own learning to keep abreast of developments in the marketplace. The emphasis on 'learning' rather than 'education' is highly significant because it reduces the traditional preoccupation with structures and institutions, and instead focuses on the individual (Tuijnman and Bostrom, 2002). Indeed, according to Boshier, 'if lifelong education was an instrument for democracy, lifelong learning is almost entirely preoccupied with the cash register' (Boshier, 1998: 5). The shift in dis-course from 'education' to 'learning' also reflects the trend to privatise education and training and to organise it primarily in relation to market needs (Walters, 2000). Thus the danger is that if knowledge is a commodity that is being marketed, lifelong learning may exacerbate the gap between the knowledge-haves and knowledge-have-nots. This makes it very difficult for the needs of those with less economic, political and cultural power to be accurately heard and acted upon in ways that deal with the true depth of the problem (Apple, 2001).

Historical perspectives: adult higher education and manpower training in China

The Chinese government is explicit about the link between education and eco-nomic development to serve the nation's modernisation programme (Hayhoe, 1992). It has long viewed adult education as critical to the economic develop-ment and modernisation process by providing necessary and qualified man-power. Higher education, particularly adult higher education, was structured to serve the needs of economic development in China, and was organised to match the political environment and economic conditions. Adult higher education played a very important role in training employed personnel, enhancing the quality of current workers, and scientists, government officials and industrial leaders. Thus, China's education policy-makers and educators in recent years adopted the concept of lifelong learning to address primarily the needs of economic growth and increased productivity, with less importance attached to creating conditions of social progress. By accepting human capital perspectives in lifelong learning, China's education policy-makers hoped to form a long-term policy, which in turn could provide the well-trained talents needed to compete in the global economy (Liu, 2008; Wang, 2011; Tan, 2008).

When China launched economic reforms and decided to open the door to foreign investment following the third Plenary of the Eleventh Congress of the Chinese Communist Party (CCP) in December 1978, the country lacked the skilled and professional people needed for its modernisation in the new era. Between the mid-1960s and 1976, the proportion of technicians in the industrial labour force declined from 4 per cent to 2.6 per cent (Naughton, 1995). The national college entrance examination was resumed after ten years of radical ideology, and the first group of students started their undergraduate studies in the spring of 1978. Despite the efforts made and the leap in enrolment in universities and colleges, China experienced a huge shortfall of places for post-secondary education in the 1980s owing to the increasing demand for higher education (Kuang and Shi, 2009).

Seeing the future potential, the government launched reforms for adult higher education. The First National Conference of Adult Education was held in 1986 to discuss the role of adult education in economic development. In the following year the government released the first policy initiative on adult education entitled 'Decision on Development and Reform of Adult Education' which pronounced that the advancement of education levels of the whole society was critical to the cause of social modernisation (State Council, 1987). The Chinese government attempted to develop adult higher education in the service of modernisation. Most universities and colleges also set up schools of adult education to coordinate all higher education programmes for adult students and to assure the quality of the programmes. China's adult education entered into a new era of rapid growth.

The year 1993 witnessed the beginning of the comprehensive refurbishment of China's adult higher education. The Outline for Reform and Development of Education in China issued by the CCP and the State Council on 13 February stated clearly that adult education is a newly developed system which would lead to lifelong education from traditional education, and it called for building a lifelong learning system with its focus on providing continuing education and on-the-job training programmes (CCPCC and State Council, 1993). As a result, the Committee of Continuing Education in Higher Education Institutions was formed by the central government. In anticipation of the changes in the new millennium, the Ministry of Education in December 1998 proposed an '*Action plan to revitalize education towards the twenty-first century*' to establish a lifelong learning system by 2010 (MoE, 1998). The term 'lifelong learning' as opposed to 'adult education' began to infiltrate Chinese policy documents, and the government adopted the framework of lifelong learning, reflecting the international trend.

The development of higher education in the late 1990s marked a dramatic policy change shifting from elite higher education to mass higher education (Liu, 2008; Zha, 2011). In 1998, the Chinese government decided to increase the ratio of gross enrolment from 9 per cent to 15 per cent by 2010 (CCPCC and State Council, 1998). However the goal was accomplished by 2003. As a result, the Ministry of Education called upon adult institutions of higher education to shift their focus from offering degree-oriented programmes to launching continuing professional education programmes. With the emphasis on continuing education, universities in China started to rename their schools of adult education as schools of continuing education. Not only did this change provide a new opportunity to expand the sector, but it also had implications for, and an impact on, the adult higher education system, institutional structure, business operations and programme development (Liu, 2009; Hao, 2010).

Restructuring China's adult higher education: strategies and responses

The new strategies adopted by China's universities to restructure adult education were designed to operate under market mechanisms with more authority and flexibility to provide programmes that meet the needs of the market. The first type of strategic response adopted by Chinese universities was to restructure the adult higher education system. The massification of higher education provided an opportunity to revamp the adult higher education system; this developed into much broader areas to incorporate online education and included continuing professional education.

Adult higher education was traditionally considered as a university extension by offering degree programmes to working adults. Historically, this was the most important part of the adult higher education system. Most universities set up a school of adult education in the late 1980s and early 1990s to coordinate all award-bearing programmes for working adults. Although the main objectives were aimed at providing working adults with higher education opportunities in a part-time mode, many university adult education units also enrolled secondary school graduates who had failed the national college entrance examination in a full-time mode (Liu, 2012). While the latter operation was terminated in 76 universities under the Ministry of Education in 2006, the adult education sector continued to offer part-time degree programmes to working adults. Some schools of adult education even established the Academy of Self-study Examination to offer preparatory courses for students taking the self-study higher education examinations. China claimed to have built the largest self-study higher education system in the world, which allowed adult students to complete their post-secondary studies by following the study outline provided by the examination authority. The flexibility of the system permitted adult students to conduct their study in their spare time and at their own pace (Sun, 2008; Yan and Huang, 2009).

Online education – once an independent unit in China's higher education system – was included under the umbrella of adult education, with the merger intended to strengthen its role to offer academic degree programmes off-campus. Since adult education institutions were allowed to only enrol part-time students, online programmes offered in a full-time mode could supplement traditional adult education by providing a hybrid study mode. The combination of part-time face-to-face teaching and full-time online learning did not violate the government's policy of limiting adult education institutions from offering full-time academic programmes. And, even more importantly, this approach increased the meeting times between teachers and students both face-to-face and online, thus delivering better teaching outcomes.

Commencing in 1999 when 67 universities were given the green light to launch programmes online, online education enrolled over one million students annually. The programmes offered through online education ranged from a higher diploma, to a two-year top-up Bachelor degree for those who already had a higher diploma, to a four-year university degree, and to postgraduate courses. Differing from other academic programmes, universities were given autonomy to admit students for online programmes based on their own criteria, to set up the subjects without seeking approval from the Ministry of Education, to decide the tuition fees with more flexibility, to grant awards (which usually needed to be authorised by the Ministry of Education), and to allow students to accumulate their credits in a certain period. These factors contributed to the high-speed development of online education, which has become one major area for further expansion of the university adult education sector.

However, the prime area for expansion and growth was continuing professional education, which became an engine for the further development of adult higher education. Continuing professional education began in the late 1980s when the development of the economy required more seasoned managers to run the growing business and professional operation for almost all specialisations. Although China has made impressive gains in human resource development after more than two decades into the reform of the market economy, the nation is still facing a critical shortage of well-trained managers and professionals. One major reason behind the scarcity of human resources was attributed to the fact that the investment in human capital in China was even below the average of most developing countries such as India, Thailand, Brazil and Mexico (Heckman, 2003). However, market-driven economic reforms could provide people with incentives to invest in human capital, since talented professionals could move freely in the labour market with the opportunity of a better salary and promotion.

Tsinghua University in Beijing provides the most prominent example in developing continuing professional education programmes. Tsinghua started to operate China's first school of continuing education in 1986. In the ten years since Tsinghua launched the reform in 2003 to focus on continuing professional and executive programmes as the core operation of adult education, more than one million participants have attended various professional development programmes offered by the school. Tsinghua's continuing education sector has also grown in size since 2003, and the total number of staff members has increased more than ten-fold over the past decade. The development in this area also became a phenomenon nationwide – with the rapid expansion of continuing professional education programmes, this sector generated additional tuition fees for universities.

Thus, the second type of strategic response adopted by Chinese universities was to establish a business-oriented organisation to implement a corporate-style management. With the arrival of the 'Customer Century' in higher education, the university's adult education sector re-engineered its structure to fit the new, changing environment.

A flat, centre-based structure was promoted and set up along the lines of professional business management to support its reformed operation. This centre-based operation was streamlined in line with the practice of the business community. Tsinghua University's School of Continuing Education started its reform in 2003 to stop degree programmes for adults and to only run professional development programmes, and by spring 2008 the school had 15 business centres. At Zhejiang University's School of Adult Education, ten centres were established following its restructuring in 2007 to focus on training for the different professions, trades and industries, while traditional adult education and online education to offer academic degree programmes continued to operate. Three centres were formed at Sun Yat-sen University's School of Higher Adult Education to specialise in academic programmes for adult students, online education and professional development programmes. Although different universities had adopted various approaches, the operations in general tended to be more programme-based than department-based, and a head was usually appointed to lead one or two programmes with a high degree of autonomy and flexibility. This eliminated unnecessary layers between the top management and front lines, allowing greater flexibility to react to changes in a timely and effective manner.

The adult higher education sector even established a training centre in partnership with private companies for the purpose of seeking financial back-up for the operations. The primary consideration for the collaboration was the lack of funding from the university. But this has broad implications – this type of university–industry alliance would enable the adult education sector to link the educational service with the market closely and even help introduce corporate governance into its operations. This newly established flat, centre-based structure provided flexibility and accountability in order to maintain a balance between the transfer of authority and responsibilities. Thus, the devolved budgeting system was implemented so that programme teams could make sound decisions in the self-funding operation. Each business unit comprised a programme centre which provided different kinds of professional development programmes for the specialised fields. It also functioned as a budget unit which was responsible for its own financial outcome and generating sufficient revenue to sustain its own growth.

However, financial benefits, not social benefits, were taken into consideration as the most important factor in launching the programmes as a result of the restructuring. Thus, university adult education was no longer like an education institution, since the different business units in the university adult education sector franchised educational agents to run programmes without sufficient supervision and monitoring. This type of operation generated increasing complaints from adult students that universities only cared about generating revenue, and this has also harmed the reputation of adult higher education in China. According to a news report, Tsinghua University's School of Continuing Education was sued by an entrepreneur who enrolled in its programme, alleging the false promise of advertising prominent faculty staff and small class sizes, but the school claimed that the programme was run by the agent and not the school, even though the programme was advertised under the name of the school.

There was little doubt that the centre-based, corporate-style structures gave staff much more freedom than they ever had before. The empowerment of employees became a common structural and cultural characteristic of entrepreneurial education organisations. Thus, the reform and change of the management style opened a new chapter for the organisation with the market demands and needs taking an increasingly salient position in the outlook of the significant decision-makers. However, the restructuring of China's adult higher education clearly showed that executive and professional education is treated by universities as a mere cash machine, and the importance of social justice in the field of lifelong learning has not been given equal weight in the restructuring process. Some of the potential dangers in this situation have been highlighted with reference to adult higher education in Taiyuan and their impact on student motivation and outcomes (Wang and Morgan, 2009).

The third strategy adopted by the Chinese universities was to offer more flexible and relevant curricula to meet the changing needs of students and society. With the introduction of the centre-based structure and the underpinning of the entrepreneurial culture, programme teams in the adult higher education sector were empowered to look into the opportunities and work with academics and professionals to develop the most needed courses. At the institutional level, the university's adult education sector was given more authority to launch both continuing professional education and online academic programmes. They were required to form an academic committee to be responsible for curriculum development, and which functioned as an advisory board to make academic decisions.

With the fiercely competitive environment in China's adult higher education sector, universities were required to reverse the traditional way of developing courses. This should have started from feeding information about learner needs back to the top management, and then developing and adjusting programmes according to the identified needs and wants. Thus, the designing of market-oriented and outcome-based curricula was crucial in the process of successfully launching adult higher education programmes demanded by the market. While various channels of developing programmes were employed, three approaches were considered as the most important to capitalise on following three kinds of resources: academic staff in the university, experts in the professional bodies and international cooperation (Liu, 2008).

First, the sector attempted to react proactively to market needs and to closely link the university with the business community. Researchers for programme development kept abreast of the changing environment for professional training, and fed back information about market demands through periodic surveys. With the support from the university's academic staff in the programme and curriculum design, the adult and continuing education sector quickly introduced high-quality programmes. By giving sincere consideration to the needs from the perspective of the business community, authoritative experts in the related field not only included the latest research results in China and abroad, but also integrated theory and practice with a focus on practical application, when designing the curriculum of such programmes.

The second common approach used in launching the market-oriented programmes was to use the knowledge of experts in the field and the professional bodies, since they understood the trends in the field and the market needs. The school maintained direct communication channels with the training departments of some professional bodies, and even involved them in designing the programmes.

International partnership was the third approach to offer adult and continuing education programmes. International cooperation was an important aspect of educational development in China. During the twentieth century Chinese educators encountered varied foreign influences and became more proactive in using them to pioneer their own national path towards educational development (Ding, 2001). The impact of globalisation on China has served as a very important way to provide professionals with better learning opportunities. International partners include some leading universities and professional bodies worldwide. Almost all cooperative programmes with overseas partners had one thing in common: the adult and continuing education sector was unable to locate experts in China to help it develop, or was not allowed to develop due to government regulation.

In developing continuing professional education programmes, adult higher education institutions involved more experts in various professional bodies and associations than academics. As a result, there were better interrelations between theory and application in the programme designed for professional adult students. However, there were some concerns in the process of designing and launching market-oriented programmes. First, the market-oriented approach to the development of courses with its particular attention to the changing environment in the fields may backfire. In many circumstances, the life-span of programmes depends on the short-lived needs of the industry. Second, there are the increasingly strong – but not always positive – influences on the content of programmes by educational agents and students. These may in the end dictate this buying and selling relationship and determine the supply–demand chain. Thus, the university adult higher education sector may only focus on the financial gain in running such programmes but completely overlook academic values that may not be appreciated by their clients/students. This could also completely transform the university as a social institution.

Historical perspectives: adult higher and continuing education in Hong Kong

Hong Kong has also played a role in higher and continuing education in China, whether in the colonial period or since 1997. Its geographical position and historical function as a bridge between East and West dictates that this would be so (Young and Zhang, 2008). For example, the University of Hong Kong from its inception in 1912 articulated a mission to serve the peoples of China as well as Hong Kong and the region. Such historical links, however, and indeed the resumption of sovereignty, have not impacted upon the way in which Hong Kong's higher education institutions have been viewed in China. That is, they are regarded in the same way as any other overseas provider in terms of offering degree programmes in Mainland China. Thus, in order to offer degree-awarding programmes they have to partner with a mainland educational institution and seek Ministry of Education approval.

There was also a particular challenge for Hong Kong's higher education institutions after 1997 in that they were generally well regarded internationally, but little known nationally. Thus, a conscious process was undertaken to project their reputation within China. This coincided with a move towards internationalisation generally in Hong Kong's higher education institutions and for the attraction of overseas students to study in Hong Kong (UGC, 1996, 2002, 2010). This has been a successful endeavour such that the leading Hong Kong universities now attract the best mainland students on the basis of their school-leaving examinations and compete for the best students with leading Chinese higher education institutions such as Tsinghua, Peking and Fudan. Moreover, since there is good scholarship support available for such students, this does contribute in a small way to social justice, since the top students can be attracted and admitted on a needs-blind basis. This is particularly important given that Hong Kong is not a cheap place for students although it is certainly less expensive for students than moving to the United States, Australia, the UK or Europe.

Hong Kong's higher and continuing education sector

Hong Kong has a robust tertiary education sector, although the number of students admitted is relatively small compared with the demand for places. As mentioned above, the Hong Kong institutions rate highly on various international ranking such as THE, QS, etc. in both global terms and in terms of Asia (Altbach and Postiglione, 2012). There are eight publicly funded universities and two other self-financed university institutions. In addition, these institutions have strong continuing education units and there is a private sector of tertiary education provision in a number of post-secondary colleges and other private colleges (Cribbin, 2002). The universities funded by the Universities Grant Committee are subject to its coordination of the sector and periodic reviews of the system. Following the 1996 review (UGC, 1996), there was a specific aim to internationalise the sector both in terms of attracting overseas students, including those from Mainland China, to Hong Kong as well as ensuring that Hong Kong students had the opportunity to undertake part of their studies overseas. This policy has been very successful and the target or quota for such numbers of overseas students has progressively risen to 20 per cent of the total numbers and many of the institutions have made significant progress, with some even exceeding that figure. Even so, in terms of being a destination for overseas students, the numbers are relatively small given that the sector is relatively small compared with cities such as London, New York, Boston, Shanghai, Beijing and Singapore.

Since about 2004, the Hong Kong government has begun to articulate a policy of Hong Kong as a higher education hub, later refined as a regional education hub, and has therefore promoted the notion of Hong Kong as a serious player in the business of international education or transnational education. The reality in this context is that the numbers of overseas students in Hong Kong are relatively small if using volume as a yardstick by which to judge the success of the hub policy. Nevertheless, in terms of quality provision a strong case may be argued for the success of the policy. Indeed, Hong Kong, judged by the international rankings, where half its university sector is in the world top 200, can in this sense be described as a higher education hub for quality provision. In another sense, there is a very significant presence in Hong Kong of overseas institutions offering their courses. Occasionally, this is on a direct basis but more often it is in partnership with the continuing education units of the universities or a private operator. Indeed, it is the university continuing education sector that tends to dominate this provision. For example, the University of Hong Kong School of Professional and Continuing Education (HKU SPACE) has more than 30 international partners, and a significant proportion of its degree and above level offerings are for international programmes. Thus, as an import hub for higher education, Hong Kong is a significant player (Cribbin, 2011).

In terms of the system as a whole, student numbers in international degree programmes being studied in Hong Kong are about 40 per cent of the total degree places in Hong Kong. Historically, the numbers of students who were able to undertake degree-level study in Hong Kong has been severely limited when compared with the demand. Indeed, the former secondary school system itself was a bottleneck so that many students were not able to have the opportunity after junior secondary school to study to obtain the qualifications necessary for degree-level entry, yet they were fully capable of so doing. This led to very significant demand for part-time study by working adults in the past 20 years although the recent education reforms in Hong Kong are now changing that balance. This is because the government promoted an expansion of full-time, post-school, post-secondary education from the year 2000 which was achieved by the establishment of community colleges offering Associate Degree and Higher Diploma programmes. While these were intended to be awards in their own right, most students perceived them as routes to access degree-level study after completion, and indeed HKU SPACE's own figures are that some 70 per cent of Associate Degree and 50 per cent of Higher Diploma holders proceed to degree-level study after their awards. The government has also promoted this by progressively providing 'senior-year places' in the publicly funded universities. There are now some 4,000 such places available to enable such articulation. There are also a number of self-financed degrees, and these include overseas degrees that may be studied full-time in Hong Kong through the university continuing units and others. It is likely therefore that the demand for undergraduate degree study on a part-time basis for working adults may well decline as more and more school leavers are able to progress directly to first-degree studies.

There has also been a major reform in the Hong Kong education system such that the 'British' system of 5+2 secondary education has been replaced by a six-year secondary curriculum leading to a Diploma of Secondary Education which is now the entry point for four-year university degrees as opposed to the former 'colonial' three-year honours degree system. This extensive reform also opens the bottleneck that previously existed such that only around one-third of students after five years of junior secondary education (to Hong Kong Certificate of Education HKCE level) were able to proceed to the final two years to Hong Kong A level. Now all students may achieve the Diploma and aspire to higher education, as indeed do the parents for their children. The pool of students seeking to enter higher education has therefore expanded significantly, although it should also be stressed that this is a somewhat temporary phenomenon given that the school-leaving age cohort is set to decline by some 40 per cent over the next ten years. Thus, there is an element of cynicism in Hong Kong's higher education policy with the government promoting expansion of self-financed degree places, essentially by private operators (including the university CE units), in the knowledge that many institutions will inevitably fail because the demand will drop through the demographic decline. Nevertheless, it should be emphasised that the Hong Kong system has seen a rapid expansion of availability of higher education from some 30 per cent of the school-leaving age group in the year 2000 to close to 70 per cent by 2012, although it should be acknowledged that this is still less than some other competing Asian economies such as Korea and Singapore (Lee and Cribbin, 2011).

In parallel, the government also introduced the Qualifications Framework (QF) in 2008. The development of the QF bears some similarity to frameworks in other advanced economies but was promoted at a time when the then Education and Manpower Bureau spanned both education (including tertiary education) and the vocational sector. The development of the QF was heavily influenced by the vocational sector and driven by perceived industrial needs in relation to training, rather than the needs of the higher education sector which uses other criteria. Subsequently, the two parts of the Bureau split with the Education Bureau now dealing with the school and higher education sectors, and the manpower portfolio being subsumed in the Labour and Welfare Bureau. This has resulted in a framework which combines both the academic and vocational sectors and which, from the perspective of the higher education institutions, is a case of the 'vocational tail wagging the academic dog'.

The system is premised on prescribing all the qualifications in terms of level plus credit plus title. There is thus far not too much difficulty with the definition of levels (using the outcomes-based learning approach with defined intended learning outcomes), but the introduction into the framework of titles has been more influenced by vocational sector needs, as has that for credits which is based on a 1,200 learning-hour model being equivalent to a full year of learning. This is certainly more apt for the vocational sector and may, when it is fully introduced, be problematic for the higher education sector. To date, the self-accrediting university sector places awards directly on the Qualifications Register, whereas the continuing education sector has to do so via the accreditation agencies. Essentially, the higher education sector in the eight funded universities is already quite regulated given the extent of government funding via the University Grants Committee. The numbers admitted to the universities have been capped at 15,000 per year and within that figure targets are set for each academic programme. The situation is now more relaxed at taught postgraduate level but these courses have to be self-financing. Moreover, in 1996, the government ruled that the continuing education sector must be self-financing and initially this was possible, partly because there was a 'light touch' in the sense of regulation and trust was given by the government to the university continuing education sector in particular which flourished in this context. However, this drew criticism from the private sector operators who were more tightly regulated, and, of course, the result has been not that the burden of regulation of the private sector has been lessened but that the burden of regulation on the university continuing education sector has been increased to provide a 'level playing field'. Hence, we can see a case of marketisation and regulation in operation.

References have been made to the significant penetration of the Hong Kong higher education market by overseas providers, usually in collaboration with a local institution or private sector entity. Again, the regulation in this sector has been relatively light under the Non-local Higher and Professional Education (Regulation) Ordinance but the implementation of this Ordinance has been significantly tightened in the past two years such that there is now quite significant intervention, by the Education Bureau which administers the Ordinance, in the affairs of such programmers. A parallel development in the past two years has been a system of non-local accreditation available to overseas institutions and their local partners such that the partnership and the programmes are subject to an accreditation process by a Hong Kong quality assurance agency, the Hong Kong Council for Accreditation of Academic and Vocational Qualifications (HKCAAVQ). This is a costly and intensive exercise but one that institutions feel may be necessary. The end result is that the qualifications concerned, provided they are successfully accredited, may appear on the Qualifications Register which is the public face of the Qualifications Framework and carries details of all locally accredited courses. There are advantages involved for such programmers to undergo this accreditation process in that it entitles students on those courses to be eligible for the same range of grants and loans as students at a local university. Such courses may also enrol overseas students with a caveat that this has not yet included students from Mainland China, largely because the Ministry of Education in Beijing has yet to be convinced of the value and quality for mainland students to be able to study overseas programmes in Hong Kong.

This potential development is somewhat related to the education hub policy mentioned earlier and also other government policies that relate to the development of 'pillar' industries, which includes educational services. These are seen therefore as a priority by the government for expansion either in attracting students to Hong Kong or exporting Hong Kong education services overseas, particularly to the mainland. There are, however, as yet few concrete results to be seen from this policy objective as far as education is concerned. In this context, it may also be relevant to note that the government manpower projections are showing that the proportion of the workforce with higher education qualifications is increasing quite rapidly and this is reflected in the government manpower projection to 2018 and beyond (Manpower Survey, 2012).

Another related area is that government is also making available to overseas institutions the ability to apply for land grants and loans to develop campuses. This is somewhat parallel to the situation in Singapore which has been rather more successful in establishing it as an education hub than has Hong Kong, certainly in terms of the numbers of overseas students attracted and overseas institutions in operation.

Hong Kong adult higher education and continuing education initiatives in China

Because of the strong links between Hong Kong and China and the rapid development of the Chinese economy since 1980, many of the Hong Kong institutions have links with Chinese institutions and a number of the universities have joint operations in Mainland China either for the development of campuses, the offering of programmes or, in the case of the University of Hong Kong, the opening of a hospital which will also facilitate the teaching of medical students. Nevertheless, given that such links require a mainland partner, it is the case that not all such partnerships have worked well. Moreover, in terms of continuing education there is the issue that continuing adult education in China has historically been perceived as remedial education and so establishing lifelong learning and continuing professional education programmes as high-level activities has proved challenging in Mainland China.

The principal feature of higher education provision in Mainland China since the year 2000 has been one of rapid expansion. The numbers involved are almost breath-taking and yet this has not always had good results, since the expansion of quantity has not always been matched by expansion in quality, and one result has been serious graduate unemployment in a number of major cities because the studies undertaken have not fitted the graduates for employment (Li and Morgan, 2011).

The expansion of opportunities within China itself has also been matched by a significant expansion of numbers of students going overseas. These graduates on return are often in higher demand than graduates of some of the institutions that have opened up to meet demand (Li, 2011; Morgan and Wu, 2011; Li *et al.*, 2011). Indeed, there is also recent evidence that Chinese students are going overseas at even earlier ages (Zha, 2011). However, there is also some evidence that this pattern may not be as pronounced as in the past where a recent article cites the fact that the '*Sea Turtles*' or '*HaiGui*' are no longer in such demand (*Economist*, 2013).

It is certainly the case that some Hong Kong higher education institution collaborations in Mainland China have not always been successful, but equally there are a number of successful partnerships that have been initiated: for example, by the Hong Kong Baptist University via its International College in Zhuhai in collaboration with Beijing Normal University; the University of Hong Kong MBA programme in collaboration with Fudan University in Shanghai and a Master of Finance programmed with Peking; and initiatives by the Polytechnic University and the Open University. The Chinese University, the University of Science and Technology and the University of Hong Kong have also forged research partnerships with mainland partners.

HKU SPACE has also forged a number of institutional partnerships, some of which have been successful and some of which have not, and has established with a mainland partner, the Suzhou Global College where both the Hong Kong University Associate Degrees and the Dazhuan qualification are offered, and those students do successfully articulate to overseas programmes. More recently however, the emphasis in HKU SPACE has been on the provision of management training/executive programmes that do not lead to degree awards but rather to postgraduate diploma/certificate awards which can be offered directly and appear to be building up with some success. Nevertheless, as stated earlier, the Ministry of Education in China is still wary of overseas awards. There are well-established precedents such as the University of Nottingham at Ningbo and the University of Liverpool with Xian Jiaotong University in Suzhou, as well as an extensive range of individual programme partnerships (Stanfield and Wang, 2012). Nevertheless, the Ministry is concerned about the quality of overseas programmes offered in Mainland China and is not yet convinced that overseas programmes being offered in Hong Kong should be available to mainland students. However, with the rapidly expanding availability of online courses and/or blended learning courses, it may only be a matter of time before the situation changes. Hong Kong is well placed to offer more opportunities to mainland students if and when this occurs.

Conclusion: the notions of social justice in Hong Kong and China

There are similarities and differences between Hong Kong and China in terms of higher and continuing education. For China, there is a long history and tradition of study with both the traditions of the Confucian era and the Imperial Examinations as well as 'Shu Yuan' academies from the Tang and Song Dynasties (Hayhoe and Liu, 2010). This has been supplemented by the Western influence in universities developing since the late nineteenth century. These institutions suffered vicissitudes through the civil war and revolutionary period, and particularly during the Cultural Revolution. These were, nevertheless, elitist systems although open to all talents, particularly given the nationwide examinations for all schools, the *Gaokao*, established since the Revolution. The other feature is massive expansion since 1999 and, while this has opened up opportunities for many, it should also be noted that the private sector has played a role.

> China's higher education expansion would not have been tenable without private higher education, despite the latter's shortcomings in providing a quality of instruction as high as that of public universities. While private higher education remained relatively weak and in a marginal position it helped decrease the financial pressure on government and also expanded access to higher education.
>
> (Postiglione, 2010)

Thus, social justice may be seen in the expansion of opportunity but it has nevertheless been accompanied by a 'user-pays' element to make it a reality. There has also been the well-known exodus of students from Mainland China to overseas universities, particularly the United States, the United Kingdom and Australia, to seek qualifications, and statistics show that the return rate of such students has not been very large (Zha, 2011).

In the context of a close link between adult higher education and manpower training, the traditional functions of an educational system have also changed. Governments in general shy away from their responsibilities for adult learning and from financing continuing education. As in many other countries, China no longer considers that human capital development should be solely the responsibility of the government, and market forces are replacing state forces as the major drivers for the development of adult and continuing education (Liu, 2012). As a result, adult higher education has become a consumption item, and adult higher education institutions are the suppliers in the market which aim to meet market demands for manpower training. This market-driven approach to adult education and training is concerned mainly with developing the economy (Walters, 2000). As Bleiklie pointed out, 'the idea of the university as a community of scholars, students or disciplines, and as a public agency to some extent yielded to the idea of the university as a corporate enterprise' (Bleiklie, 2002: 30). Therefore, the strategies and responses to policy changes adopted by university adult higher education in China have been consistent with the global trend of marketisation in higher education. This latest development in China's adult higher education has strengthened the role of higher education in human capital development, but weakened its traditional social functions and values.

In Hong Kong by contrast, there was the strong element of the British tradition from the colonial era where higher and continuing education was generally elitist. This was reinforced by a school system on a 5+2 model which permitted only about one-third of students to progress to the stage of attaining university matriculation qualifications and where the number of funded university places was then not sufficient even for this small group. Thus, overseas opportunities were one way of this being circumvented while, as we have seen over the past 20 years, part-time education offered by the continuing education sector has been a pathway to degree qualification. Nevertheless, while the small, government-funded sector is generally needs blind owing to the availability of grants, loans and scholarships, the other routes are clearly a user-pays element. In that sense there is a contrast also where in Hong Kong the continuing education sector, perhaps influenced by its extra-mural origins, was regarded as a high-level provider so that the route to qualifications via continuing education was respected. In China, however, continuing education has been regarded as remedial because of its origins and this perception is still an element now, even though there are more routes to higher education via continuing education. A further contrast is that in China much of the expansion and the work of continuing education has been domestically sourced, while in Hong Kong most of the higher level continuing education to degree level has been provided by overseas universities via their export of educational programmes. A further area of contrast therefore is that the Hong Kong experience has been much more open to overseas influence and globalisation as would be expected in the 'world city', whereas China has been more inward-looking and suspicious of overseas awards.

Moreover, it is also ironic that as China opens up more to global influences, and more particularly increases its outward investment, there is a need for it to have more experience of the world via the continuing education courses and management training that could be made available. In both cases there has been a perceived need for a highly educated workforce but, whereas China would be principally sourcing this internally, Hong Kong has been prepared to source and search for talent on a wider basis. In addition, in China generally there is more of a contrast between the highly developed east coast and the less developed interior in terms of opportunity, whereas Hong Kong, as a compact territory, has been more open to opportunity generally. From a social justice perspective however, while government policy has sought to make opportunities available, there has nevertheless been a strong element of the 'user pays' in terms of the expansion of opportunity in both higher and continuing education.

References

Altbach, P. and Postiglione, G. (2012), Hong Kong's academic advantage, *International Higher Education*, 66(4): 22–27.

Apple, M.W. (2001), Comparing neo-liberal projects and inequality in education, *Comparative Education*, 37(4): 409–423.

Bleiklie, I. (2002), Explaining change in higher education policy, in Trowler, P.R. (ed.) *Higher Education Policy and Institutional Change*, Buckingham: SRHE and Open University Press, pp. 24–45.

Boshier, R. (1998), Edgar Faure after 25 years: Down but not out, in Holford, J., Jarvis, P. and Griffin, C. (eds) *International Perspectives on Lifelong Learning*, London: Kogan, pp. 35–55.

Chinese Communist Party Central Committee (CCPCC) and State Council (1993), *The Outline for Reform and Development of Education in China* (in Chinese), Beijing: CCPCC and State Council.

CCPCC and State Council (1998), *Decision on Deepening Educational Reforms and Comprehensively Promoting Quality-oriented Education* (in Chinese), Beijing: CCPCC and State Council.

Coffield, F. (1999), Breaking the consensus: Lifelong learning as social control, *British Educational Research Journal*, 25(4): 479–499.

Cribbin, J. (2002), Competition and collaboration: Hong Kong providers and partners, in Cribbin, J. and Kennedy, P. (eds) *Lifelong Learning in Action: Hong Kong practitioners' perspectives*, Hong Kong: Hong Kong University Press, pp. 35–55.

Cribbin, J. (2011), Education reform in Hong Kong: Implications for higher education and lifelong learning, in Morgan, W.J. and Wu, B. (eds) *Higher Education Reform in China: Beyond the expansion*, London and New York: Routledge, pp. 139–153.

Ding, G. (2001), Nationalization and internationalization: Two turning points in China's education in the twentieth century, in Peterson, G., Hayhoe, R. and Lu, Y.L. (eds) *Education, Culture, and Identity in Twentieth-century China*, Hong Kong: Hong Kong University Press, pp. 161–186.

Economist (2013), Plight of the sea turtles, *Economist*, 6 July, pp. 32–33.

Faure, E., Herrera, F., Kaddoura, A.R., Lopes, H., Petrovsky, A.V., Rahenema, M. and Ward, F.C. (1972), *Learning To Be: The world of education today and tomorrow*, Paris: UNESCO.

Ge, D. (2008), Non-traditional higher education in China: Evolution, developments and implications, *International Journal of Continuing Education and Lifelong Learning*, 1(1): 23–34.

Gustavsson, B. (1997), Life-long learning reconsidered, in Walters, S. (ed.) *Globalization, Adult Education and Training*, London: Zed Books, pp. 237–249.

Hao, K. (2010), Development and system construction of continuing education in China, *International Journal of Continuing Education and Lifelong Learning*, 3(1): 1–16.

Harris, R. and Simons, M. (2004), Adult and vocational educator: Their changing work and professional development, in Kell, P., Shore, S. and Singh, M. (eds) *Adult Education at 21st Century*, New York: Peter Lang, pp. 137–152.

Hayhoe, R. (ed.) (1992), *Education and Modernization: The Chinese experience*, Oxford: Pergamon Press.

Hayhoe, R.V. and Liu, J. (2010), China's universities, cross-border education and dialogue among civilizations, in Chapman, D., Cummings, W. and Postiglione, G. (eds) *Crossing Borders in East Asian Higher Education*, Hong Kong: Springer/CERC, pp. 47–72.

Heckman, J.J. (2003), China's investment in human capital, *Economic Development and Cultural Change*, 51(4): 795–804.

Kuang, Y. and Shi, W. (2009), Developments of China's vocational education in the past thirty years: In retrospect and analysis, *International Journal of Continuing Education and Lifelong Learning*, 2(1): 15–32.

Lee, N. and Cribbin, J. (2011), Lifelong learning in Hong Kong: Marketisation and per-sonalisation of lifelong education, *International Journal of Continuing Education and Lifelong Learning*, 4(1): 49–72.

Li, F. and Morgan, W.J. (2011), Private higher education in China: Problems and possibilities, in Morgan, W.J. and Wu, B. (eds) *Higher Education Reform in China: Beyond the expansion*, London and New York: Routledge, pp. 66–78.

Li, F., Morgan, W.J. and Ding, X. (2011), The labour market for graduates in China, in Morgan, W.J. and Wu, B. (eds) *Higher Education Reform in China: Beyond the expansion*, London and New York: Routledge, pp. 93–108.

Li, J. (2011), Equity, institutional change and civil society – The student experience in China's move to mass higher education, in Hayhoe, R., Li, J., Liu, J. and Zhe, Q. *Portraits of 21st Century Chinese Universities: In the move to mass higher education*, Hong Kong: Springer/CERC, pp. 58–90.

Liu, J. (2010), China's universities, cross-border education, and dialogue among civilizations, in Chapman, D., Cummings, W. and Postiglione, G. (eds) *Crossing Borders in East Asian Higher Education*, Hong Kong: Springer/CERC, pp. 77–100.

Liu, N. (2008), Restructuring China's adult and continuing education: An examination of driving forces behind the reform, *Research in Post-Compulsory Education*, 13(1): 107–121.

Liu, N. (2009), Decentralisation and marketisation of China's adult and continuing education: A Chinese case study, *International Journal of Educational Development*, 29(3): 212–218.

Liu, N. (2012), Transforming China's adult and continuing education, in Elliot, G., Fourali, C. and Issler, S. (eds) *Education and Social Change*, London: Bloomsbury, pp. 175–186.

Manpower Survey (2012), HK Government Manpower projection. Available online at: www.lwb.gov.hk/report/mp2018_en.pdf (accessed July 2013).

Martin, I. (2000), Reconstituting the agora: Towards an alternative politics of lifelong learning, in Sork, T., Chapman, V. and Clair, R. St (eds) *Proceeding of the 41st Adult Education Research Conference*, Vancouver, Canada, July. Department of Educational Studies, Vancouver, BC: University of British Columbia, pp. 255–260.

Ministry of Education (MoE) (1998), *Action Plan to Revitalize Education towards the Twenty-first Century*, Beijing: MoE.

Morgan, W.J. and Wu, B. (2011), Introduction, in Morgan, W.J. and Wu, B. (eds) *Higher Education Reform in China: Beyond the expansion*, London and New York: Routledge, pp. 1–10.

Naughton, B. (1995), *Growing out of the Plan*, Cambridge: Cambridge University Press.

Organisation for Economic Cooperation and Development (OECD) (1996), *Lifelong Learning for All: Meeting of the education committee at ministerial level*, Paris: OECD, 1: 16–17.

Postiglione, G. (2010), East Asian knowledge systems: Driving ahead amid borderless higher education, in Chapman, D., Cummings, W. and Postiglione, G. (eds) *Crossing Borders in East Asian Higher Education*, Hong Kong: Springer/CERC, pp. 25–46.

Stanfield, D. and Wang, Q. (2012), Full scale branch campuses in China, *International Higher Education*, 69(3): 1–5.

State Council (1987), *Decision on Development and Reform of Adult Education* (in Chinese), Beijing: State Council.

Sun, X. (2008), The legislation of lifelong education in China, *International Journal of Continuing Education and Lifelong Learning*, 1(1): 1–10.

Tan, S. (2008), Continuing education in China: Evolution, developments and trends, *International Journal of Continuing Education and Lifelong Learning*, 1(1): 11–22.

Tuijnman, A. and Bostrom, A. (2002), Changing notions of lifelong education and lifelong learning, *International Review of Education*, 48(1/2): 93–110.

University Grants Committee (UGC) (1996), *Higher Education in Hong Kong*, a report by the University Grants Committee, Hong Kong: UGC.

University Grants Committee (UGC) (2002), *Higher Education in Hong Kong*, a report of the University Grants Committee, Hong Kong: UGC.

University Grants Committee (UGC) (2010), *Aspiration for the Higher Education System in Hong Kong*, a report of the University Grants Committee, Hong Kong: UGC.

Walters, S. (2000), Globalization, adult education, and development, in Stromquist, N.P. and Monkman, K. (eds) *Globalization and Education*, Lanham, MD: Rowman & Littlefield.

Wang, N. (2011), Adult higher education in China: Problems and potential, in Morgan, W.J. and Wu, B (eds) *Higher Education Reform in China: Beyond the expansion*, London and New York: Routledge, pp. 30–47.

Wang, N. and Morgan, W.J. (2009), Student motivations, quality and status in adult higher education (AHE) in China, *International Journal of Lifelong Education*, 28(4): 493–491.

Yan, J. and Huang, C. (2009), Developments of continuing education in research universities in China: Opportunities and challenges, *International Journal of Continuing Education and Lifelong Learning*, 1(2): 1–18.

Young, E. and Zhang, W. (2008), Joining hands to make a difference, *International Journal of Continuing Education and Lifelong Learning*, 1(1): iii–v.

Zha, Q. (2011), The study-abroad fever among Chinese students, *International Higher Education*, 69(3): 15–17.

8 Social justice and higher education financing in Hong Kong

Peter P. Yuen, Ngok Lee, Stephanie W. Lee and Jason K.Y. Chan

Introduction

For some time, Hong Kong has been regarded as a society with relatively high fluidity in social mobility (Chan *et al.*, 1995). Its education system has often been credited as contributing significantly to this phenomenon (Luk *et al.*, 2009). While the education system in Hong Kong still ranks among the best in the world in terms of the cognitive skills and educational attainment of its students (Ho, 2013), as well as the rankings of its universities (QS, 2013), the popular mood on these issues appears to be changing. Some critics (e.g. Ho *et al.*, 2005) regard Hong Kong's tertiary education system as too elitist, placing Hong Kong far behind the majority of developed economies in terms of participation rate in tertiary education, the percentage of its workforce with tertiary qualifications, as well as its performance in helping disadvantaged young people to succeed. There is a persistent popular perception that social mobility in terms of access to good university education and good professional occupations is still strongly related to family background, that the middle class in Hong Kong is shrinking, and that social immobility and downward mobility are on the rise.(Lui, 2010; Ho, 2012; Hong Kong Institute of Education, 2013). The Hong Kong Special Administrative Region Government (HKSARG) counter-argues that it has increased tertiary education participation in a major way by encouraging the development of self-financing tertiary education through a number of policy measures (Education Bureau, 2013).

This chapter examines the question of social justice in higher education in Hong Kong. It assesses the extent to which government policies and measures in support of students in both publicly funded and self-financing tertiary institutions are in line with the generally accepted norm on social justice in terms of access, equity and participation. It describes, first, the Hong Kong tertiary education system – the publicly funded sector (institutions under the aegis of the University Grants Committee (UGC)), and the self-financing sector (subsidiary colleges under UGC-funded universities as well as independent self-financing institutions) – and the associated funding policies and mechanisms. It reviews data and studies relevant to social mobility/social justice and higher education in Hong Kong. It then examines the concept of social justice in higher education, as well as practices in selected countries. A review of relevant government policies regarding the supply and financing of tertiary education, as well as data pertinent to social mobility/social justice and higher education in Hong Kong, are presented subsequently. Views collected through focus group discussions or group chat in smart phone messenger applications and interviews from undergraduate students and key personnel in the tertiary institutions from both the UGC sector and the self-financing sector are included, with a view to shedding light on the students' social background, their academic performance, their ability to succeed in completing their Bachelor's degree, in obtaining gainful employment (or continuing to undertake postgraduate studies), and the effectiveness of various financial assistance and other programmes in helping students overcome different types of personal and academic problems. Conclusions are then drawn using various perspectives of social justice (Gale, 2000).

The Hong Kong context

Hong Kong, with a population of over seven million, has been a Special Administrative Region of the People's Republic of China since 1 July 1997. Around 95 per cent of the population is ethnically Chinese. Other major ethnic groups include Indonesians, Filipinos, Thais, Americans, Indians, Canadians, Nepalese, Pakistanis, Malaysians, Australians and British (Information Services Department, 2014). It has a relatively high per capita GDP of US$35,214 (in 2012), but a high-income disparity (Gini Coefficient 0.54 in 2011) (Census and Statistics Department of Government of the Hong Kong Special Administrative Region, 2015). Since the territory was under British administration prior to 1997 for over 100 years its education system resembles that in the UK.

Primary and secondary education

In Hong Kong, the government provides nine years' free and compulsory primary and junior secondary education to all school-aged children attending public sector schools. Starting from the 2008/2009 school year, senior secondary education is also provided free through public sector schools. Such a regime provides opportunities for all students to receive 12 years of free primary and secondary schooling. Since 2012 there has been only one public examination leading to the Hong Kong Diploma of Secondary Education (DSE), which is the secondary education graduation examination as well as the higher education entrance examination. In theory, no one, under this system, is denied the opportunity of receiving primary and secondary education and the opportunity to compete for a tertiary education place because of financial reasons. However, critics have pointed out that students from ethnic minority backgrounds often have difficulties getting into universities because of poor performance in the Chinese language (Niroula, 2014).

Publicly funded HE institutions

There are eight degree-awarding institutions funded by the University Grants Committee (UGC), which provide each year 15,000 first-year first-degree places. There is also the Academy of Performing Arts, which is also publicly funded and degree granting, but not under the aegis of the UGC. Approximately 18 per cent of the relevant age group is awarded a publicly funded university place. These institutions are well resourced and some are among Asia Pacific's best universities in terms of their teaching and research achievements. According to the QS Asia University Rankings 2013, the Hong Kong University of Science and Technology and the University of Hong Kong are ranked number one and two in Asia. The Chinese University of Hong Kong, the City University of Hong Kong and the Hong Kong Polytechnic University are also within the top 200 in the world (QS, 2013). Since places are limited, only students with relatively high grades in their DSE examination are admitted to these institutions.

In addition to offering degree and postgraduate studies, a small number of UGC-funded institutions, together with institutions under the Vocational Training Council, also offer publicly funded sub-degree programmes – mostly Higher Diplomas. The UGC also funds a limited number (currently 2,000 a year, to be increased gradually to 4,000) of senior year undergraduate places (places in the third and fourth year of an undergraduate degree programme) to UGC-funded institutions for graduates of publicly funded and self-financing sub-degree programmes to articulate to the publicly funded degree programmes. Since the number of such places is limited (approximately 10 per cent of the sub-degree graduate population), only students with very high grades are able to obtain such a place.

Self-financing HE institutions

Conscious of the relatively low tertiary education participation rate in Hong Kong, the Hong Kong Special Administrative Region Government (HKSARG) in 2000 initiated a policy to set a tertiary education participation rate of 60 per cent in the relevant age group. This policy has led to a rapid growth in the number of self-financing post-secondary programmes – initially Associate Degrees and Higher Diplomas, and later on Bachelor's Degrees – offered by the continuing education arm of some of the UGC-funded institutions as well as independent institutions. The post-secondary participation rate doubled in five years' time: from 33 per cent in 2001/01 academic year to 66 per cent in the 2005/06 academic year. The rate then levelled off in the 2006/07 academic year, and is now maintained at above 60 per cent (Ng *et al.*, 2013) (see Figure 8.1).

A total of 27 institutions are currently accredited to provide full-time self-financing sub-degree and degree (including top-up degree) programmes in the 2013/2014 academic year. The number of first-year intake places offered by the publicly funded sector and the self-financing sector for 2013 is shown in Table 8.1.

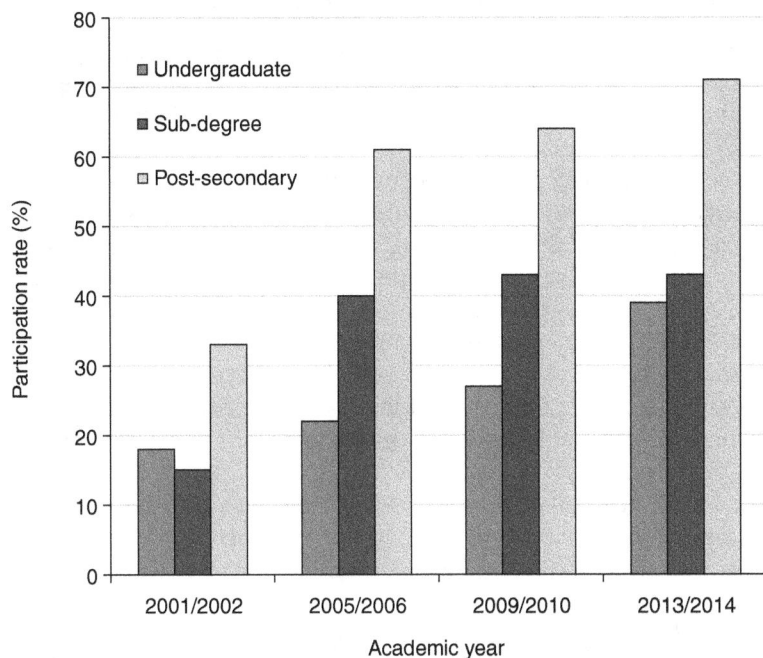

Figure 8.1 Post-secondary education participation rate (2001–2013) (source: Concourse for Self-financing Post-secondary Education (www.cspe.edu.hk/content/Statistics)).

Table 8.1 Number of first-year intake places in 2013

Programmes	Number of places
Undergraduate degree	
Publicly funded	15,200
Self-financing	7,200
Sub-degree	
Publicly funded	10,000
Self-financing	29,000
Publicly funded total	*25,200*
Self-financing total	*36,200*

Source: Education Bureau and Information Portal for Accredited Post-secondary Programmes.[1]

The self-financing sector is currently larger than the publicly funded sector in terms of the number of intake places (Education Bureau, 2013). In general, students admitted to these self-financing programmes have lower grades in their DSE examination than those admitted to the publicly funded institutions.

Social justice and higher education in other countries

While there seems to be no simple and universally accepted definition of social justice (Nelson *et al.*, 2012), in the context of higher education, the literature suggests that it generally involves the assurance of access, equity and participation of young persons in post-secondary education as well as enhancing performance and experience of disadvantaged students (James, 2007, 2008; Nelson *et al.*, 2012). Access generally refers to the availability of post-secondary places, as well as the consideration of possible factors such as religion, culture of students, and the geographical proximity of institutions. Equity often refers to equal opportunity access to higher education, and the removal of barriers – physical, financial, social, political and cultural – for disadvantaged students. Participation is often the outcome measurement for access as well as having mechanisms that can enhance students' experience and improve the probability of their being successful in their studies and in securing employment. It has been suggested that measures to support social justice in higher education include strengthening student preparation by enhancing links between K-12 and post-secondary education, pricing tuition fees close to real costs and providing direct student aid, limiting public subsidies to wealthy private schools, and substituting public direct student assistance for institutional support (Haveman and Smeeding, 2006).

Studies in the USA and Australia have found that the majority of university students, especially those attending élite universities, are from the highest quartile in terms of socio-economic status (SES) (Haveman and Smeeding, 2006; Scull and Cuthill, 2010).This inequality carries over to postgraduation stage. Findings have indicated that students from higher SES families and élite universities are more likely to secure higher paying jobs and to have better career prospects (Craven, 2012). Different countries have adopted various measures to counter such phenomena. The commonly adopted measures include increasing the number of university places, providing financial assistance for students, and providing special support for students from less privileged families.

In Australia, for example, the number of university places was greatly increased by converting Colleges of Higher Advanced Education (CAE) into universities (Nelson *et al.*, 2012). In the USA, the establishment of community colleges throughout the country was an attempt to increase the participation rate (21st Century Commission on the Future of Community Colleges, 2012). In addition, other initiatives, such as the California Master Plan, provide for collaboration between community colleges and universities whereby students who began at the community colleges (and who are likely to be from low socio-economic background) are given priority to transfer to a four-year degree-awarding institution (Liu, 2011).

Regarding the removal of financial barriers, in Australia, for example, the Higher Education Contribution Scheme (HECS) was introduced, allowing students to opt for up-front tuition fee payment upon graduation or deferred payment upon securing postgraduation employment with income exceeding a minimum threshold (Nelson *et al.*, 2012).

The introduction of the Higher Education Participation and Partnerships Program (HEPPP), also in Australia, is another example involving the provision of funding to institutions to increase access and retention of low SES students. Similarly, in the United Kingdom, the Higher Education Funding Council's Widening Participation Programme provides specific funding for activities undertaken by institutions to engage low SES students in academic and non-academic activities (Nelson *et al.*, 2012).

Social justice and higher education in Hong Kong

The following sections assess the extent to which the Hong Kong Government's policies and measures relating to the funding and delivery of both publicly funded and self-financing tertiary programmes are in line with generally accepted norms on social justice. It first reviews the government's supply-side policies – policies involving the funding and regulation of tertiary education institutions. It then reviews its demand-side policies – policies targeting students directly – and seeks to answer the following questions: Does the rapid growth of self-financing tertiary institutions significantly improve equity? Is the current funding model of institutions fair in the sense that students from low-income families (including recent immigrants and those from ethnic minorities) are benefiting as much as those from middle-class families? Are the Government Grant and Loan Schemes effective in ensuring that no qualified students will be denied tertiary education opportunities because of financial reasons?

Supply-side funding

It is not by accident that some of the Hong Kong universities are ranked among the top universities in the world. They are funded generously by the UGC. In the year 2012/2013, the total funding to the eight UGC-funded institutions was HK$18,920 million, which was 5 per cent of total government expenditure and 24.3 per cent of total government expenditure on education. The average annual student unit cost in a publicly funded university in 2011/2012 amounted to HK$247,000, which is approximately five times the average annual tuition fee charged by self-financing institutions. In addition to recurrent funding, capital projects carried out by institutions are supported by capital grants from the UGC. Furthermore, a HK$18 billion Research Endowment Fund was estab-lished in 2009 to provide stable research funding for the eight UGC-funded institutions (UGC, 2013). In contrast, self-financing institutions receive no recurrent funding. They need to borrow money for capital projects. Their aca-demic staff is not entitled to apply for research funds of the UGC. There is some support from the government to self-financing institutions such as land grants at nominal premiums, interest-free start-up loans, a HK$3.5 billion fund for scholarships and quality enhancement projects (Education Bureau, 2013), and a HK$965 million subsidy scheme for designated professions/sectors (Information Services Department, 2014). However, the difference in terms of funding levels between the UGC sector and the self-financing sector is enormous.

The interesting question is whether students from low socio-economic families are benefiting from this public supply-side funding to the same extent as students from the middle and upper classes. As pointed out earlier, studies have shown that in many countries the majority of university students, especially those attending élite universities, are from families with a high household income (Haveman and Sneeding, 2006; Lee, 2011).

In Hong Kong there is an indication that the most prestigious university, the University of Hong Kong (HKU), tends to recruit more students from better-off families. Close to 40 per cent of the fathers of the HKU's students have post-secondary education (Cedars, 2012). If the other two top universities are included – the University of Hong Kong, the Chinese University of Hong Kong and the Hong Kong University of Science and Technology, fewer than 25 per cent of students have a parent who has tertiary education. 25 per cent or more of students have parents who have only primary education or less. At other schools, such as Hong Kong Polytechnic University, fewer than 10 per cent of students have college-educated parents. 40 per cent have parents with primary or no education (Lee, 2011).

While no survey data are available regarding family background of students in self-financing institutions, interviews with student counsellors and students from both the UGC-funded and self-financing institutions were conducted. Based on the amount of grants and loans awarded to students in the two sectors, on whether they live in public housing (which is a reliable indicator that they are from lower income groups), on the need to do part-time work, on whether they consider their learning environment at home inadequate and on the number of financial hardship cases that counsellors had to deal with, it is observed that while many students in the public-funding sector are from low-income families, there appear to be more students in the self-financing sector from worse-off families.

The above suggests that while many students in the UGC sector are from low-income families and are benefiting from the generous UGC funding, there are many more students from low-income families studying in self-financing institutions who are excluded from such funding.

Supply-side policies

Not only is there a huge discrepancy in public funding support to institutions, but the associated regulatory policies for self-financing institutions also prevent them from competing effectively with the public-funded institutions. There appears to be no government concerted effort to nurture the development of some self-financing institutions into strong universities, so that their graduates would not be disadvantaged in the job market.

Land is granted to self-financing institutions at a nominal premium, which is extremely important, given that property prices, whether to let or purchase, in

Hong Kong are among the most expensive in the world (World Property Channel, 2014; Ho, 2014). However, the available plots for self-financing institutions to bid have been mostly small, including vacant primary school premises, scattered in different geographic locations, thus limiting the capacity for these institutions to further develop.

Capital projects are financed by loans, not grants. A significant portion of students' fees, therefore, has to be spent on loan repayment and not on learning and student development activities. This is particularly difficult for the better quality institutions that invested heavily in capital projects in order to provide a high-quality campus for their students and faculties.

The accreditation body for institutions not under the aegis of UGC, the Hong Kong Council for Academic Accreditation and Vocational Qualifications, was criticised by the government's Audit Commission for being inefficient and having rather serious governance and management problems (Audit Commission, 2012: 19). A long lead time is generally required for programmes to be validated, resulting in unnecessary delay in programme offerings. This can be quite detrimental for self-financing institutions which have to respond rapidly to market forces.

The ordinance that regulates independent self-financing institutions – Post-Secondary Colleges Ordinance (CAP 320)[2] – is extremely antiquated, and not conducive to the development of modern private universities that require autonomy and flexibility. There is no private university ordinance. In general, self-financing colleges are required to be registered under CAP 320 and be observed for an indefinite period before it can be considered for 'university' status. Apart from the Open University of Hong Kong (which was established by the government), so far only one self-financing institution, Shue Yan, has been conferred a university title, more than 30 years after it registered as a Post-secondary College. There are no objective standards or straightforward pathways for self-financing institutions to become private universities. Without a university title, these institutions are severely handicapped in their ability to attract good students, good academic staff, donors, and to command respect in the community. In short, the current environment is not conducive to the development of high-quality private universities.

The general public's perception from the Opinion Survey on the Public Ranking of Universities in Hong Kong 2014 shows that the self-financing universities – Open University of Hong Kong and Shue Yan University – rank consistently below almost all publicly funded institutions (POP, 2014). Graduates of these institutions are often disadvantaged in the job market as a result of such popular perception. Interview data also show that more students from the self-financing sector have intentions to pursue further studies than students from the publicly funded sector. This may be interpreted as students' perception that the qualification obtained from self-financing institutions is not well regarded by the community, and would like to remedy it by pursuing further study in a publicly funded institution.

Limited funding also prevents self-financing institutions from providing better and more comprehensive support services to their students. Interviews with staff from self-financing institutions in charge of student support services suggest that while self-financing institutions do try to provide support services, the level of service rendered is not comparable to that in the publicly funded sector. Examples given include the number of emergency grants for needy students, library resources and financial support for students with mental health problems.

A number of initiatives were launched by the government recently to provide support to secondary schools to offer special classes for non-Chinese-speaking ethnic minority students in learning the Chinese language, aiming at bridging these students to mainstream Chinese language subjects, which are required for entrance to local post-secondary institutions (HKSARG, 2014).

Demand-side funding

Given the absence of recurrent funding from the government, tuition fees of self-financed programmes are generally much higher than similar programmes in publicly funded institutions (see Table 8.2). For some programmes the difference can be more than double. Higher fees with lower prestige severely hamper self-financing institutions' ability to attract good students.

The government, however, has made available various financial assistance schemes to assist students in both the publicly funded and self-financing sectors. The Student Financial Assistance Agency (SFAA) of HKSARG administers the following schemes: Tertiary Student Finance Scheme for Publicly funded Programmes (TSFS); Financial Assistance Scheme for Post-secondary Students (FASP); Non-means-tested Loan Scheme for Full-time Tertiary Students (NLSFT); and Non-means-tested Loan Scheme for Post-secondary Students (NLSPS) (SFAA, 2009). A comparison of the schemes for students in the two sectors is presented in Table 8.3.

Table 8.2 Annual tuition fees of full-time courses by founding source and programme (2013/2014)

Funding source	Programme	Tuition fee (HK$)
Publicly funded		
UGC-funded institutions	Degree	$42,100
	Sub-degree	$15,040–$31,575
Vocational Training Council	Higher diploma	$29,500–$30,250
Academy for Performing Arts	Degree	$42,100
	Advanced Diploma	$31,575
Self-financing		
	Associated Degree	$35,800–$76,250
	Higher Diploma	$41,000–$79,200
	Degree	$52,000–$99,200
	Top-up Degree	$52,000–$99,200

Source: Education Bureau and Information Portal for Accredited Post-secondary Programmes.[3]

Table 8.3 Student financing assistance schemes

Item	Tertiary Student Finance Scheme – publicly funded programmes (TSFS)	Financial Assistance Scheme for Post-secondary Students (FASP)
Eligibility	Registered as a full-time student in publicly funded institutions.	Full-time students aged 30 or below who are engaged in locally accredited self-financed post-secondary education programmes leading to a qualification at the sub-degree level or degree.
Form of financial assistance	Provided in the form of grant and/or loan. The grant is for covering tuition fees, academic expenses and compulsory union fees. The loan is for living expenses and is interest-bearing at 1% per annum chargeable from the commencement of the repayment period. Eligible students who do not pass the means test for a full grant may receive partial grants according to a sliding scale.	Same.
Maximum level of financial assistance	Tuition fee, academic expenses and compulsory union fees: the maximum grant for a student is equal to the tuition fee.	Tuition fee maximum: HK$68,110 for 2013/2014. Academic expenses maximum: HK$4,700 for 2013/2014.
Loan repayment	The living expenses loan borrowed by students and the interest accrued thereon are repayable in 15 years by 180 equal monthly instalments, or in a shorter repayment period by equal monthly instalments as agreed by the SFAA.	Same.

Item	Non-means-tested Loan Scheme for Full-time Tertiary Students (NLSFT)	Non-means-tested Loan Scheme for Post-secondary Students (NLSPS)
Eligibility	Full-time students enrolled in the recognised courses offered by the institutions under the TSFS.	Full-time students engaged in a locally accredited self-financing post-secondary education programme at sub-degree (i.e. associate degree or higher diploma) or degree level.
Lifetime maximum ceiling	A lifetime loan limit is imposed upon students eligible for receiving loans under the NLSFT and NLSPS. The loan limit will be price-adjusted annually. The lifetime loan limit for the 2013/2014 academic year is HK$312,300.	Same.
Current interest rate	Both NLSFT and NLSPS operate on a full-cost-recovery basis. Interest rate is set at the HKSARG's no-gain-no-loss rate which is currently 1.395% per annum.	Same.
Loan repayment	Both NLSFT and NLSPS loan(s) borrowed and the interest accrued thereon are repayable in 15 years by 180 equal monthly instalments upon completion of the programmes.	Same.

Sources: combination of Student Financial Assistance Agency (www.sfaa.gov.hk/eng/schemes/pst.htm) and University Grant Committee (www.ugc.edu.hk/eng/doc/ugc/publication/report/her2010/annex-f.pdf).

There is also a recently launched subsidy scheme for ethnic minority students in secondary schools for sitting Chinese examinations under the General Certificate of Secondary Education (GCSE), the International General Certificate of Secondary Education (IGCSE) and the General Certificate of Education (GCE). The results are accepted as an alternative Chinese-language qualification for consideration for admission to local post-secondary institutions (HKSARG, 2014).

In general, the schemes for students in publicly funded and self-financing programmes are quite comparable. The schemes for students in publicly funded programmes offer greater flexibility than those for students in the self-financing sector. Interviews with students from the two sectors indicate that the majority of the students in both sectors are recipients of one or more of these schemes, and that students in both sectors are appreciative of these financial assistance programmes, without which many will find it impossible to continue their studies. Many, especially those from self-financing institutions, are concerned about debt repayment, which normally commences on 1 December of the year of graduation.

Furthermore, interview data also show that students from the publicly funded sector tended to choose programmes mainly because they were able to fulfil specific admission requirements, whereas students from the self-financing sector tended to be able to choose programmes based on interest.

Conclusion

The above analyses show that access to higher education in Hong Kong is, in the main, merit-based – students with better grades are admitted to better universities. While there appears to be some correlation between admissions to top universities and socio-economic background, the problem does not appear to be too serious, since many students from lower socio-economic status are still able to gain access to these prestigious universities. There are a number of schemes in place to assist students from low SES families.

Government policies and measures to encourage the growth of the self-financing tertiary education sector as an attempt to promote greater social justice have achieved only limited success. The most prominent achievement is the boosting of the tertiary education participation rate in a very significant manner.

On the equity front, the amount of public resources spent on helping self-financing sub-degree and degree students, the majority of whom are from low SES families, is only a small fraction of what is being spent on students in publicly funded universities. The Hong Kong Government does not appear to have a coherent plan to nurture self-financing institutions into strong institutions of higher learning, which can command the same level of respect from the community as those given to publicly funded universities, so that the graduates of these institutions will not be disadvantaged in the employment market. Currently, the probability of graduates of self-financing institutions succeeding later in life is likely to be much lower than their counterparts in publicly funded institutions because of the public perception of self-financing institutions in Hong Kong.

Regarding measures to enhance disadvantaged students' experience and performance, the HKSARG's initiatives are not too sophisticated, especially for those attending self-financing institutions. Not much thought has been put into tackling personal/family problems of students while attending the institution, as well as postgraduation difficulties with loan repayments.

As for the way forward, first, the concepts of access, equity and participation should be more carefully defined and considered by the Hong Kong Government to guide the design of its strategies and actions. Second, student loan repayment amounts should be made progressive; that is, low-income graduates should only be required to repay a lower percentage of their debt compared to higher income groups. Those earning incomes lower than a stipulated threshold should not be required to pay off their debt until their income exceeds a minimum amount. This will certainly alleviate their financial burden, since such graduates are less likely than their affluent counterparts to secure high-income employment. Third, a more coherent set of strategies and policies needs to be in place to nurture the self-financing institutions, at least the more promising ones if not all, so that they can become strong institutions of higher learning, producing graduates who can compete successfully in the employment market with their counterparts from public universities.

Notes

1 Information from the Education Bureau at: www.edb.gov.hk/en/edu-system/post-secondary/local-higher-edu/publicly-funded-programmmes/index.html; and Information Portal for Accredited Post-secondary Programmes at: www.ipass.gov.hk/edb/index.php/en/home/institutions.

2 Chapter 320: Post Secondary Colleges Ordinance at: www.legislation.gov.hk/blis_pdf.nsf/6799165D2FEE3FA94825755E0033E532/67DEABE9E9A7D68C482575EE0060 38C7?OpenDocument&bt=0.

3 Detailed information is available at: www.edb.gov.hk/en/edu-system/postsecondary/local-higher-edu/publicly-funded-programmmes/index.html; and www.ipass.gov.hk/edb/index.php/en/home/programmes.

References

21st Century Commission on the Future of Community Colleges (2012), *Reclaiming the American Dream*, Washington, DC: 21st Century Commission on the Future of Community Colleges.

Audit Commission (2012), *Hong Kong Council for Accreditation of Academic and Vocational Qualifications*, Report 58, Hong Kong: Audit Commission. Available online at: www.aud.gov.hk/pdf_e/e58ch02.pdf (accessed 28 July 2013).

Cedars (2012), *A Profile of New Full-time Undergraduate Students 2011–2012, Cedars*, The University of Hong Kong. Available online at: http://cedars.hku.hk/publication/UGprofile/UG1112_fullwebversion.pdf (accessed 8 July 2013).

Census and Statistics Department of Government of the Hong Kong Administrative Region (2015), *National Income and Balance of Payments*. Available online at: www.censtatd.gov.hk/hkstat/sub/so50.jsp (accessed 1 April 2015).

Chan, T.W., Lui, T.L. and Wong, T.W.P. (1995), A comparative analysis of social mobility in Hong Kong, *European Sociological Review*, 11(2): 135–155.

Craven, A. (2012), Social justice and higher education, *Perspectives: Policy and Practice in Higher Education*, 16(1): 23–28.

Education Bureau (2013), *Post-secondary Education: Overview*, Hong Kong: Education Bureau. Available online at: www.edb.gov.hk/en/edu-system/postsecondary/index.html (accessed 8 July 2013).

142 *P.P. Yuen* et al.

Education and Manpower Bureau (2006), *Review of the Post-secondary Education Sector*, Hong Kong: Education and Manpower Bureau. Available online at: www.edb.gov.hk/attachment/en/about-edb/press/consultation/review_report.pdf(accessed 8 July 2013).

Gale, T. (2000), Rethinking social justice in schools: How will we recognize it when we see it?, *International Journal of Inclusive Education*, 4(3): 253–269.

Haveman, R. and Smeeding, T.M. (2006), The role of higher education in social mobility, *Future of Children*, 16(2): 125–150.

Ho, H.K. (2013), Hong Kong's education 'superpower', *China Daily* (Hong Kong Edition), 8 January, p. 3.

Ho, L.S., Morris, P. and Chung, Y.P. (2005). *Education Reform and the Quest for Excellence: The Hong Kong Story*, Hong Kong: Hong Kong University Press.

Ho, S.M. (2012), Increasing social mobility, education opportunities in HK, *China Daily* (Hong Kong Edition), 19 December. Available online at: www.chinadaily.com.cn/hkedition.

Ho, S.M. (2013), Urgent need for more government-funded undergraduate quotas. *China Daily*, 19 January. Available online at: www.chinadaily.com.cn/hkedition.

Hong Kong Federation of Youth Groups (2013),The daily needs and financial pressures of young people with government loans, *Youth Study Series*, No. 49, Hong Kong: Hong Kong Federation of Youth Groups.

Hong Kong Institute of Education (2013), Hong Kong youth envision tougher road in moving upward: Survey finds. Available online at: www.ied.edu.hk/media/news.php?id=20130430 (accessed 8 July 2013).

Hong Kong Special Administrative Region Government (HKSARG) (2014), *Initiatives in the 2014 Policy Address – Support for ethnic minorities*, Government Logistic Department, www.policyaddress.gov.hk/2014/eng/EM.html (accessed 26 September 2014).

Information Portal for Accredited Post-secondary Programmes (iPASS) (2013a), www.ipass.gov.hk/edb/index.php/en/home/ (accessed 19 July 2013).

Information Portal for Accredited Post-secondary Programmes (iPASS) (2013b), *Support Measures for Institutions*. Available online at: www.ipass.gov.hk/edb/index.php/en/home/support_insti (accessed 19 July 2013).

Information Services Department (2014), Study subsidy scheme for designated professions/sectors launched, Hong Kong: Information Services Department. Available online at: www.info.gov.hk/gia/general/201407/24/P201407240232.htm (accessed 24 July 2014).

James, R. (2007), *Social Equity in a Mass, Globalised Higher Education Environment: The unresolved issue of widening access to university*, Melbourne, Australia: University of Melbourne.

James, R. (2008), *Participation and Equity: A review of the participation in higher education of people from low socioeconomic backgrounds and Indigenous people*, Melbourne, Australia: University of Melbourne.

Lee, J.Z. (2010), Family background and access to higher education in China, slides at Central Policy Unit of the HKSAR Government's website. Available online at: www.cpu.gov.hk/doc/en/events_conferences_seminars/20111216%20James%20Z%20LEE.pdf.

Liu, A. (2011), Unravelling the myth of meritocracy within the context of US higher education, *Higher Education*, 62: 383–397.

Lui, T.L. (2010), Who gets ahead (or stay behind): Life chances and social mobility in Hong Kong, *Public Policy Digest*, Issue 3. Available online at: www.ugc.edu.hk/eng/doc/rgc/publication/ppd/ppd3.pdf (accessed 8 July 2013).

Luk, B.H.K., Lin, A., Choi, P.K. and Wong, P.M. (2009), Education reforms and social mobility: Rethinking the history of Hong Kong education, in Siu, H.F. and Agnes, S.K. (eds) *Hong Kong Mobile: Making a global population*, Hong Kong: Hong Kong University Press, pp. 293–325.

Nelson, K., Creagh, T. and Clarke, J. (2012), Social justice and equity issues in the higher education context. Available online at: http://safeguardingstudentlearning.net/wp-content/uploads/2012/05/OLT_MSLE_Project-Literature-Analysis_June12draft3.pdf (accessed 20 July 2013).

Ng, P., Chan, J.K.Y., Wong, P. and Mak, C. (2013), A conceptual management model of strategic enrolment, graduation, and articulation (SEGA) in self-financing tertiary education in Hong Kong, *EDULEARN13, The 5th Annual International Conference on Education and New Learning Technologies*, Barcelona, 1–3 July.

Niroula, A. (2014), Hong Kong's ethnic minority students lag in Chinese language skills. *South China Morning Post*, 21 July. Available online at: www.scmp.com/.

Public Opinion Programme (POP) (2014), *Opinion Survey on the Public Ranking of Universities in Hong Kong 2014*, Hong Kong: University of Hong Kong.

Quacquarelli Symonds (QS) (2013), QS World University Rankings. Available online at: www.topuniversities.com/qs-world-university-rankings (accessed 8 July 2013).

Scull, S. and Cuthill, M. (2010), Engaged outreach: Using community engagement to facilitate access to higher education for people from low socio-economic backgrounds, *Higher Education Research and Development*, 29(1): 59–74.

Stokes, G. and Edmonds, A. (1990), Dawkins and the labor tradition: Instrumentalism and centralism in federal ALP higher education policy 1942–1988, *Australian Journal of Political Science*, 25(1): 15.

Student Financial Assistance Agency (SFAA) (2009), *Welcome Message*. Available online at: www.sfaa.gov.hk/eng/about/welcome.htm (accessed 17 July 2013).

Student Financial Assistance Agency (SFAA) (2013), Tertiary student finance scheme. Available online at: www.sfaa.gov.hk/eng/schemes(accessed 20 July 2013).

World Property Channel (2014), HS prime retail rent. Available online at: www.world-propertychannel.com/news-assets/HS-Prime-Retail-Rent-Q4-2013.JPG (accessed 26 September 2014).

Yorke, M. and Thomas, L. (2003), Improving the retention of students from lower socio-economic groups, *Journal of Higher Education Policy and Management*, 25(1): 63.

9 Taiwanese adult learners with self-regulated learning difficulties

The social justice perspective

Cheng-Yen Wang

Introduction

Self-regulated learning (SRL) is a pattern of self-learning and is a key competency through which to achieve the ideal of *Education for All* and in developing a
learning society. Adult learners' literacy of SRL therefore becomes a factor
affecting social justice and equality in education. In Taiwan the values of lifelong learning and of social justice have been the essences of culture since the
age of Confucius. Accordingly, from the constitution to major acts concerning
education, assuring the right to learning and to social justice has been legislated.
This chapter uses empirical data collection via a questionnaire survey
($N = 1,495$), followed by semi-structured interviews ($N = 45$). The author sampled
adult learners in formal, non-formal and informal education to reveal both their
difficulties as a whole and in the six dimensions of SRL, comparing seven social
demographic variables with the national norms set up previously. The findings,
based on qualitative and quantitative analyses, indicate Taiwan's experiences
and suggest recommendations for supporting adult learners' literacy of SRL to
protect and enhance social justice. These Taiwanese experiences should also be
helpful for other countries and societies, and the purpose of this chapter is to
explore them from the perspective of social justice.

The ideal, *Education for All*, has been promoted by the United Nations Educational, Scientific and Cultural Organization (UNESCO) since the 1990s and has
become an educational principle in most countries. Education in this sense not
only means compulsory education but also opportunities for continuing education.
Adult education and lifelong learning, especially, have been advocated to achieve
the above ideal and to meet the principle. According to this, learning is seen as an
individual basic right which has to be protected by government. An individual's
learning right must not be affected because of any social demographic particularities such as age, gender, race, occupation, religion, educational level, economic
income or residence location. The state should also provide compensatory education to those who are comparatively disadvantaged by such particularities in an
attempt to achieve educational equality, at least in opportunity. Namely, for
achieving social justice, such equality is the necessary condition. Social justice is a
significant issue in educational sociology and practices. In a democratic society,

the necessity of studying fair opportunity in education from the perspective of social justice and equality is also emphasised (Anderson, 2007).

The educational issues in social justice may be shown in multiple facets. For example, Satz (2007) notes that educational inequalities include not only disparities in funding per pupil but also in class size, teacher qualifications, and resources such as books, laboratories, libraries, computers and curricula, as well as the physical condition of the school and the safety of students within it. Again, social justice, equality and inclusion are complex and interlinked concepts, and feature prominently in Scottish social policy discourse (Riddell, 2009). For example, it is recommended that children with additional or exceptional problems (e.g. autistic children) need more rather than less support, redistribution of resources and recognition; but policies need to be couched within a discourse of rights rather than individual needs. The target group could be expanded to the public, as the problem of race shows (Garratt, 2011), or to general citizenship (Satz, 2007). For instance, Dyson (2011) points out that if the work of school were aligned with wider social strategies, the limited impacts on social justice of services in school could be enhanced. This raises questions about how school systems are governed and about what kind of society schools are expected to help build. Therefore, stakeholders who may aim at an education for social justice are composed of different kinds of providers. There are three main theories on which education for social justice is based. These are critical pedagogy, globalisation theory and cultural studies (Hytten, 2006). The diversity of education for social justice should also be noted.

Education and social justice in Taiwan

Taiwan is a democratic country and the importance of equal opportunity in education has been of traditional concern. In June 2014 Taiwan's population was 23,392,036, living chiefly on the west coast of the small island of 36,193 square km in East Asia. The ethnic composition of the population is 97 per cent Han Chinese, 2 per cent Aboriginals and 1 per cent others. Table 9.1 provides some further statistics of Taiwan's population at the end of April 2013.

Table 9.1 Some updated statistics of Taiwan's population

Category	Item	No.	%
Gender	Male	11,677,390	50.04
	Female	11,658,190	49.96
Age group	0–14	3,393,167	14.54
	15–64	17,313,532	74.19
	Over 65	2,628,881	11.27
Babies born[1]	–	15,506	8.08

Source: Department of Household Registration (2014).

Note
1 Babies born denotes the period April 2012 to April 2013. There was a decrease of 10.91 per cent compared with the previous year.

The above reveals several important features of the Taiwanese population. The sex ratio was 100.16:100 male to female and the difference in numbers between the sexes is therefore small. As to the birth rate, between April 2012 and April 2013 the crude number was 8.08 per million, a fall of 10.91 per cent compared with the previous time period. The Taiwanese birth rate has declined steadily over several years and this trend has had a serious impact on school education owing to the fall in pupil numbers. Regarding different age groups, those aged 15 to 64, the majority of the population, provide the workforce. The percentage of the population aged over 65 was 11.27 per cent and this has obviously increased over recent years. Accordingly, Taiwan is an ageing society and this has contributed to the strong demand for adult education of all types.

The rights of different minorities are highlighted both in the legislation and in practice in Taiwan. For instance, in terms of central and local governmental institutions, there are responsible departments set up to serve ethnic and other minorities. In the Executive Yuan, the highest governmental administration department, there are the Ministry of Labour, the Veterans' Affairs Council, the Council of Indigenous People and the Hakka Affairs Council. Accordingly, there are also responsible departments in local governments to protect and enhance the welfare and rights of minorities. The Ministry of Education (MOE), the highest government department responsible for national education policy-making and policy implementation, has overall responsibility for Education for All, including the disabled, the elderly, the illiterate, indigenous people, and people living in remote or otherwise disadvantaged areas. This shows that the spirit and culture of equality is rooted in Taiwanese society and government.

There are two visions advocated by the MoE. These are to cultivate excellent and creative people culturally; and to improve Taiwan's international competitiveness economically. In order to achieve these strategic visions, 12 themes have been identified covering the different stages of education in the system (MoE, 2014). In terms of education for the minorities with special needs, a new population has recently come to Taiwan. This comprises foreign females married to Taiwanese males who are usually from the lower socio-economic class themselves disadvantaged both educationally and economically. Such females are known as *New Taiwanese*, *New Immigrants* or *New Residents*. The latter term is used officially to avoid implications of social bias against them. In June 2014, there were 107,247 females who had become citizens of Taiwan through marriage. Most come from South Asia, with women from Vietnam, Indonesia, the Philippines and Thailand predominant. Table 9.2 shows the changes in numbers of these New Residents over the past five years (Department of Household Registration, 2014).

As Table 9.2 notes, although the numbers of New Residents from the four countries seem to have declined over the past five years, the total number of this population is over 200,000 in the past 20 years. It is a significant number comparable with the total of the indigenous Taiwanese (not Han Chinese). The social and economic issues that have resulted are now on the relevant policy agendas of the Taiwanese government and its different governmental departments.

Table 9.2 The numbers of new residents from four countries in five years (2009–2013)

	2009	2010	2011	2012	2013	Total
Vietnam	7,421	5,732	4,386	4,129	3,680	25,348
Indonesia	1,058	866	719	633	530	3,806
Philippine	316	272	235	298	272	1,393
Thailand	102	70	70	31	50	323
Total	8,897	6,940	5,410	5,091	4,532	30,870

Source: Department of Household Registration (2014).

For example, such families resulting from mixed marriages provide a great number of social and cultural challenges for the couples, their children and other relatives. Education is seen as a key strategy to support them in facing these challenges successfully, and therefore these families have become target groups for different government departments. Since most of the husbands and their parents are themselves disadvantaged socially and economically, compensatory education is the first priority for them and for the New Residents. This is a critical challenge for the achievement of social justice in Taiwan, and in adapting to a multicultural society. Consequently, the MoE provides adult basic education for New Residents via its Department of Lifelong Education aimed at improving competencies in literacy, and in language and culture generally. In addition, there are also extra informal curricula and activities for pupils from such families to enhance their learning, provided by the K-12 Education Administration of the MoE. The education of New Residents, their children and families is an important current policy focus which provides a signal of official determination to assure educational equality and social justice in Taiwan.

The remainder of this chapter analyses specific issues of educational equality and social justice in Taiwan, and refers especially to adult education which is a main field for UNESCO in promoting the vision of *Education for All*.

Lifelong education, self-regulated learning and social justice

Since lifelong education is the main target and self-learning is the core strategy to conduct lifelong learning, one pattern of self-learning (i.e. self-regulated learning (SRL)) will be the major topic of this chapter. Accordingly, adult learners who have difficulties in SRL are the focus of this chapter, and how to support their learning is the core issue considered. Most importantly, the chapter also explores these issues from the perspective of social justice. Recently, Taiwan's central government has tried to formulate policy to meet the demands of an ageing society but there are still disadvantages to be addressed (Lin and Huang, 2013). The policy is one of the strategies to assure social justice to elderly Taiwanese who are disadvantaged because of their age. However, there are still drawbacks to be resolved. Both the concept of learning right and that of social justice are familiar terms in traditional Chinese educational thought and practice since ancient times. These two ideas are actually not imported into Chinese thought, but developed there originally.

Learning right as a traditional value

Assuring educational equality is originally an essential part of Chinese culture. For instance, Confucius was a great educator and is seen as the Model Teacher for those who succeeded him. Over 3,000 years ago, Confucius said education should not be discriminated according to the differences in learners' origins. He also stressed that teaching had to be conducted according to learners' characteristics. Compared with modern educational thought, such ideas are both original and still up to date. The first shows Confucius' idea on equality and therefore social justice. It has been absorbed into Chinese culture and has also affected educational philosophy and practice in Taiwan.

The idea of learning right and how to protect it may be seen in different dimensions of education. Power and Taylor (2013) argue that social justice can be conceptualised in ways that have complex and multi-faceted implications for public and private sphere involvement. In terms of education, providers of the public and private sphere are all stakeholders who can assure the right of learning to have social justice (Jauhiainen and Alho-Malmelin, 2004) and consider education as a religion in the learning society. There has been a strong faith in the power of education to create and maintain many kinds of progress in society: social cohesion and order, economic growth, equality, justice and so on. Accordingly, social capital may be created through protecting lifelong learning for everyone and it has become an active phenomenon in most countries. In practice, associations between education and social capital may be found in most developed countries in individual-level analysis (Green, 2011), and social capital can be developed and recovered through community-based learning, as McIntyre (2012) found out via semi-structured interviews in Scotland. The relationship between education and human capital as well as social capital has been a significant issue, especially from the perspective of social policy (Morgan, 2012).

Legislation of major acts

The assurance of educational equality to achieve social justice in Taiwan may be found in relevant laws and acts. The Constitution is the mother of all kinds of laws. In Taiwan's Constitution, Article 159 regulates directly that all citizens' educational opportunities be equal. The Education Basic Act, revised on 11 December 2013, may be seen as the foundation law of all the educational legislations. Its Article 3 directly cites the two Confucian ideas described above to emphasise the significance of equality. Its Article 3 also regulates that education cannot differ because of learners' diverse social demographic variables, while Article 4 highlights that education for those who are disadvantaged in social and economic backgrounds has to be supported. The Lifelong Learning Act, revised on 18 June 2014, is the special act for lifelong learning in Taiwan. Its Article 20 regulates that education for disadvantaged citizens has to be supported, similar to Article 4 of the Education Basic Law. In Taiwan, the Supplementary Act, revised on 30 January, 2013, specifically regulates supplementary education for those who are disadvantaged in different backgrounds. The Act also signifies the emphasis on educational equality in Taiwan. The other example is the Special Education Act, revised on 23 January 2013, which is enacted for citizens who have special education needs, not only limited to school education but also including continuing and higher education. The Act also shows the core value of equality in Taiwan's educational systems. In addition, the Gender Equality Education Act, revised on 11 December 2013, was legislated to assure educational equality for the different genders and it is also a banner to show Taiwan's advance in basic human rights. Accordingly, from the Constitution to other relevant laws in Taiwan, the value and significance of equality in education to the Taiwanese are clearly pointed out.

Legislation is merely the basic educational construction rather than the panacea. The critical factor is whether there is correspondent policy-making and effective policy implementation to carry out the targets of the above legislations. Actually, one of the problems of Taiwan's educational policy-making is that although there is regulation in legislation, there is no concrete policy plan or effective policy implementation to meet the objectives of laws. The gap always depends on different levels of citizen representatives and different lobby groups to put pressure on the government's institutions to do that. However, as with most democratic countries, the above problem is a not an unusual phenomenon.

Self-regulated learning for adult learners

Self-regulated learning (SRL) is a concrete pattern of self-learning, a fundamental strategy for conducting lifelong learning. For adults who have difficulties in SRL, their right to lifelong learning would be faced by obstacles and result in inequality in educational opportunity and outcomes. Accordingly, how to cultivate the individual adult's SRL to continue his or her lifelong learning is a key strategy to achieve the target of social justice and, furthermore, the strategy can be carried out in different contexts. For example, equity and lifelong learning may also be achieved through the workplace learning provided by different firms (Riddell *et al.*, 2009). Besides, a diversity of students in higher education cannot be taken simply as an indicator of greater 'equality' within the system (Archer, 2007). It actually covers a great number of complicated factors. SRL is different from class-based learning, which may be more competitive with other classmates rather than with oneself. Nash (2004) emphasises that critical sociology of education has abandoned equality of educational opportunities as an imperfect objective, recognising it as one that is fully compatible with the competitive ideology of liberalism. Through the better literacy offered by SRL, one would be able to become more competitive in different learning contexts and hence be able to avoid inequality in education.

Compared with their younger counterparts, adult learners have a greater requirement to be self-learners and hence SRL has been recommended as an effective learning strategy. According to the summative definition of Boekaerts (1999), SRL is seen as the extent of an individual's active involvement in the learning process in aspects of meta-cognition, cognition, affection and behaviour. SRL is focused on how an individual initiates, changes and continues his or her learning and the process of transference. Accordingly, through SRL, an individual has to play a main role to control and manage the learning process rather than be only a negative follower. For adults who have comparatively more personal available conditions to learn actively and independently, SRL seems to be a helpful strategy.

There has been less research on SRL in the field of adult education compared with conventional educational psychology. For instance, in the limited literature, Trawick (1998) employed a questionnaire survey to collect data from students who had experienced academic failure in American community colleges. The results show that there are many students utilising SRL strategy and SRL has a significant positive correlation with the expectancy of academic achievement. Namely, SRL has positive effects on the academic achievement (Morris *et al.*, 1998) of sampled adults in the workplace and they explored the relationship between SRL and task performance. They found that SRL and task level could explain 33 per cent variance in performance. This implies that SRL is one of the crucial contributors to task performance. Therefore, they recommended that SRL is important and can be taught in the workplace. Winne (1996) also pointed out that SRL has been seen as 'a developable aptitude'. It can be developed and enriched via instruction and experience for the individual.

SRL is composed of many different elements of learning strategies. Zimmerman and his colleagues employed 14 items to concretely define SRL (Zimmerman, 1989; Zimmerman and Pons, 1986).[1] Zimmerman (1989) further developed a structured interview form based on the above 14 items and to formulate a checking list of SRL. The author developed a scale to evaluate adults' SRL in Taiwan and set up a norm reference framework based on seven social demographic variables of adults (Wang, 2007). The scale had been proved to be valid and reliable. It is the first instrument for evaluating SRL in Taiwan and has been applied in many domestic studies. The instrument has 28 items in six dimensions: (1) Improvement of learning process; (2) Seeking learning materials; (3) Control on learning contents; (4) Self-encouragement in learning; (5) Positive self-concept; and (6) Searching for learning partners. The instrument was also used to diagnose adult learners' difficulties in SRL's six dimensions and their items via questionnaire surveys and individual face-to-face semi-structured interviews for data collection.

Supporting adult learners with difficulties in self-regulated learning

The needs of adult learners with difficulties in SRL were explored from an empirical study. Two stages of data collection were conducted. In the first stage, the scale of SRL revised by the author was used to measure adult learners in three types of continuing learning (i.e. formal, non-formal and informal education in the three areas: the north, central and south of Taiwan) through stratified random sampling. The numbers of samples are listed in Table 9.3.

Table 9.3 shows the subjects sampled from three types of continuing education and three areas of Taiwan. The total number of subjects was 1,495. The subjects' grades in the total SRL scale and six dimensions were referred to the norms based on seven social demographic variables as mentioned earlier to find out the subjects whose grades were comparatively lower and who had left contact information to be interviewed. In total, 45 subjects had face-to-face semi-structured interviews in the second stage via purposeful sampling. Table 9.4 lists the subjects from three types of continuing learning.

As Table 9.4 indicates, there were 45 subjects sampled intentionally in three types of continuing learning and they were also from different areas of Taiwan. These subjects were disadvantaged in SRL as a whole and in its six dimensions, compared with their counterparts in seven norms based on social demographic variables. The face-to-face semi-structured interviews were conducted by three trained research assistants with professional backgrounds in adult education. Each interview took one and a half to two hours, and the SRL scale was employed item by item as the instrument for identifying their difficulties. Data collected via interviews were dealt with to be transcribed for analyses. Based on the Nvivo software analysis, the contents of the interviews are shown statistically in Table 9.5.

In Table 9.5, 'Sources' refers to the numbers of interviewees who responded to the questions on the scale, and 'References' are the 45 interviewees who responded to the SRL. There are six dimensions of SRL and these were used to interview the subjects on what they feel about each item according to their own

Table 9.3 The distribution of SRL learners by region and type

Region	Formal	Non-formal	Informal
North	156	155	178
Central	120	177	200
South	163	158	182
Total	*439*	*490*	*566*

Source: author's own survey ($N=1,495$).

Table 9.4 The numbers of subjects for semi-structured interviews

Formal education	Non-formal education	Informal education
15	15	15

Note
$N=45$.

Table 9.5 Node summary report of contents of interviews

Item	Sources	References
Improvement of learning process	38	41
Observe the process	1	1
Improve learning effectively	22	40
Look for better methods	16	21
Seeking learning materials	38	56
The Internet	32	78
Traditional media	14	22
Books	14	20
Control on learning contents	33	68
Catch the point of contents	32	68
Summarise the contents	13	21
Self-encouragement in learning	38	40
Encourage myself in learning	19	32
Praise myself in learning	1	1
Positive self-concept	35	39
Be optimistic	25	29
Be confident	19	25
Be active	29	54
Searching for learning partners	33	53
Partners make learning happy	4	10
Friends to improve learning	13	35

experiences. Since the interviews were conducted face to face and one to one, research assistants were able to explain the meaning of items if the subjects did not understand them.

If the numbers were greater, the subjects' difficulties would be larger in SRL, as shown in Table 9.5. In the whole SRL, 38 subjects mentioned that they had difficulties in three dimensions: improvement of the learning process, seeking learning materials, and self-encouragement in learning. The results imply that most subjects experience problems with these three dimensions of SRL, although the difference is not so significant from the other three dimensions. With regard to the numbers of references, the largest is on control of learning content (68), followed by seeking learning materials (56), and searching for learning partners (53). The results show that the three dimensions of SRL are highlighted most frequently by the subjects who have most difficulties with them.

In the dimension of improvement of learning process, how to improve learning effectively is the most difficult (22, 40), followed by how to look for better methods (16, 21) for the majority of subjects. In the dimension of seeking learning materials, most subjects have difficulty in using the Internet (32, 78). As for traditional media like television, broadcasting and books, the numbers of difficulties are similar. In the dimension of control of learning content, most subjects experience difficulties in catching the points of content (32, 68), followed by summarising (13, 21). In the dimension of self-encouragement in learning, most subjects have difficulties in encouraging themselves in learning (19, 32). In the dimension of positive self-concept, the majority of subjects evaluate themselves as less optimistic, confident and active. In the dimension of searching for learning partners, most subjects have difficulty in making friends to improve their learning (13, 35). The above findings and the comparatively larger numbers are valuable for formulating the following strategies as recommendations of this chapter.

From enriching SRL to enhancing social justice

SRL is the fundamental literacy for adults' lifelong learning, and enriching such literacy would be the crucial step to enhance social justice and equality in education. Based on the Taiwanese experiences given above, the following strategies may be helpful in meeting the demands on social justice.

First, the literacy of knowing how is critical for lifelong learning for adults. In Taiwan's educational practices, grade, rank and memory are largely focused on, especially at the stages of elementary and secondary education. Knowing how has been emphasised only recently, as creativity is one of the educational objectives of primary schools. Therefore, for adult learners, particularly those over the age of 60, the literacy of knowing how is very limited and results in their difficulty in continuing learning. In order to compensate for this, support in developing the capacity of knowing how should be necessary for all adult learners in formal and non-formal education institutions. It could be arranged at the early stage of the curriculum or in programmes to enhance basic literacy. Such courses should also be open to the adult public for self-learners via informal education.

The objective of adult learning is principally to meet the needs of daily life and this is quite different from traditional school education. Utility is therefore generally part of the target agenda of adult education. Besides the above, in other courses teachers should be expected to transmit the literacy of knowing how in their teaching and therefore teacher education should include this in its own curriculum (Reynolds and Brown, 2010). Accordingly, if the literacy of knowing how can be learned via each course in formal and non-formal education, adult learners would be much more likely to enhance their competency in self-learning. If the literacy of knowing how could be rooted in this way, adult learners would have less difficulty with SRL and this would contribute greatly to achieving both educational equality and social justice.

Enhancing learning guidance to the disadvantaged

Learning guidance plays a significant role in formal and non-formal education institutions for adult learners, but in Taiwan the service is seriously insufficient. It is argued that the literacy of knowing how and self-learning are not innate abilities, but must be learned from an early life by everyone. Accordingly, those who are disadvantaged in SRL for social demographic reasons require the extra service of learning guidance provided by educational institutions. No matter when they need it, or when their tutors recommend them to accept it, learning guidance provided by professionals needs to be made available. In Taiwan, such a service has been advocated in policy discussions but is still rarely found in practice. As to the educational guidance profession itself, there is still much room for Taiwan to catch up with the pioneer countries.

Expanding Internet literacy to older adults

In the information society, the Internet is a necessary tool for all, but not everyone has either access to it or the capacity to use it effectively. Taiwan has a competitive industry in technologies of information, communications and electronics in the global market. How to apply these technologies to education has therefore been a hot topic in school education and in lifelong learning. For instance, there are two open universities in Taiwan which provide distance learning to adults via multiple media and the Internet. In order to bridge the digital divide, Taiwan's Ministry of Education has set up many Digital Opportunity Centres in disadvantaged areas to provide basic knowledge and skills to access the Internet and use computers. These Centres help adults, who are generally aged over 55, improve their basic competencies in using the Internet. Since research shows that the majority of adult learners have difficulty in employing the Internet to seek data, Taiwan's Ministry of Education could extend the successful experiences of the Digital Opportunity Centres to older adults to enhance their computer literacy and knowledge of the Internet.

Conclusion

To achieve social justice via lifelong learning for adults is the main target of different tracks and patterns of education. To meet such a target requires the collaboration of different partners. Gewirtz (2006) contextualises social justice in education from three perspectives: (1) Cognition of the multi-dimensional nature of justice and the potential for conflict among different facets of justice; (2) An attention to the ways in which justice is mediated by the other norms and constraints that motivate actors; (3) A consideration of the contradictions among different facets of justice. Accordingly, since the concept of social justice is complex, more interaction and dialogue among different partners would be helpful for educational equality. For example, well-being via lifelong learning could be the common value for different partners. Zapke (2013) raises the social perspectives that lifelong education must advance well-being through social justice to enrich personal subjective well-being. The point implies that through social justice in lifelong learning, individual well-being could possibly be improved. Both social justice and well-being are now advocated in modern society and lifelong learning could be a critical strategy to achieve them.

Education for All has been an ideal for developing a learning society and the individual learning right is the key and basic condition by which to achieve the vision. *Education for All* also implies that to assure the individual learning right is a fundamental signal of educational equality and commitment to social justice. Since self-learning is the critical competency for lifelong learning, whether an individual has such a capacity is a crucial factor affecting his or her achievement of social justice in education. Therefore, SRL, a concrete pattern of self-learning, has been identified in this chapter to explore the issue of social justice in the context of Taiwan.

According to the empirical data collected through questionnaire surveys and semi-structured interviews, I have revealed adult learners' difficulties in the whole of SRL and in its six specific dimensions. Based on the findings, recommendations have been formulated to support adult learners' SRL. If their capacity in SRL can be enhanced, then adult learners would become more competent in conducting lifelong learning and in realising social justice. Adult learners who were identified as disadvantaged according to seven social demographic variables in SRL would have a clear picture of their learning characteristics. This would enable educational advisers and educational institutions to plan adaptive teaching and learning supports for them through learner-oriented teaching and educational services. Because of the diversity of adult learners, customising teaching to individuals' learning needs would be a strategy for achieving the ideal of *Education for All*. It is also in the spirit of enhancing educational equality and ensuring social justice. The findings and experiences of Taiwan explored in this chapter should be of value to other societies, including Mainland China, Hong Kong and Macau, since *Education for All* has become a common value in education policy throughout the world.

Notes

1 They include: (1) Self-evaluation; (2) Organisation and transformation; (3) Goal setting and planning; (4) Information seeking; (5) Making records and checking; (6) Surroundings arrangement; (7) Self-arrangement of result; (8) Reviewing and remembering; (9) Seeking peers' help; (10) Seeking teachers' help; (11) Seeking adults' help; (12) Reviewing tests; (13) Reviewing textbooks; (14) Reviewing notebooks.

References

Anderson, E. (2007), Fair opportunity in education: A democratic equality perspective, *Ethics*, 117: 595–622.

Archer, L. (2007), Diversity, equality and higher education: A critical reflection on the ab/uses of equity discourse within widening participation, *Teaching in Higher Education*, 12(5–6): 635–653.

Boekaerts, M. (1999), Self-regulated learning: Where we are today?, *International Journal of Educational Research*, 31: 445–457.

Chang, B. (2013), Education for social change: Highlander education in the Appalachian Mountains and study circles in Sweden, *International Journal of Lifelong Education*, 32(6): 705–723.

Department of Household Registration (2014), Household statistics analysis (April 2013). Available online at: www.ris.gov.tw/en/web/ris3-english/home (accessed 30 July 2014).

Dyson, A. (2011), Full service and extended schools, disadvantaged, and social justice, *Cambridge Journal of Education*, 41(2): 177–193.

Garratt, D. (2011), Equality, difference and absent presence of 'race' in citizenship education, *London Review of Education*, 9(1): 27–39.

Gewirtz, S. (2006), Towards a contextualized analysis of social justice in education, *Educational Philosophy and Theory*, 38(1): 69–81.

Green, A. (2011), Lifelong learning, equality and social cohesion, *European Journal of Education*, 46(2): 228–243.

Hytten, K. (2006), Education for social justice: Provocations and challenges, *Educational Theory*, 56(2): 231–236.

Jauhiainen, A. and Alho-Malmelin, M. (2004), Education as a religion in the learning society, *International Journal of Lifelong Education*, 23(5): 459–474.

Lin, Y. and Huang, C. (2013), Policies and practices in educational gerontology in Taiwan, *Educational Gerontology*, 39(4): 228–240.

McIntyre, J. (2012), The development and recovery of social capital through community-based adult learning, *International Journal of Lifelong Learning*, 31(5): 607–621.

Ministry of Education (MoE) (2014), MoE policy blueprint. Available online at: http://english.moe.gov.tw/ct.asp?xItem=15708&ctNode=11410&mp=1(accessed 29 July 2014).

Morgan, J.W. (2012), Human capital, social policy and education, *Journal of Educational Development*, 33(2): 217–220.

Morris, D.R., Gredler, M.E. and Schwartz, L.S. (1998), The role of self-regulated learning in an industrial training environment, paper presented at the Annual Conference of the American Educational Research Association, San Diego, 13–17 April.

Nash, R. (2004), Equality of educational opportunity: In defence of a traditional concept, *Educational Philosophy and Theory*, 36(4): 361–377.

Power, S. and Taylor, C. (2013), Social justice and education in the public and private spheres, *Oxford Review of Education*, 39(4): 464–479.

Reynolds, R. and Brown, J. (2010), Social justice and school linkages in teacher education programmes, *European Journal of Teacher Education*, 33(4): 405–419.

Riddell, S. (2009), Social justice, equality and inclusion in Scottish education, *Discourse: Studies in the Cultural Politics of Education*, 30(3): 283–296.

Riddell, S., Ahlgren, L. and Weedon, E. (2009), Equity and lifelong learning: Lessons from workplace learning in Scottish SMEs, *International Journal of Lifelong Education*, 28(6): 777–795.

Satz, D. (2007), Equality, adequacy and education for citizenship, *Ethics*, 117: 625–648.

Trawick, L.V. (1998), Relationships among cognitive-motivational processes and academic failure, paper presented at the Annual Conference of the American Education Research Association, New Orleans, 5–9 April.

Wang, C. (2007), Analysis of individual differences in social demographic variables to set up adult self-regulated learning literacy norm and implications to adult online learning, *Journal of Lifelong Learning Society*, 3(1): 105–115.

Winne, P.H. (1996), A meta-cognitive view of individual differences in self-regulated learning, *Learning and Individual Differences*, 8(4): 327–354.

Zapke, N. (2013), Lifelong education for subjective well-being: How do engagement and active citizenship contribute?, *International Journal of Lifelong Education*, 32(5): 639–652.

Zimmerman, B.J. (1989), A social cognitive view of self-regulated academic learning, *Journal of Educational Psychology*, 81(3): 329–339.

Zimmerman, B.J. and Pons, M.M. (1986), Development of a structural interview for assessing student use of self-regulated learning strategies, *American Educational Research. Journal*, 23(4): 614–628.

Index

For Product Safety Concerns and Information please contact our EU
representative GPSR@taylorandfrancis.com
Taylor & Francis Verlag GmbH, Kaufingerstraße 24, 80331 München, Germany